before OPRAH

before OPRAH

Ruth Lyons,
The Woman Who Created Talk TV

Michael A. Banks

ORANGE FRAZER PRESS
Wilmington, Ohio

ISBN 978-1933197-494
Copyright©2009 Michael A. Banks

Additional copies of *Before Oprah: Ruth Lyons, The Woman Who Created Talk TV* may be ordered directly from:
Orange Frazer Press
P.O. Box 214
Wilmington, OH 45177

Telephone 1.800.852.9332 for price and shipping information.
Website: *www.orangefrazer.com*

Design: Jeff Fulwiler

Library of Congress Cataloging-in-Publication Data

Banks, Michael A.
  Before Oprah : Ruth Lyons, the woman who created talk TV/
by Michael A. Banks.
      p. cm.
  Includes bibliographical references and index.
  ISBN 978-1-933197-49-4
1. Lyons, Ruth, 1905-1988. 2. Women broadcasters--Ohio--Biography.
3. Television broadcasting--Ohio--Biography.
4. Businesswomen--Ohio--Biography. I. Title.
  PN1992.4.L9B36 2009
  791.4502'8092--dc22
  [B]
                              2008053826

For Debra Morner, who toughed it out through three in a row with me.

Table of contents

Introduction

The woman who created talk TV

It would be appropriate if I could say that my earliest memory of television was Ruth Lyons. But I can't say that, as my first memories of television are of a Western movie and *Peter Pan*, circa 1955. Ruth Lyons was on television (and radio) at the time, but if I saw her then it just didn't register.

I do remember her in 1959, though. On a boring summer afternoon I walked next-door to my Aunt Ramona's house where the television was on and tuned to Channel 5 (WLWT) and *The 50-50 Club*. It was pretty quiet, but it beat soap operas. Many times that summer I walked next door and watched *The 50-50 Club,* even for a time being caught up in whatever soap opera followed.

Eventually, I started watching *The 50-50 Club* at home—intermittently, of course, because boys (like girls) have lots of outdoor duties involving riding bicycles, playing the usual kid games, and exploring the neighborhood.

Naturally, I didn't watch television in school (unheard of when I was in the lower grades). But when we had a weekday off school, I would sometimes remember the show and watch it. After a time, *The 50-50 Club* became associated in my mind with a pleasant afternoon with nothing to do. And sometimes they did interesting (read: *funny*) things on the show. At least it wasn't all boring, and it was something to do.

A few years later I would tune to Ruth Lyons (as everyone called *The 50-50 Club*) in my first car by default, thanks to the station having a 50,000-watt, clear-channel signal. Most of us didn't have FM receivers in our cars. (*Argh!* Nothing but classical music!) Other radio stations faded in and out, and crackled and popped with static, but not WLW. Eventually I got an 8-track tape player and FM radio got hip, so I missed the final days of *The 50-50 Club*. I wasn't the primary demographic at the time, anyway.

Decades later I look back fondly on those early days of local media. It turned out that WLW and WLWT were pioneers in broadcasting on a national level, as I discovered when I began writing magazine articles on local history, and rediscovered while researching the biography of Powel Crosley, Jr.

As with Crosley and other bits of Cincinnati legend and lore, there was no full-length book about Ruth Lyons, certainly none that told all of her story, for good or bad. I decided that such a book should exist, and you hold it in your hands.

As time goes by and events recede ever more deeply into the past, facts are lost. In books, magazine articles, and newspaper stories, some facts get blurred or omitted. Others are replaced by what an author thinks he remembers. Half-memories that have little to do with reality are often set down as history. The truth gets shuffled as deadlines loom. And on occasion, somebody passes along a made-up story, because they wish it had happened that way, or because it makes them seem a better storyteller.

For these reasons, I went to as many primary sources as I could in doing the research for this book. Paramount among the sources were reports contemporary to the times, and people who were there. Occasionally one story or report would conflict with another. In such cases I sought out a third source to verify one or the other. My hope is that I've found the right facts and organized them clearly without introducing inaccuracies. For any errors that may have made it into the text, my apologies.

Michael A. Banks
Cincinnati, Ohio
Spring, 2009

before OPRAH

mother knows best

It's just before noon on a weekday in 1960. In homes across the Midwest—in Cincinnati, Dayton, Columbus, and Indianapolis—dish towels are put away, vacuum cleaners shut off, and the televisions turned on. Time for Ruth Lyons.

Music by the Cliff Lash Orchestra fills some five million living rooms and kitchens as an announcer cheerily booms, *The 50-50 Club!* The camera pans across the studio audience of 150, most of whom are women, and zooms in on

Ruth's audience was never sure who might show up on stage, but she made every occasion seem special.

Lyons, a well-dressed, energetic woman with an immaculate, gray-blonde coiffure. She holds a microphone disguised as a floral bouquet and sings "Let Me Entertain You," her traditional opener.

The live program, originating from Crosley Broadcasting's WLW-T studio in Cincinnati, is simulcast, so television viewers and radio listeners alike settle back for ninety minutes of . . . something different.

There's likely to be a special guest who will join Ruth on her rocking couch for a lively or serious chat. It could be a Hollywood star—maybe Peter Nero, Lorne Greene, Phyllis Diller, or Tony Randall. It might be the governor of Ohio, or perhaps a local author with her first book. It might even be Bob Hope. Guest or no guest, the audience can count on music, chatter among Ruth and her sidekicks, prizes, jokes, and most of all, the host holding forth on whatever strikes her fancy that day. It might be politics, her husband's wardrobe, religion, crime, race issues, housekeeping—just about anything.

Ruth introduces one of the show's regular performers, Marian Spelman, who sings a love ballad Lyons penned years ago. A few minutes later, the audience waves to the accompaniment of "The Waving Song," a *50-50 Club* tradition. Most of the women wear white gloves, another of the show's traditions.

With the program now underway, Ruth begins a witty repartee with her band director, Cliff Lash (something David Letterman and Paul Shaffer would be doing forty years later). She interrupts their conversation, though, when she sees a six-foot reproduction of a sponsor's print ad at the far end of the stage. The ad—for Serta mattresses—features a woman who looks as if she hasn't slept in a week.

Ruth hurries across the stage, high heels clicking. She grabs the life-size reproduction and shakes it.

"Who is this woman?" she asks.

The audience laughs.

"I will not have that on this show!" Ruth proclaims. "It looks too much like me and I won't have it!"

More laughter and applause.

"Look at that—I call this negative advertising. I mean, the very thought of putting a face like that with the name 'Serta' affects my soul!"

"I am primarily a businesswoman, not a girl trying to get her name in lights."—Ruth Lyons

Ruth gestures to someone offstage.

"Bill," she beckons, "I want to talk to you like a mother. Now come here!"

Appearing somewhat abashed, a young man in a checked suit walks onto the set. He is *50-50 Club* producer Bill Gustin. On any other show, you'd never see the producer.

"How many times have I asked you to get this woman out of here, and keep her out?" Ruth asks, tapping the Serta advertisement with her free hand.

Gustin opens his mouth to speak, but the host rolls right over him.

"We've sold Serta mattresses for nine hundred years," Ruth says. Gustin nods in agreement. "And we don't need this horrible, negative approach that you have to look like this before you buy a mattress."

Now, Gustin shakes his head "no," and Ruth adds, "Why, it would scare the salesman to death if you came in looking like the model."

He nods again.

Lyons tells her producer to raise his right hand. Gustin stares at her in surprise for a second before raising his hand.

"Now," she orders, "repeat after me: I promise . . ."

"I promise," the producer echoes.

"To get this woman out of the studio and never let her back in . . ."

"To get this woman out of the studio and never let her back in . . ."

"So help me!" Ruth stabs the air with her microphone bouquet.

"So help me," Gustin finishes.

There's more applause and laughter as Gustin picks up the cardboard display in apparent defeat.

"But what are the agency men going to say?" he asks.

"The *agency* men!" Ruth replies in mock outrage. She shoves the sign and Gustin offstage, shouting "Out, out!"

Many in the audience may be wondering if Serta will pull its ads from future shows. Not a chance. The extemporaneous bit of theater more than fulfills Ruth's obligation to the sponsor. She's delivered three full minutes of exposure for the price of a one-minute spot—a commercial that any other show would have disposed of in thirty seconds, if not less.

Now, rather than picking up where she left off when she attacked the Serta ad, Ruth selects a bottle of steak sauce from an armload of products her handsome sidekick, Bob Braun, holds for her. (Braun, a singer and Arthur Godfrey talent scout winner, is one of several regulars on the show. Others include a varying cast of female singers and WLW veteran newsman, Peter Grant.) Ruth ad-libs praise for the sauce, which she really has used. Her rule is absolute: She won't take on an advertiser unless she personally likes the product.

Just to make sure her audience is paying attention, Ruth plucks another product from the consumer treasure trove in Braun's arms—a pink plastic container of Gentle Fels dish detergent—and drops it on the tiled floor with an exaggerated flourish. There are gasps of surprise; glass is still standard packaging for liquid products in 1960.

"See, you can drop that if your hands get slippery," she says, "and it'll never break. You don't lose any—and it scares 'em to death every time I do that!"

Smiling, Ruth picks up the bottle and pats it.

"Stock up, kids. It's really worth it!"

She pitches other sponsor products for several more minutes, getting all the commercials "out of the way" so she can host her show uninterrupted. This is the rhythm of *The 50-50 Club*. Advertisements happen whenever and however Ruth Lyons feels like doing them.

When she tells her audience, "Stock up," they do. It's not uncommon for sponsors to call WLW's ad director, confessing they can't keep up with the demand after advertising on *The 50-50 Club*, which is why Serta didn't pull its ads and why sponsors lucky enough to get on the show spend more than $2 million a year for the privilege, while others wait in line.

RUTH LYONS HAD THE POWER to throw a sponsor off her show (literally, in the case of Serta's sleep-deprived standup), yet she was savvy enough to know the same sponsor would pay for more ad time the next day. She might do a three-second plug for Folger's coffee, saying, "I had a great cup of Folger's this morning," and the next day take viewers through the coffee's harvest, roasting and packaging process—getting the same network rates for each spot.

She liked to say, "I'm just a housewife with a radio program." (And, later, a television program.) In reality, Ruth Lyons was an institution, a woman who knew the minds of the millions of women in her audience and involved them in the conversation, whatever the subject, whether they were at home in front of their TVs or in the studio seats. She prompted the show's singers, on-air announcers, and guests to join in the discussion as well.

The 50-50 Club had all the elements of a variety show, thanks to the talents of its host. Ruth was a singer, songwriter and musician who broke into broadcasting on the strength of her piano playing ability. Though she wasn't vocally gifted, her albums sold thousands of copies. But above all, Ruth liked to talk. The topic might be as light as the clouds drifting in the sky on a sunny afternoon. If the darker events of the day moved her, she spoke her mind. A crime wave might spark a thirty-minute diatribe.

Racism bothered her. From her studio couch, she spoke out against racist acts, like the time her male companion opened the door to get in a cab, saw the driver was black, then slammed the door shut and stepped back away from the vehicle. Ruth hailed the next black cab driver she saw and rode with him. The next day, she recalled her conversation with the cabbie, and her audience shared Ruth's disgust when she noted that the driver had shrugged and said, "It happens all the time." (During the tumultuous Civil Rights Movement that began in the 1950s, Lyons danced with African-American singer Arthur Lee Conley on her show.)

On or off the air, Ruth held the same opinions. And she apparently wielded as much power in the boardroom as she did on her show, often butting heads with top management as a member of Crosley (later AVCO) Broadcasting's programming committees. She always won. More than once, she bested the combined might of AVCO and Procter & Gamble.

Ruth Lyons was an innovator whose show would influence the future careers of David Letterman, Jane Pauley, Nick Clooney, Phil Donahue, and the Tri-state's most notorious TV personality, Jerry Springer. *The 50-50 Club* was live television with enough material every day to fill more than the ninety minutes allotted it.

Ruth, however, never put business ahead of family. She was, first and foremost, a mother to her daughter Candy. As she once told an interviewer, "I have only two major interests in life: my family and my job, in that order." Thus, child-rearing, marriage, and homemaking were frequent topics.

She also had a strong maternal bond with her fans—they could count on her to care about the world, to give voice to their thoughts and to offer good advice. Many of them called her "Mother," a nickname that originated among the seventy or so cast and crew members of *The 50-50 Club*.

RUTH'S MATERNAL INSTINCTS also took over when she observed the plight of children in hospitals—children alone, perhaps for the first time, and without anything they could call their own. She made a plea for donations to provide each child with a toy or some other object of comfort to help them through their ordeals. The charity she established remains active today, seventy years later.

To her millions of fans, Ruth Lyons was mother, homemaker, business-woman, entertainer, and friend. She embodied the best of each role, sharing her life with her audience even as she privately endured a heart-breaking tragedy of the worst kind. There were things no one knew except her family and closest friends—nothing criminal or scandalous, but private nonetheless. Eight years of her life seemingly all but disappeared from history, and for another seven years she lived a kind of divided existence. For the star of *The 50-50 Club*, it all began in Cincinnati's East End in 1905.

east end kid

Ruth Lyons's original debut caused mild debate. Her mother's doctor, Dr. George W. Prugh, recorded that Ruth Evelyne Reeves was born at her parents' home at 2077 Eastern Avenue on October 3, 1905. Her mother insisted that Ruth was born the following day, October 4. Does a mother confuse such a laborious event? In time, Ruth chose her mother's version and October 4 it was.

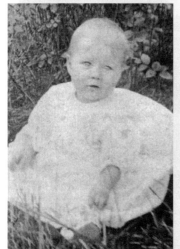

For six years in her young life, Ruth was a solo act, and she liked the attention.

The neighborhood where Ruth was born was more definite. Known as Cincinnati's East End, it began at the edge of downtown and ran eastward for five miles, its major feature being Eastern Avenue. For a mile or so after leaving the city, Eastern maintained a comfortable distance between itself and the Ohio River, which it paralleled. At that point the land behind it rose sharply and forced the roadway closer and closer to the river. In less than two miles, the street was squeezed onto a narrow shelf of land, the Ohio River on one side and almost unclimbable hills on the other.

This shoreline niche was but a few hundred feet wide for most of its length, leaving on either side of the street just enough room for a house with a small yard, plus a line of railroad tracks at the base of the hills. The rare cross street ran a block or less before it was terminated by either rocky hillside or water. Throughout its length, Eastern Avenue followed a great bend in the river, persistently curving toward the shore and urging the traveler ever closer to its edge.

Industry dominated the street for the first two miles out of downtown. Metal shops, machinists, planking mills, tanneries, and tire recappers raised a din and odor unique to the area. A huge complex called the Fulton rail yard covered land that a century later would be a park, and farther out was the East End Gas Works, adjacent to the Cincinnati Consolidated Street Railway Company's immense repair shop.

A few sagging houses peered from between grimy factory buildings but most residents had long since joined the eastward migration encouraged by the influx of industry and abetted by horse cars and electric trolley lines.

As 19th century developers pushed ever farther from the city, they created in effect a geographically isolated village—a village one street wide and four miles long. Its main street, Eastern Avenue, was its only connection with the outside world. To find a bridge or ferry across the Ohio, one had to go downtown.

In four cobblestoned miles, only three streets challenged the hills, struggling up the steep slopes for a couple hundred feet or so to Columbia Parkway or Macmillan Avenue before collapsing in exhaustion, as did most of the humans and horses who ascended them.

So situated, the East End stood nearly independent of the city. The trolley lines provided smooth passage to city or country, but most East End residents had no need to leave their village. The neat frame houses along Eastern Avenue were interspersed with shops, churches, and a grade school. Jobs were available with the industries at the city end of the avenue, and the Eastern residents found a full life in their very backyards.

It was the kind of neighborhood that accumulated large families.

People who settled in the area tended to stay, as did their families, who grew to be large extended families. Thus, within just a few blocks, a child could visit her grandparents, uncles, aunts, and family friends who might some day become relatives by marriage.

The Reeves family had lived on Eastern Avenue for decades, beginning with Ruth's paternal great-grandfather, who had moved to the East End from rural Kentucky in 1855. The family he brought with him included a young son named James Morris Reeves, Ruth's paternal grandfather, and when James Morris Reeves married, it was to a girl who lived barely a block from his home. Then he and his wife, Mary Hirst Reeves, moved into a house literally around the corner from both their families. His brothers also married neighborhood girls and settled nearby.

The males of the next generation—including Ruth's father, Samuel Spencer Reeves—followed the tradition of marrying a local girl and staying close to home. Samuel Reeves was a quiet, witty man with an unusual ability to perform complex calculations in his head. Born in 1871 and educated in Cincinnati public schools, he became a railroad rate clerk, an occupation that made good use of his abilities. It also involved no heavy lifting, which appealed to his less-than-energetic nature.

Samuel—as his father and uncles before him—lived with his parents until he was well into adulthood. He was 28 and still with them when a riverboat pilot named Thomas Jefferson Henry moved his family from the river town of Newport, Kentucky, to a house half a block from the Reeves's home. Henry's daughter, Margaret, was 23 and by current social standards a spinster although she didn't look the part. She was tall and slender, a delicate beauty worthy of the family nickname "Doll." Samuel, a handsome man himself, was immediately taken with her, and she with him.

They lingered in courtship for nearly three years, two birds reluctant to leave their nests, and still uncertain as to whether they were ready, they married in 1902 at Eastern Avenue's Sixth Presbyterian Church, just a few blocks west of their homes. Both sets of parents breathed a sigh of relief.

Predictably, the couple moved into an apartment close to his parents' home and his job at the Fulton rail yard. Within a year, Margaret gave birth to a son, Morris Jefferson Reeves. The delivery was difficult and the child died two days after birth. Margaret recovered, and despite the earlier tragedy, she became pregnant again early in 1905. This time there were no problems. Ruth Evelyne Reeves was born a plump, apple-cheeked baby with light blue eyes.

THIS TIME, TRAGEDY CAME in the form of losing their house. The situation may have been due to expenses associated with the new baby, but more likely was caused by Samuel Spencer Reeves's poor talents regarding personal finance. He treated dollars like orphans, seemingly bent on finding new homes for as many of them as possible.

He spent money on expensive gifts for his wife and daughter for no reason other than to surprise them, and in later years Ruth and her mother often returned such gifts to the downtown stores from whence they came. Otherwise, there might have been times when they would have gone without food.

For a temporary solution, Samuel looked to family. He carried what belongings he and Margaret shared just a few doors east to a spare room in his parents' house and settled in with his wife and daughter until he could "get on his feet."

Living in close quarters created friction between Margaret Henry Reeves and her mother-in-law, inevitable because the latter was a strong-willed woman who enjoyed her role as matriarch. Saturday was the older woman's designated baking day, while Monday was reserved for laundry, and other days similarly appointed. But Margaret baked and did her laundry on whatever days pleased her, ignoring the obvious good example of her elder.

This fit Margaret Henry Reeves's reputation as a non-conformist. Easygoing like her husband, she showed other contrasts to her mother-in-law, among them stressing the churchly values of generosity and compassion more than religion's restrictive aspects. Grandmother Reeves, on the other hand, lived by fervent religious principles. Drinking, smoking, gambling, and dancing were sins, as were plays and musicals, or any entertainment other than religious music.

ALTHOUGH GRANDMOTHER REEVES was strict and unyielding, Ruth remembered her with fondness. She admired her grandmother for being well-read and informed, and was impressed with her precise schedule. The old woman rose at precisely 4 a. m. every morning to do housework. Then it was on to market, after which she either called on relatives or perhaps distributed food to the poor.

She was a charter member of the Women's Christian Temperance Union and the self-appointed moral guardian of both her family and a wide swath of the neighborhood as well. Her skirmishes with saloon-keepers were legendary. While working men from Eastern Avenue's sawmills, machine shops, and factories sometimes spent their entire week's pay in taverns on a Saturday night, Mary Reeves saw this as money laid at the very altar of evil.

One of these dens of iniquity was owned by a neighbor, an Irishman named Pat Bains. One day, she called on Bains and drew him a picture of damage left by his offensive trade. She was so persuasive that Bains limited his over-indulgers to a certain number of beers each, no matter how loud their protests. Over the years and almost apologetically, he became good friends with the Reeves family.

Her grandmother's persuasiveness seemed to rub off on Ruth, and Ruth also absorbed her WCTU attitudes; she was a teetotaler all her life and later joined the organization. But Ruth was still her own person. She took up smoking and embraced show business. Perhaps these rebellions, such as they were, came from her mother's side of the family.

As a child, she was drawn to music, a talent manifest in the Reeves family; her father and grandfather sang in church, and her uncles played piano and organ. Ruth traced her interest in music to her mother, Margaret, who placed the 3-year-old Ruth on a table and sang to her while she did her ironing. The slender, fair-haired little girl memorized the songs and repeated them without being asked, and she enjoyed the attention she received.

It wasn't as if she didn't get noticed on her own. She was a solo act for the first six years of her life, used to lots of attention from her parents, grandparents, aunts, and uncles. Singing merely brought her more of a good thing.

When she was 6, she began taking piano lessons and discovered that she had perfect pitch. Soon, she was picking out melodies after listening to songs on records. (Ruth's parents had the first phonograph in the neighborhood, and a large collection of records, heavy on opera.)

It was only natural that Ruth was attracted to the musical theater. When she was old enough, she used the ten-cent allowance she received for housework and chores to take in the Saturday afternoon shows in the gilded opulence of Keith's Vaudeville Theater in downtown Cincinnati.

She collected sheet music, but after carfare and admission, she had no money left for a show's sheet music. Her father indulgently bought it for her at a downtown music store and brought it home every Monday evening.

IN 1910, RUTH AND HER PARENTS again moved into a home of their own, a two-story, two-family house at 2081 Eastern Avenue, still only half a block from her grandparents, James and Mary Reeves. Ruth's sister, Rose Jayne, was born here in 1911, the same year Ruth started first grade at the Highland Public School. (An odd name for a school located in the flood plain of the Ohio River, but there it was.)

Ruth adopted a motherly attitude toward Rose Jayne because in helping care for her, Ruth shared the spotlight. As a child, Rose had a roguish nature that frequently got her into trouble—both in the neighborhood and at school. Ruth rescued Rose when she could and tried teaching and correcting her sister. It seemed as if Rose wasn't being watched as closely as Ruth was at her age, so Ruth resolved to make up for it, although to no avail.

In her teen years, Rose was an underachiever, more concerned with the cutting edge of fashion than academics or music. Ruth protected her as much as possible while Rose put up a solid resistance. Once Ruth established herself in the role of big sister and substitute mother, it was easy to expand her mothering to the entire neighborhood, which she did, even to the point of supervising boys' marble games. And while some childhood friends considered her bossy, they usually followed her lead. The confidence she picked up from her grandmother, along with her own qualities of persuasion, helped shape her as a leader.

It helped that three of her cousins were her best friends and almost constant companions. They were Bud, Mary and Persis Reeves, who lived—where else?— half a block east at 2150 Eastern Avenue. (They were the children of her father's bookkeeper brother, George. Her other uncle was a bartender who lived in the city.) But Ruth was clever in dealing with people on her own, too. When she was given the particularly tedious weekly chore of polishing a long staircase, she came up with a Tom Sawyer-like scheme to get her friends to do the work. She paid them in penny candy and as they toiled she sat at the top of the staircase and told stories, each of which ended with a cliff-hanger.

She was still subcontracting this portion of her housework a year or so later when her allowance increased to a quarter a week. To keep her domestic helpers interested, she added the reward of taking one of them with her to Keith's each Saturday. She paid their admission, but her companion paid the nickel carfare.

RUTH RARELY TRAVELED more than a half-dozen miles from home—into the city for shopping or to a Reds game, to see a show, or spend a day at Coney Island. To get to the amusement park, she went into the city and boarded the sidewheeler excursion steamboat *Island Queen* for a leisurely seven-mile cruise upriver to Coney, passing her neighborhood on the way. After a long day at the park, the Island Queen carried the holiday travelers back downriver to Cincinnati, an onboard orchestra playing for those with enough energy left to dance.

The most important things in Ruth's life—church, school, family, and friends—were within blocks of her home. Her Grandfather Reeves was an elder in the church, and her family was involved in every church activity—a tremendous commitment of time. The Sixth Presbyterian Church held five different services on Sunday. Christmas, the New Year, Easter, and other holidays called for special services. There were church suppers throughout the year, and choir practice. Adding weddings, funerals, and committee meetings, one could easily devote a dozen weeks a year to the church. Ruth's involvement included accompanying choirs and playing solos. With her father and uncles, she formed a church quartet. The only way she could have put more into church would have been to take over the pulpit.

School took up twice as much time—more, if one were involved in extracurricular activities. Ruth happily walked or roller-skated the mile from home, no matter the weather. She would have preferred to ride a bicycle, but the family couldn't afford one.

Her grades were nearly perfect, but she sweated each test and report card as if her entire future depended on it. She took advantage of every opportunity to put her creative talents to work. She wrote and acted in school plays, played piano for school programs as often as she could, and every child in the school knew who she was.

SHE WAS BLESSED WITH BOUNDLESS energy, as if she drew vigor from all the attention her activities brought her. If nothing was happening, she made things happen. She volunteered to play small concerts at the Home for Incurables. Entering her teens during World War I she enlisted her friends to help with a Red Cross project supplying servicemen with cigarettes. She baked fudge for the Red Cross and sold it door-to-door, and made cloth bandages, as well as gift packages for the boys "over there."

From first through eighth grades, she had been a star in both academic and musical activities at Highland Public School, and to cap off her neighborhood school career, she wrote and starred in her first musical play. Not surprisingly, she graduated at the top of her class. Within the safe confines of her neighborhood, she had accomplished everything significant. Now it was time to move onto a new, larger stage: high school.

Ruth's freshman class would be the first to occupy Cincinnati's newly built

East High School. This impressive temple of public education sprawled over a twenty-seven-acre, park-like campus. In addition to the standard academic accommodations, it featured agricultural buildings and an industrial arts unit housing the school's own electrical power plant. Massive indoor and outdoor athletic complexes, the equal of the finest of their European counterparts, rose at the edge of campus.

The school's architecture—which included an arched entry bridge and bell tower housing a bell from a sunken riverboat—was impressive enough that photos and drawings of it were shown at exhibitions in London and Paris.

When Ruth crossed the symbolic bridge and stepped into East High for the first time in September of 1919, she entered a work in progress. Details like door handles and lockers were not yet installed, nor were most of the electric lights. There was no lab equipment, classroom doors were missing, and students with bugles—substituting for bells—signaled the beginning and end of class periods. (The year after Ruth Reeves graduated, the name of the school was changed to Withrow High School, in honor of a prominent Cincinnati medical doctor who had led the drive to build the school. The move to change the name began when a number of local businessmen suggested that "East High" might be connected, euphoniously, with New York's notorious East Side tenement slums.)

Ruth and her friends found it all hilarious. The faculty of ninety squared their collective shoulders, and picking their way past workmen and around materials piled in dim hallways and classrooms, set about the business of training young minds.

RUTH'S FIRST PRIORITY was to make sure she didn't miss out on anything musical. She studied violin and viola, and played in both junior and senior orchestras. There were several choruses, a glee club, and dancing classes that needed piano accompaniment, and she signed on, somehow finding the time to play for an evening adult dance class.

Incidental to all of this, her college preparatory program included two weekly music classes. In what time she had left, she turned her attention to traditional subjects—English, history, Latin, algebra, and science. She neither liked nor did well in science, and after the first year was able to drop it in favor of Spanish. (A personal conflict with the science teacher simplified the choice.)

The years immediately following the Great War were years of economic recovery in America. But in Europe and elsewhere they were years of reconstruction—cities, factories, shops, and the very infrastructure of a technological society were literally rising from rubble.

Multinational corporations with European interests, such as the Ford Motor Company and Reichhold Chemical, had men on the spot, supervising the rebuilding of destroyed factories, hiring new workforces, and attending to the thousands of details in recreating commercial empires.

For those with capital, in the right sorts of businesses, endless opportunity waited in the post-War ruins. Just as "damnyankee" businessmen flocked south to aid in and profit from the post-Civil War Reconstruction, so did a new generation of opportunists flock to Europe—financiers, traders, and others who could turn the needs of devastated nations into profit.

At the same time, the 1920s saw the release of a pent-up demand for European travel. For too many years, the scions of wealthy families had been denied their tours of Europe. Families accustomed to wintering (or summering) on the continent were ready to resume their vacations. And thousands of people wished to visit relatives not seen in a decade or more. The demand for European travel was particularly strong in Cincinnati, with its heavy German and Irish population, multinational corporations like P&G, and opportunistic investors.

The Provident Bank of Cincinnati was among the city's more accomplished organizations when it came to foreign transactions, money conversion, and related matters. In the course of its diverse dealings overseas, both before and after the world war, the bank had built up an impressive body of knowledge on conditions, travel, and accommodations in countries around the world. And its officers had an enviable list of commercial contacts in major foreign cities.

Accordingly, Provident Bank established a Travel Department, with the experienced manager of the bank's Foreign Department in charge. An assistant manager was needed to help set up and operate the travel agency, and Samuel Spencer Reeves was tapped for the job.

However lax he may have been in handling his own money, Samuel Reeves was a paragon when it came to handling the money of others. For more than twenty years he had done an exemplary job of dealing with the complex and ever-changing world of railroad shipping rates. He had worked his way up to freight expediter, his work brought him into contact with businesses of all kinds, and he was not unknown in the banking community.

That summer the Reeves family packed up and moved to a comfortable two-story house on Peabody Avenue in Madisonville, in a new development at the eastern edge of the city. Seven miles out from East High School, Madisonville was a pleasant community of tree-lined streets, with a compact business district and a nearby hospital. Samuel still brought surprise gifts home, but Ruth and Margaret no longer felt that they had to return all his little extravagances.

Ruth remained without a bicycle, but in the new neighborhood there were fewer places to go, and shops were within walking distance. Most trips were far enough to take the streetcar—to school, downtown on Saturdays to shop or take in a show, and Sundays for church in the old neighborhood.

Even with the heavy load at school, Ruth maintained her church activities. Sunday was the only day Ruth saw her whole family, and besides, church offered music. In the spring of 1921, the second half of Ruth's sophomore year, there was more music than usual. That was when her church helped sponsor one of evangelist Billy Sunday's famous "Sawdust Trail" campaigns.

Billy Sunday was the Billy Graham of the early 1900s, but more conservative—and energetic—than Graham. In the days before mass media and mega-auditoriums, the only way to reach large numbers of people was to go to them. Most evangelists were guest speakers in churches, or traveled with large, circus-size tents in which they preached their messages. Billy Sunday went for larger crowds. He persuaded churchmen in cities like Boston, Kansas City, Cincinnati, and Detroit to build huge temporary tabernacles, capable of holding 20,000 people or more. He would hold several services each day for a month in such a tabernacle, and when he moved on to his next crusade, the tabernacle was torn down and the lumber sold for salvage.

The Billy Sunday campaign traveled with a staff of nearly thirty musicians and crew members, plus advance men who were particularly good at lining up newspaper coverage of the meetings. Music was a key element in Sunday's evangelism, because Sunday knew that many people would come to evening meetings just for the music. Once they were there, he hoped to sway them with his powers of persuasion. There were so few other opportunities for entertainment that in most places a Billy Sunday campaign was almost as good as a traveling circus come to town.

The music was certainly an attraction for Ruth. Where else could she meet so many professional musicians? She got to know several of Sunday's orchestra, including Homer "Rody" Rodeheaver, Billy Sunday's "warm-up man" and musical director. Ruth was pleased, even flattered, that the musicians accepted her. She admired them not so much for their association with Sunday as for the fact that they were professionals who made their livelihood with music. Something of a celebrity in the commercial music world, Rodeheaver became one of Ruth's ardent fans, once her radio career took off.

"Radio career" was a concept that didn't even exist in 1921, let alone something to which Ruth Reeves might aspire. Like the majority of America's 105 million citizens, she knew little or nothing about radio, or the wireless, as it was sometimes called. There were only 60,000 radio receivers in the entire country, and finding something to tune in was a real challenge.

But a Cincinnati auto accessories manufacturer named Powel Crosley, Jr. was about to bring radios to the millions—and give them something to listen to. Even as that 1921 Billy Sunday revival was being conducted, Powel Crosley, Jr., with the help of two University of Cincinnati engineering students, was designing his first radio. When Ruth began her junior year at East High, Crosley was selling radios at the rate of 5,000 per month. As she finished her junior year, Crosley's station WLW went on the air, and people were buying 5,000 Crosley sets per day. At the time, these things meant nothing to Ruth, but before the decade was out they would mean everything.

RUTH'S SENIOR YEAR went much like the two before it: a flurry of classes, rehearsals, dances, lessons, church—and trying to keep an eye on Rose. Rose had grown into a slender, dark-haired beauty who lacked focus and, in truth, Ruth was too busy to monitor her sister's life, try as she might.

She had other worries. During the winter of 1922-'23, Ruth spent quite a bit of time serving detention for something completely out of character for her: she was frequently late for her first class. The reason had to do with her father. Late in 1922 Samuel Reeves came down with pneumonia and was off work for four months. Ruth had little experience with serious illness, and had certainly never seen her father so ill. Her maternal grandparents had died when she was too young to be touched by the events. Her Grandfather Reeves had passed away in 1919, but he was very elderly, and his death was expected.

Ruth worried until she convinced herself that he had something more serious than pneumonia, and that Dr. Prugh wasn't telling the family what it was. The obsession drove her to travel several miles by streetcar every morning from Peabody Avenue to her old neighborhood where she pumped the doctor for information. It was as if she felt responsible for making certain no mistakes were made, and that her father got the best possible care.

Ruth's conviction that her father was suffering from something fatal, perhaps the dreaded tuberculosis, could not be shaken. She was sure it wasn't pneumonia because a neighbor lady much older than her father had contracted pneumonia, yet she was up and around in just a few weeks.

Dr. Prugh assured her time and again that Samuel Reeves would recover. Exasperated, he finally told her that with all her rushing about and worrying he was more concerned about Ruth herself than her father.

Her father recovered, but Ruth convinced herself that the neighbor had recovered more quickly because she was treated by an osteopathic physician. For the rest of her life she was a cheerleader for osteopathy.

HER SENIOR-YEAR ACTIVITIES reached a crescendo as she was elected co-editor of the school yearbook, started a girls' club called the Kalidasa Klub (apparently named after the classic Indian poet and dramatist of that name), and launched plans for a school musical review. Naturally, she would write the script, direct, and play the musical accompaniment.

East High School's principal advised her that the school board would not permit such a show. So she made an appointment with the superintendent of schools and, with a persuasiveness honed by practice, convinced the superintendent to permit the show. It was all very presumptuous for an 18-year-old, but she had the talent to back herself up. The musical became an annual tradition that continued for over fifty years as "The Sounds of Withrow."

The variety show was a fitting finale to her high school career. In the 1923 East High yearbook, a page titled "Who's Which and Why" crowned her with several superlatives. In addition to being the "Girl who has done most for East," she was "Fastest Talker," "Most Musical," "Slangiest," "Wittiest," "Peppiest," and "Ablest Manager." Each of these described Ruth perfectly, though "Ablest Manager" may have also been a comment on her habit of trying to take charge of everything. It was also predicted that she would become a famous author and songwriter.

Bearing those titles, her diploma, and well-wishes from relatives and friends, she set her sights on college. Only one thing was missing: the great romance of her life. She had hoped he might appear during her high school years. At one point she even took an astronomy course, thinking evening classes could be romantic. But, save for the occasional shooting star, no sparks flew. She seemed to entirely miss the point that she just didn't have time for romance.

Her sentimental ties to East High were not diminished by that void, as these opening lines from a lengthy poem she wrote upon graduation demonstrate:

> *Night of graduation, came,*
> *From the brow of every Senior*
> *Gone was every trace of Sorrow,*
> *With a smile of joy and triumph,*
> *With a look of exultation,*
> *As for one, who, in a vision,*
> *Sees what is to be, and is not,*
> *So he stood and viewed the future.*

Just after graduation, in June of 1923, the Reeves family returned to the East End. Though Samuel Reeves had recovered, he was weakened and the long commute downtown to his job was too much for him. He missed quite a bit of work, and the lost income meant the cost of living in Madisonville was too high. So the family found a roomy two-story house at 332 Tusculum Avenue, three miles east of the rest of the Reeves family. It was a block from Eastern and a small but thriving business district.

The move inspired Ruth to do something uncharacteristic and impetuous. Throughout grade and high school, she had wished for a bicycle and her desire was so strong that she came up with a scheme to get one. She and her sister would conduct a sale from the front porch of their Madisonville house. They would get rid of things they felt were no longer needed, and at the same time lighten the moving load.

Surely their parents would approve. Still, the sisters prudently waited until both parents had gone before starting the sale. With any luck, the sale would be over before their mother even knew of it. They strung rope across the porch to display their merchandise. Pots and pans were the first items to go up, followed by old dresses. They posted For Sale signs, and with the help of a neighbor boy on a bicycle spreading the word, sold out their stock in almost no time. Encouraged by their success, the girls added some of their mother's old dresses and hats to their second-hand shop. Then they threw in her winter coat, which, Ruth explained, "we thought unbecoming on her."

They did well financially, but their parents weren't as thrilled as the girls had hoped. And Ruth did not buy a bicycle. "In all," she later explained, "the sale netted us $28.50—plus the worst scolding my mother and father ever administered to me. And—the worst blow of all—the $28.50 was appropriated by them to help pay the moving bill."

Once they were settled into the house on Tusculum Avenue, Ruth and Rose tromped up one street and down another, thoroughly exploring the area. They were especially interested in a former polo field called Turkey Bottoms. Bordered by the Little Miami and Ohio rivers, the flat, grassy plain was a growing aviation center, soon to be the area's major airfield and the site of two airplane factories. (Today it is known as Lunken Airport.)

Ruth was interested in more than airplanes. As she explained it, "We lived not too far from Lunken Airport, and many of the student pilots roomed near us. And so we became very interested in flying, that is to say, the pilots."

Another discovery interested her even more. He was 20-year-old John D. Lyons, III. Johnny lived a few doors north of Ruth on Tusculum Avenue, and his father owned a shoe store on Main Street in Cincinnati. Bored with school, Johnny had dropped out in 1918 after finishing the eighth grade, then went to work as a clerk in his father's store.

Tall and handsome, with a ready smile, curly dark hair, and a subtle sense of humor, young Johnny attracted Ruth from the moment they met. Like Ruth's father, he had an ability with numbers, which made him even more interesting.

The two dated frequently throughout the summer. They took long walks in nearby Alms Park and learned to play tennis. Many evenings they lounged at the soda fountain at Snyder's Drug Store at the corner of Tusculum and Eastern Avenue, and on sunny days when Johnny wasn't working and Ruth had no musical commitments, they went to the beach.

Ruth began to think about him cautiously, but seriously.

high hopes

She made good grades, but academics to Ruth were almost an afterthought.

That summer, Ruth easily passed the University of Cincinnati's entrance exams. Money wasn't a problem, at least not from her perspective. Samuel Reeves had returned to work and, like the fathers of everyone else she knew, had paid her tuition and bought her books. It was difficult for Ruth to imagine her father lacking in anything, certainly not money for her college education.

She went out with Johnny Lyons, but she didn't devote all of her free time to him. Ruth felt that his close friends, and even some of their own crowd, regarded her as "Johnny's girl." She wanted people to know and like her as Ruth Reeves, not as an extension of someone else, even though most young women of her era saw themselves as the extension of husband or boyfriend.

Although Ruth had much to think about on the eve of college, she made time for friends and had long talks about the future, school, boys, and the many other topics girlfriends share. Two of her best friends lived in the neighborhood, one next door and the other across the street. Church and home life filled the rest of the summer. She never did get a bicycle, though.

Through her neighborhood, church and school connections, Ruth knew several UC students before she ever set foot on the Clifton campus. Thus, she approached college with confidence, at least socially. If nothing else, she could easily gather enough friends for a lunchtime bridge game. Some elements of college life, however, remained question marks—sororities, for instance.

She needn't have been concerned. UC was waiting for her with open arms. "I was welcomed by six sororities," Ruth wrote in her memoirs. "My reputation for activities had preceded me." One girlfriend urged her to pledge Kappa Kappa Gamma. Her two neighborhood girlfriends wanted her for Theta Phi Alpha. In the end, she surprised everyone by pledging Delta Delta Delta along with two high school classmates.

Ruth was pleased to be a "Tri Delt," but as a new pledge she didn't like being under the control of older sisters in the sorority hierarchy. So she started her own club, the Checker Board Society, composed of three East High grads from each UC sorority. "We had great fun and a sense of camaraderie that was left over from high school days," she recalled. Initially, UC's dean of women didn't like the idea of Ruth's private club any more than the principal of East High liked her school musical idea. Ruth, however, was successful in lobbying the dean to have the Checker Board Society recognized on campus along with the university-sanctioned associations.

Academics were almost an afterthought. She made good grades, taking a general course load. And for her mother's benefit, she gave lip-service to becoming a teacher. Margaret Reeves wanted her daughter to go to college with a definite career goal, and regarded teaching as a proper vocation for a woman, but long-term planning was never high on Ruth's list of priorities. She engaged the present completely, attending classes and church,

> "In college, I was interested in boys, modern music, playing the piano, languages, boys, clothes, eradication of intolerance and class distinction, boys, tennis, and boys."—Ruth Lyons

participating in social events, and playing and writing music. She accepted an appointment as the humor editor of UC's yearbook, *The Cincinnatian*, and was sought out for her musical abilities, winning first prize in music on Honors Day with what she described as a "plaintive little song" titled "Great White Moon."

A student musical comedy troupe calling themselves the Fresh Painters asked Ruth to write the entire musical score for a play titled *Lemme Alone*. She accepted the assignment, although it felt like baking a cake for someone else to ice. Unlike her previous musicals, this one wasn't her personal showcase. Ruth shrugged off compliments on the score, saying she hadn't done her best because she wrote better when she composed both the lyrics and the music.

The student production ran for a week in a downtown theater and featured Libby Holman, a UC senior who would become one of Cincinnati's more notable exports. In the 1930s, Holman built a career as a notorious torch singer and turned one of Ruth's songs for *Lemme Alone*, "Bungalow Blues," into a hit. In later years, the press loosely credited Ruth with both the lyrics and the music, but she never protested.

Between classes and meetings, Ruth also wrote new songs for her Tri Delta sorority, as well as songs and skits for other organizations. Never one to shy away from the spotlight, she was always the person playing piano at fraternity and sorority parties. And she was dating new boys she met on campus—boys who were, as Ruth put it, "very attentive."

Johnny Lyons, who worked at his father's shoe store downtown, just wasn't as exciting as some of the fraternity boys, destined to become attorneys and doctors and corporate business leaders. Ruth had tennis dates, went out dancing, took in musicals, and enjoyed opera at the zoo. She always dressed well, because everyone on campus was well-dressed and it pleased her to look sharp. She had never been sloppy, but now she paid closer attention to fashion as well as appearance. Money was tight, but she and her younger sister Rose swapped items to expand their wardrobes. Ruth also got her hair cut short and let it hang straight, just down to her collar, with a casual part and bangs combed aside. It wasn't quite the chic "helmet" cut many women wore in the 1920s, but her hair looked more brilliantly blonde and accentuated her long cheeks and blue eyes.

Ruth's enthusiasm for college life knew no bounds until something happened that caused her to have second thoughts about sorority life. She described the incident as "my first encounter with snobbery, intolerance, and prejudice."

"While working on the music for the Fresh Painters," she related, "I met a very fine Jewish boy. He was a wonderful musician and very handsome. He invited me to a dance and I accepted gladly. Later, when talking with some of my older sorority sisters, I mentioned with whom I was going. You cannot imagine what a crisis they made of it! But I went anyway, and enjoyed the evening thoroughly."

The reaction to her new friend was not unusual for the times. Nevertheless, Ruth seems to have been caught off-guard by it. Nothing up to that point in her life had caused her to consider religious or ethnic minorities as people apart from the mainstream. She would resist prejudice the rest of her days, at times quite publicly.

She was equally surprised and hurt when her Tri Delta sisters gave the thumbs-down to a girl Ruth had proposed for membership in the sorority; they judged Ruth's candidate unacceptable because the girl's parents had divorced ten years earlier. They did give a thumbs-up to Ruth's proposal that the sorority donate excess money in its treasury to the Catherine Booth Home for Unwed Mothers—"For who can tell," she asked, "which one of us may someday need it?"

Backing off a bit from sorority activities, Ruth began tutoring a high school boy who was doing make-up work to earn credit for a class he had failed. With the extra money, she took in shows at the Schubert and Cox theaters, where stock players and touring troupes put on plays such as *Daughters of Music* and *Candide*.

Meanwhile, Samuel Reeves's health had become uncertain, and though no one at home talked about it, Ruth's father also was struggling financially.

When it came time to register for another fall term, she decided to find a job instead.

"School seemed so futile, so meaningless . . . I could not envision spending another year just having fun," she wrote.

RUTH HAD AN ULTERIOR MOTIVE as well. She wanted to get her teeth capped. Her front teeth had large, unsightly fillings of plain amalgam, and she'd been sensitive about them for several years. She hated the way they stood out when she smiled, and was sure they ruined her appearance. (Photos taken from her late high school years through 1925 show her with a closed-mouth smile.)

Whether her self-consciousness evolved gradually, or a remark she wasn't intended to hear made her look at herself more critically, no one can say. But during or just after her freshman year at UC, her smile became an intolerable embarrassment. Something had to be done about it.

It's unlikely that her father would have been willing (or able) to pay for an expensive cosmetic procedure along with college—particularly when money was so tight. But if Ruth earned her own money, she could spend it as she wished.

"After thinking about it," she said, "I realized that music was the one thing I knew best."

The largest music store in the city was Willis Music Company, owned by the famous Schirmer Music Publishing Company of New York. In those days, music stores sold not only instruments and supplies, but also phonographs, cylinders and discs of music to play on them. They also sold sheet music.

Sheet music was big business, and had been since the late 19th century. Nearly every household had some sort of musical instrument, often a piano, and many people bought sheet music to sing a cappella. Learning and listening to the latest songs was a popular pastime, and live music was much preferred over the tinny sounds that came out of phonograph horns.

Cincinnati was a major sheet music printing center. Thus, folks in the Queen City not only had access to an unusually large selection of sheet music, they also got the latest tunes before other Midwestern towns. Like other specialty shops, music stores employed sales clerks to serve customers. In addition to sales, clerks demonstrated what they sold by playing songs on the piano. And when not otherwise occupied, they arranged stock and kept the atmosphere lively with music.

Ruth was a good pianist, and she was persuasive. So one summer day she took the streetcar downtown to the Willis Music Company on Main Street. Though no "Help Wanted" sign was posted among the banners and sheet music covers in Willis's display windows, she confidently breezed in and asked the bow-tied manager for a job. He allowed Ruth to demonstrate her skills, but was reluctant to hire a young girl. However, one of the store's pianists, another woman, was leaving to get married, so Ruth was offered the job on a temporary basis. How long she remained would depend on her sales ability; her musical talents were obvious.

There was a predictable uproar when Ruth broke the news at home. Her parents tried talk her out of abandoning school, but she stood fast. Her sorority sisters were equally unhappy—so unhappy, according to Ruth, they persuaded the national president of Tri Delta to take a train to Cincinnati from Boston to offer her a full scholarship. But she wouldn't be swayed. Now that she had secured a job, she was committed to going through with the dental work.

In her memoirs, Ruth said working at Willis Music changed the course of her life. She met people she wouldn't have encountered outside the music store.

She was pleasantly surprised, for instance, to learn so many members of the Cincinnati Symphony liked popular as well as classical music. The symphony's concertmaster dropped by the store regularly to have her play the entire score of the hit musical, *No, No, Nannette*. As with Rodeheaver and the other Billy Sunday musicians, the fellowship of professionals was flattering and reassuring. They spoke the same language, and they respected her abilities.

Another of her professional acquaintances was Howard Hafford, a popular local tenor and recording artist much in demand for society parties. Hafford observed Ruth's playing and one day brought in a piece of sheet music she'd never seen. He gave it to her and asked her to "sight-read" it—in other words, play the song without looking over the notes first. The tune, titled "The Devil's Love Song," was written in the most difficult key possible. Ruth labored through most of the tricky number, assuming that Hafford was trying to trip her up for laughs. But the singer was so impressed by her work, he asked her to be his accompanist. Hafford always had work, and it paid well. Ruth could count on $25 to $50 for a few hours' work in posh private homes. Sometimes she would back up both Hafford and popular singer Irene Webber. (Another popular American singer, Jane Froman, would get her start on the very same local party and tea circuit a few years later.)

RUTH WORKED HER DAY JOB and the evening gigs well into 1925, then left Willis Music abruptly, telling people she was exhausted and ill because she had "tried to do too much." But she wasn't sick. She had accumulated enough money to fix her teeth. After a two-month hiatus, during which she saw only her dentist and her family, she re-surfaced with a broad smile and greater confidence in her appearance. She began spending more time with Johnny Lyons. There would be no more dates with fraternity boys because, as much as Ruth had enjoyed her freshman year at UC, she was not going back to school. The "real world" had turned out to be more interesting.

Strangely, though, Ruth did not return to music. Instead, she took a job with the Cincinnati Public Library, another "proper" position for a single woman in the 1920s. Clarence Stanley, a manager at the library, lived next door, which might have figured in her decision, though it's also likely there was pressure at home for her to "settle down" and start a reasonable career. Perhaps the library paid more than the music store.

Ruth had worked at the Cincinnati Public Library for a year—well into 1926—when she decided to sit for a competitive examination for a position as a school librarian trainee. She passed the exam—qualifying for one of the four positions out of a field of twenty-four candidates—and reported on a Monday morning for her first day of a year-long training course. Whatever enthusiasm she had for the job, however, evaporated almost immediately.

"That first morning proved to me that I did not want to be a librarian," she wrote. "I looked around at the class, at the frustrated appearance of the others, and I thought, 'This is not for me.' So at noon I went across the street to the bank to see my father and tell him that I had left the library."

Many fathers might have been upset with a daughter who quit a perfectly acceptable job. "He was puzzled," Ruth remembered, "and since he was shorthanded in the travel department, he asked if I would like to work there. I agreed most emphatically, for I would have every Saturday afternoon free to go to the Shubert Theater." Samuel Reeves was well-acquainted with Shubert manager Nelson Trowbridge, so Ruth had free tickets to the plush theater whenever she wanted them.

She went to work as a clerk-typist at Provident Bank. It was a pleasant job, working with her father and helping the bank's clients with their exotic travel plans. As she put together itineraries and booked conveyances by land and sea, she promised herself that one day she, too, would travel to far places and see the world.

But for the time being, Ruth continued living at home, dating Johnny, and playing the piano and organ at church. In addition to getting free theater tickets on Saturdays, she was able to take a day off now and then to see whatever production the local stock company, which included Victor Jory, was performing at the Cox Theater.

It was about this time, as Ruth noted in her memoirs, that she "became aware of radio." But she must have already known about the medium for several years. She had been an accompanist for contralto Ann James in the informal studios of Cincinnati station WMH in March of 1925, a month before the station changed its call letters to WKRC. Her family also owned a cheap crystal radio receiver. Perhaps she just didn't want to date herself by talking about her early work on WMH.

In any event, there was no way anyone in Cincinnati could not know about radio. In 1926, Crosley Radio Corporation was the world's largest radio manufacturer and the city's biggest employer. Crosley's station, WLW, had been broadcasting since 1922, and now three other local stations filled the airwaves with music. One of the broadcasters was owned by a major evening newspaper, and two more had co-promotional agreements with newspapers, so radio got lots of press coverage. Every weekend, there were highly publicized remote broadcasts from the ballrooms of the city's swankiest hotels and venues like Coney Island's Moonlight Gardens.

Ruth made her second appearance on radio in 1926, thanks to her tenor friend Howard Hafford. Since Ruth had left Willis Music, Hafford had been busy making a name for himself at WSAI. Among other responsibilities, he was the featured soloist on a Saturday night program sponsored by the *Cincinnati Post* called *Midnight Entertainers*.

Ruth was thrilled when Hafford invited her to WSAI's Norwood studio, which was much larger than the WMH studio and located in the administration building of the U.S. Playing Card Company (where its famous carillon bell tower played on the hour to advise listeners of the time). U.S. Playing Card founded the radio station in 1923 to promote the game of bridge and market the company's bridge card decks and the books it published. In Cincinnati, WSAI was second only to WLW in listenership.

Ruth was surprised to find velvet drapes hanging from the studio walls and ceiling, and heavy rugs on the floor—"to seal the room and eliminate outside noise," Hafford explained. The small crowd of people and the piano in the room gave it a party-like atmosphere. There was even a buffet and punch bowl. It was a party, indeed, to which everyone came early and stayed late.

Hanging out with a gang of musicians and singers in a radio studio was fairly close to heaven for Ruth. The air was a little stuffy, with so many people and no open window or door, but that could be tolerated. She was among people she admired, people who also respected her musical talents. And everyone was helpful. She was learning about broadcasting—from the inside.

Ruth didn't hesitate when asked to play. And as the pianist, she commanded most of the attention. A couple of the musicians showed her some musical tricks and fillips she could not have learned elsewhere. It wasn't long before she was accompanying another popular WSAI singer, Norine Gibbons. And there would be others.

Chapter three

Ruth kept the job in her father's office; the family relied on her financial help. She considered the broadcasts little more than a good time. She was not an employee, and the token payment she received was just a small bonus. The important thing was that she was getting to play regularly.

The only drawback was that her mother, Margaret—and the family's little crystal set—could never tune in the station while Ruth was on the air.

on the air

Like Ruth, Johnny Lyons had experienced some recent changes in his life. Johnny was a grade school dropout but bright enough to be bored with the simple routines of his job: greeting customers and fitting shoes, taking deliveries, and putting stock on display. The prospect of taking over the store at some point in the distant 1940s or 1950s didn't excite him, and he

The home of WSAI's transmitter, which was located in Mason, and in 1925 the first to broadcast Ruth.

was not inspired by the example of his father working his way up from lowly clerk to owner.

One uneventful day, John Lyons, Sr., stepped out of the store for awhile, leaving Johnny in charge. In walked a disheveled character, eyeing the stock. Johnny could see that this fellow needed shoes, but obviously had no money. Overwhelmed by the man's situation or simply in a strange mood, he gave the man a pair of shoes.

Johnny might as well have turned in his resignation; to a retailer, giving away stock was as bad as taking cash from the till. When John Lyons, Sr., learned what his son had done, he fired him. This may seem harsh, but who's to say if it was the first time Johnny had given away stock? If there had been a running conflict between them, Johnny's act of charity might have been either a calculated provocation or the last straw.

Whatever the reason for the abrupt split, Johnny didn't stay at loose ends for long. After a few days in search of work, he found a position as a clerk for the Pearl Insurance Company. Headquartered at the upscale address of 22 Garfield Place, Pearl Insurance was a full-line casualty and life insurance operation with offices throughout the Midwest.

Here was a job in which Johnny could take advantage of his alacrity with figures and his easy-going nature. He would get to meet lots of new people. The company was large enough to offer almost endless opportunities for advancement to a "wide-awake" young man. There would be no waiting twenty years to take over, and if he was good at his job—who knew?—the company might transfer him to someplace exotic, such as Detroit or Chicago.

Meanwhile, throughout the summer of 1926, Ruth and Johnny double-dated and played bridge with his friends from work. They rarely saw Ruth's friends. Most of them returned to school at UC. The couple took in plays, listened to hot jazz, and visited their usual haunts—Coney Island, the drugstore, Ault Park, and Lunken Field. At Lunken, Ruth went for rides with flight instructors, though she wasn't interested in learning to fly. She just enjoyed the experience, even when the pilot did rolls and other aerobatics. Later, she swore off flying for life after a pilot with whom she had flown had a heart attack, crashed, and died, supposedly while dropping flowers over his mother's grave in Indiana.

Fortunately, Ruth continued to earn a few dollars playing the piano at WSAI and private parties now and then. Money was still a problem at home. Even though Provident Bank had promoted Samuel Reeves to the position of director of the Foreign and Travel Department, he had not curbed his spending. He also continued to suffer frequent bouts of illness, which meant time off work. With finances steadily worsening, the family moved from their rented two-story Tusculum Avenue house to a more modest dwelling at 3614 Morris Place just around the corner.

"I was certain that radio was just a passing fancy."—Ruth Lyons

Ruth and Johnny wanted to get married, but more problems loomed on the horizon as the new year—1927—approached. Johnny Lyons was secure in his own job. His father, however, was experiencing sharp downturns in his business. Johnny, like Ruth, still lived at home and helped out his family financially. Ruth

knew that money problems could quickly ruin a marriage, and that divorce—
with its heavy overtones of guilt and failure—still carried a social stigma, even
in the "Roaring Twenties." So, for the time being, there would be no plans for a
wedding and no announcement of an engagement, no matter how much she
and Johnny wanted to get hitched.

"I WAS CERTAIN THAT RADIO was just a passing fancy," Ruth said in 1968,
looking back on her broadcasting career. She and many others had been wrong,
of course. Commercial radio changed American society, sparking the post-
war economic recovery as thousands of factory workers, engineers, inventors,
and creative people found work in broadcasting. The demands of the industry
brought numerous companies in other fields from the brink of ruin and back to
profitability.

Radio's ability to deliver important news—often within minutes, and from
coast to coast—changed forever the way people regarded the world and their
lives. Before, when Americans relied on the local newspaper and the postal
system for their news, there was no urgency to events. Everything was old news
by the time it got to most sections of the country. With radio, the news was
immediate. The listening audience could feel as if they were a part of history as it
was being made, and immediately understand its impact. The authoritative voices
of reporters and commentators grabbed the listener's attention and put him or
her there, on the spot.

People listened to eyewitness accounts, and as the events grew more
dramatic, the announcer's voice filled with excitement, or dread, or awe. More
details would come with the newspaper and later radio reports, but there was
nothing like being in on the action, right now. Crosley Radio Corporation's slogan
was, "You're There with a Crosley!"

Radio advertising changed marketing overnight. It turned unknown brands
into household names (and, not incidentally, brought us the term "household
name"). As advertising grew more sophisticated, marketers positioned their
products by the use of famous people, places, and institutions, convincing radio
listeners that what they were selling held the keys to happiness and fulfillment.
They collected demographic information and, for the first time, targeted ads at
unsuspecting populations. It didn't take long before people were ready to believe
anything they heard on the radio. The U.S. Department of Commerce soon had

to establish the Federal Radio Commission (it would later become the Federal Communications Commission) to police this potent new medium.

Radio also revolutionized entertainment. Concerts and plays that had once been isolated events were now shared by millions. Unknown performers who would have spent years touring anonymously on the vaudeville circuit, desperately hoping to "catch on," became superstars overnight. New forms of entertainment came to America via the airwaves, most notably the soap opera, pioneered in Ruth's hometown of Cincinnati. There were learned discussions and lectures on fine art and issues of the day, although most folks preferred singing and dance music, plays, and comedy programs—and maybe the occasional guitar or swimming lesson.

Radio also gave families a reason to be together, other than to attend a church service, funeral, wedding, or holiday celebration. Often three generations gathered around the home receiver, as people had gathered around musicians or storytellers in times long before. They hummed along with popular tunes, followed their favorite comedy series or soap opera, and shushed one another as they listened with rapt attention to far-away disasters and triumphs.

Taken together—news, entertainment, advertising—radio programming helped create something America had never had: a national culture. For the first time, a country 3,000 miles wide could share customs, traditions, fashions and fads. People living in Colorado and California and South Carolina listened to dance music from New York, Cincinnati, and Chicago. The North dug the humor of the South. The West got a dose of the drama from the East, and vice-versa.

The acceptance and sharing of culture was possible, in part, because there was no face on the radio. Music, opinion, news, drama, comedy—everything was judged on its own merits. Even stereotypes of the day were recognized as part of radio's "big picture." People learned that most other folks liked what *they* liked—sharing their ambitions, fears, and strengths.

Before commercial radio, there had never been a culture unique to America, simply because the country was too big for trends, fashions, music, prejudices, and new ideas to travel quickly. With radio, culture spread across the continent in an instant.

There had never been anything like it. Radio exerted a greater influence on society and the individual than anything before or since. Not even the Internet caused such dramatic changes as radio. The Internet had familiar technological precedents from which it was derived: telephone, radio, television, computers, FAX, which it then unified into one compelling form. But radio had no precedent.

Ruth Reeves and her friends didn't think of the medium in those terms, of course. To them, the radio receiver was a wonderful, sometimes frustrating, gadget that delivered voices and music if you could tune it properly. Ruth was getting behind-the-scenes experience in the studio, but most people had little idea how radio worked or why. Nor did they care. Like the electric light or an automobile engine, the radio set in the parlor did what it was supposed to do.

Ruth knew when the red light went on in the studio, she was on the air. Nevertheless, she found it difficult to imagine an audience out there listening to her, such was the mystery of this new and powerful medium. Watching an announcer, she sometimes wondered if he felt he was speaking into a vacuum, talking to people who weren't there.

HOWARD HAFFORD WAS NEVER ONE to miss an opportunity. He had been singing on WSAI radio since 1924, while managing a minor recording career and entertaining at society functions and private parties. The wiry tenor with his stylishly slicked-back hair fit in wherever he went, and his singing made him that much more welcome.

In 1928, Crosley Broadcasting Corporation, the owner of WLW, bought WSAI and promptly moved the station from U.S. Playing Card in Norwood across town to another plant near the Camp Washington district. Crosley had recently completed an immense factory and office building there, the entire top floor of which was taken up by twin broadcast studios and transmitter equipment. Two antenna masts topped off the roof. Located on Arlington Avenue in the city's bustling northwest industrial district, Crosley Broadcasting counted among its neighbors Procter & Gamble's world headquarters and production facilities.

Personnel changes were in the works as well. Hafford found himself swimming in a bigger pond, surrounded by bigger fish. He sensed that his position was not as secure under Crosley management as it had been with U.S. Playing Card, and he was right. According to the employee grapevine, most WSAI people would be replaced by WLW staffers.

When Hafford heard that Cincinnati station WKRC had a new owner (a radio manufacturing company like Crosley), he decided to explore opportunities there. Clarence Ogden, president of the Kodel Radio Company, hired Hafford as WKRC's program director.

Ironically, WKRC had originally gone on the air in 1919 as WMH. Owned and operated by the Precision Instrument Company, the station broadcast live and recorded music to promote the sales of Precision radios. (Like other early manufacturers, Precision knew that you had to give customers a reason to buy radio receivers.)

Crosley had originally owned the Precision Equipment Company, purchasing the manufacturer in 1922 not so much to eliminate a competitor as to secure the rights to a very important and limited radio patent for which only seventeen manufacturers, including Precision, had a license. Not being able to use the technology represented by the patent would mean drastically reduced product performance—and sales. The patent's owner, RCA, refused to issue new licenses.

Because the Precision Equipment Company operated station WMH, Crosley Broadcasting found itself owning two stations. Powel Crosley could see no advantage in operating both stations at the time, so he relinquished the WMH license to the U.S. Department of Commerce.

A COUPLE OF YEARS LATER a new Cincinnati broadcaster, the Ainsworth Company, was assigned the call letters WMH. This new WMH was the station whose airwaves were first graced by Ruth Reeves early in 1925. Ainsworth sold the station to the Kodel Radio Company, and the latter changed the call letters to an acronym of its name: WKRC. Hence, the station that Crosley once owned, now became WLW's competitor.

WKRC had moved right after the sale to Kodel Radio, and the station's staff, past and present, had been less than tidy. The offices, studio—even the closets— were one big mess when Hafford took over as program director. It would take a lot of dedicated work to get things organized, and he knew just the well-organized, hard worker for the job: Ruth Reeves.

Hafford contacted Ruth and persuaded her to come to work for him at WKRC as assistant music director at $25 per week. She would also have some duties as a musician. Ruth was thrilled. She'd never made that much money, except when she played accompaniment at society parties, but that wasn't regular work anymore.

Her parents were thrilled as well. When Ruth told Johnny about it, a thought passed between them, something they dared not speak: this took them a step closer to marriage.

WKRC's new studios were located in the basement of the Hotel Alms in Walnut Hills, a couple of miles east of the University of Cincinnati. The Alms was a residential hotel and a Cincinnati landmark, even moreso with twin radio antenna towers rising from the roof of the granite and brick edifice. Newspapers as far away as Oklahoma carried the news when WKRC went on the air in March, 1926.

The original hotel was built in 1891 by Frederick Alms, who had founded the Alms & Doepke department store downtown, with William Doepke. It was rebuilt and expanded in the art deco style in 1925 at a cost of $5 million. WKRC took up the basement of the north wing, directly beneath the hotel's famous Italian Grill. Like most large hotels, the Alms had a ballroom, from which WKRC broadcast its "remotes" on the weekends. It even had its own dance band, Murray Horton's Hotel Alms orchestra.

Ruth spent the first few months sorting out the thousands of pages of sheet music and stacks of records the station had accumulated. WKRC was one of ten CBS affiliates, and had apparently let its music collections languish after signing on with the network, which provided eighty-five percent of the station's programming. Nobody had thrown out anything.

The storage situation was almost impossible. Children assigned to scatter everything and mix it all into random piles couldn't have made a more disorderly mess. As Ruth herself described it, "The first day I entered the doors of the WKRC studios, I nearly turned around and walked out. The music library that I was supposed to organize comprised stacks of music in every corner of the two studios. There was one large cupboard that was to be the library when finished. Across the hall, records were piled sky-high. To find a particular piece of music or a certain record was almost impossible. I was given a desk just inside the door, from which I operated, and I began to try to bring order out of complete chaos."

A more pleasant aspect of Ruth's job was playing piano and organ. She topped off each network program with some organ music. Programming between network shows featured local singers, and Ruth played backup for several of them.

She also pitched in to handle the telephone switchboard when needed, and generally keep the studio clean. She or the switchboard operator probably made the coffee, too. In those days, no one would have thought of anyone but "the girls" handling these domestic jobs.

The staff was small and, as Ruth would learn, often rowdy. Sometimes there was little for her to do, other than wait for a network program to end and then play the piano or organ for a few minutes. As an announcer delivered the station ID and local commercials, Ruth returned to sorting music. Early mornings were the most enjoyable, when she kicked back with the rest of the crew to listen to a new CBS disk jockey out of Washington, D.C. named Arthur Godfrey. After Godfrey came the news. Then a woman announcer read a script intended to be a female take on the news. The program was called *A Woman's Hour*.

FROM THE BEGINNING, Ruth waited for the chance to create her own show on WKRC. Just playing a few bars of anonymous music at the close of a network program wasn't enough. As an acquaintance later said, "Even then it was obvious that she knew exactly what she wanted and was willing to knock herself out to get it."

She thought *A Woman's Hour* would have been a good slot for her. But since it was taken, perhaps her musical talents could be featured. She pestered Howard Hafford almost daily, and after a few weeks he persuaded a local bakery, Rubel, to sponsor a fifteen-minute program of Ruth's piano music one evening a week.

The job would have been ideal, had it not been for several of the staff—announcers, singers, and musicians—who were prone to getting drunk. And the station manager, Eugene Mittendorf, was right there with them. Sometimes they gathered in Mittendorf's office to drink, or slipped away to the speakeasy across the street on an "errand" taking anywhere from two hours to the rest of the evening.

Furious, Ruth managed to cover for her co-workers by playing piano or organ solos. This was in addition to her show, and she wasn't getting any extra pay. In return, they pulled a variety of practical jokes on her, trying get her to start laughing in the middle of a program—a popular pastime for the staff at all radio stations. They never succeeded. They also poked fun at her WCTU beliefs, on many days covering her desk with their empty whiskey bottles.

One morning in May, 1929, the woman whose job it was to read *A Woman's Hour* called in sick. Eugene Mittendorf came to Ruth in a panic and handed her a few pages of script. "Since I was the only woman around besides the switchboard operator," she recalled, "I was told to go into the small studio and read the script."

Ruth silently read the script over and over as the clock on the wall slowly counted down the minutes until she would have to go on the air. The first few lines were a commercial message. The rest was boring. Ruth rebelled at the thought of delivering such frothy, empty statements.

She entered the studio and sat at the desk in front of a microphone. Across the desk, facing another microphone, the station announcer waited. The engineer watched through a window from the control room.

When the engineer gave the cue to begin, the announcer read the brief lead-in to the program. Without hesitation or self-consciousness, Ruth read the commercial, then a few minutes of the script. "But the content of the so-called fascinating discourse was far too saccharine and trite to make me speak with any credence," she recalled later. "So I suddenly started to converse with the stricken announcer across the table from me.

"I rattled on about anything and everything that came into my mind. The script was forgotten and I felt as though I were talking to people out there in radio land, who were interested in as many things as I was." She later confided that she abandoned the script because she thought she would be doing the show for just the one morning, so what she said wouldn't matter.

The announcer and the engineer were thunderstruck. Nobody spoke on the air without a script! They sat and stared as she talked all the way through to the end of the program, no doubt thinking about how quickly she was going to get the ax when it ended.

RUTH STOOD UP as the announcer gave the station ID, staring straight ahead. The engineer was bent over the board and wouldn't look at her.

What was I thinking? she asked herself.

The red light went out as the network feed came on and she opened the door and stepped into the hallway. She almost ran into the switchboard operator. "Miss Reeves, the boss wants to see you in his office!"

"Yes," Ruth muttered. "I suppose he does."

She walked the few steps up the hall to Eugene Mittendorf's office. The door was open, so she walked in.

"Yes, sir?" she said, standing before his desk, tensed against the storm of anger that she knew was coming.

"Miss Reeves," said Mittendorf, smiling and enjoying the suspense, "I just received a telephone call from the sponsor. He wants you to do the program every day, starting tomorrow!"

Ruth couldn't have been more surprised if he'd handed her the keys to the station. Her own show? A Ruth Reeves . . . concert? No, just Ruth Reeves, speaking her mind and sharing her thoughts and feelings with all the other women in the city. What could be better?

Ruth left the studio that evening walking on air. She returned to earth the next morning when the woman she'd replaced came in to clean out her personal belongings. There was a lot of slamming of desk drawers, muttering and glaring. Ruth felt bad for the woman, but there was nothing she could do about the situation—and she didn't know what she would do if she could have changed things.

Her parents were ecstatic and proud. Ruth's job came with a raise, which was a small portion of what the sponsor was paying the station, but it meant she could place a value on her work.

Johnny was happy for her, too. But behind his congratulations lurked just a hint of anxiety that Ruth might be going places he couldn't.

hard times

1929. A frenzied era was surging toward a stunning end, trailing a wake of personages and events that threatened to swamp history. *Lindbergh flying the Atlantic . . . William Jennings Bryan and Clarence Darrow arguing evolution and creation in a Tennessee courtroom . . . Gertrude Ederle swimming the English Channel . . . Babe Ruth setting a home run record for the ages . . . Bolsheviks and bomb scares . . . Scott and Zelda . . . Clara Bow, the "It Girl" . . . Al Capone . . . Barnstormers . . . Flappers . . . Jazz . . . Radio . . .* Everything that symbolized the endless potential and white-hot excitement of the Roaring Twenties was about to plunge into the Arctic depths of The Great Depression. A churn in the stock market earlier in the summer had a ripple effect, but the waves of warning were ignored as mere swells in the tides of finance. Few dared imagine anything worse.

Dapper Duane Snodgrass was Ruth's best friend at WKRC, and an accomplished musician, too.

In Cincinnati, October was much like any other October. Most days were cool and crisp, but the locals knew that the weather in the Ohio River Valley could take a summer-like turn at any time and without warning. The mild aberrations were simply "Cincinnati weather," and it was ironic, then, that Black Friday came during what was normally a period of gentle, persistent change. No one was prepared for the tsunami of October 29th, when the stock market crash plunged the nation into dark years of inescapable despair.

The Crash rocked the Reeves family, but with Ruth's help, they managed to stay afloat. She continued hosting *A Woman's Hour*, bringing in extra income. Her father kept his job with Provident Travel, though business was minimal; both travel and foreign commerce dropped drastically. Any bonuses he might normally have received, vanished. Samuel Reeves also lost money in the stock market—money that could have been set aside for retirement or a medical emergency. He was a bright man, but had accumulated little. Like so many others, Samuel speculated in stocks, believing the market would be his material salvation. In fact, he had come out ahead on trades several times, and each time he put a little more money into stocks. When the market crashed, he was left holding the bag—an empty one.

The Lyons family, on the other hand, was caught in a tempest. Johnny was working at Pearl Insurance and still living at home; he'd been fired by his father, but not evicted. His parents, too, needed all the financial help he could give them. John Lyons, Sr., clung to hope, stubbornly unlocking his shop each morning. But business

"I assume that my listeners are at least as intelligent as I am and have as many interests as I have, so I talk to them as equals."

slumped as the economy worsened. It had once been a truism that the well-dressed applicant stood a better chance of getting the job, but there were no longer any jobs to get. So who needed new shoes? Got holes in your soles? Take 'em to the repair shop. Learn to make do.

For Johnny Lyons and Ruth Reeves, whose families now depended upon them, the prospect of marriage grew dim.

EARLY IN OCTOBER, Kodel Radio put WKRC up for sale. At the same time, the company ordered a state-of-the-art, 5,000-watt transmitter from Western Electric at a cost of $35,000. WKRC's existing transmitter put out 1,000 watts of power, enough to cover Cincinnati and reach into several counties in Kentucky and Indiana. But the station's major competitor, WSAI, broadcast at 5,000 watts. With the resources of Crosley Broadcasting now behind it, WSAI was steadily eroding WKRC's bottom line. The transmitter was a hedge. It made WKRC a more attractive property, and until the station was sold it would be in a more competitive position in the local market.

Less than two weeks before the stock market crashed, Kodel found a pair of buyers for its Cincinnati station: a Chicago investor named J.S. Boyd and CBS employee Sam Pickard. Suspicions of irregularities in the sale, however, were voiced by several newspapers. Pickard, they pointed out, was formerly a member of the Federal Radio Commission (FRC) and had granted a number of concessions to WKRC, including assigning it to a clear channel—meaning that no other station in the country would broadcast on the same frequency. Boyd was an attorney who had frequently handled radio cases before the FRC when Pickard served on the Commission. The deal smacked of conflict of interest, among other things, but the sale went through anyway.

The new owners planned no changes in the station's operation. WKRC's new transmitter would be on the air by year's end, at which point the station's future would be driven by programming, not power. Now that all other things were literally equal, Ruth Reeves felt certain WKRC would prevail.

Radio signals carry much farther at night because of the "skywave" phenomenon, which causes radio waves to bounce off the ionosphere and travel many miles beyond their normal range. But for the present, WKRC was licensed to broadcast at 5,000 watts only during the daytime, which was just fine with Ruth. It meant that her show would reach a much larger audience—including people who formerly heard nothing at 550, WKRC's location on the AM dial (because numbers on radio dials ran left to right, beginning with 550, the station adopted the slogan, "First on your dial").

Meanwhile, for some of the more boisterous men at WKRC, it was goofing off as usual. Almost daily, the same crew took advantage of Ruth's sense of duty by leaving her stuck with their jobs for part of the afternoon while they went out to have a few drinks. She recalled one sunny afternoon when several of them stepped out to a brand-new miniature golf course a few blocks from the studio, near the UC campus, and she was left for hours to run the board, play records, make announcements, and do station breaks. She complained to the manager, who promised to give them a talking-to, but it was an empty promise. He'd been out with the rest of "the boys."

Usually an errant staff member strayed no farther than the nearest speakeasy—like one singer whose identity Ruth wouldn't divulge who spent every afternoon drinking, coming in only when his program was scheduled. "Sometimes," she remembered, "I would have to start a program while the vocalist was sent for at the bar across the street." But that wasn't always the best idea. "One time I played an entire half hour, for upon his arrival, he [the vocalist] opened his mouth and fell down, dead drunk, carrying the microphone with him."

Ruth threatened to walk out on a regular basis. "Every Saturday afternoon I tightly belted my white trench coat, packed my makeup, and proceeded to the manager's office to quit," she said. But she didn't really want to leave, and so accepted his false assurances that things would change. "He always pretended that next week would be different and that the horseplay would stop. So I went on for three years."

The rampant unprofessionalism was exacerbated by Eugene Mittendorf's mismanagement. A broadcast veteran who called the first full Reds game on WLW in 1924, Mittendorf spent almost as much time in speakeasies as his staff did. Ruth found the various inattentions of management to her advantage, however, making it easier for her to do things her own way. Any one of them could have stepped in and told her to do something differently "because women know nothing about these things." Ruth, though, knew plenty about the practical side of radio, having run things in the absence of men supposedly in charge.

Not all of the men were hopeless drunks. Ruth's best friend at WKRC, a young man named Duane Snodgrass, was an accomplished piano player, aspiring actor and classmate of Tyrone Power, Jr., at Cincinnati's famous Schuster-Martin Dramatic School. Born the same year as Power (1914), Snodgrass was hired as an announcer by WKRC less than a year after Ruth came on board. The two of them got along perfectly, musically as well as personally. Snodgrass, smooth-cheeked with a dapper mustache and long eyelashes, often joined Ruth in a program of "double piano"—a gimmick that had both of them playing the same tune, an octave apart. Originally, Ruth and the wife of one of the sponsors had performed the program, but WKRC's pranksters had proven to be too much for the other woman. When she and Ruth played "The Stars and Stripes Forever," three crew members marched back and forth in the studio dressed like the Spirit of '76.

"Their marching," recalled Ruth, "had set up such a flurry that the sponsor's wife's music blew away, and in her effort to retrieve it, all the hairpins from the bun of hair on her neck fell out. I had to play solo throughout the rest of the program." As for the sponsor's wife, "she dissolved into near hysterics and then and there renounced her musical career."

There seemed no end to the station shenanigans. On another occasion, the crew dragged a coffin (used as a stage prop) through the studio while Ruth played accompaniment for a noted basso profundo. As the singer performed "The Volga Boatman," two of the crew clowns opened the door to the studio and walked in, pulling at ropes slung over their shoulders. At the end of the ropes was the coffin with a third merrymaker inside, wearing a frilly baby's cap to top off the stunt. Ruth didn't lose her composure but the singer did. Red-faced, veins popping, he tried to continue but gave up in anger. The mischief makers had a similar effect on a trumpet or trombone soloist by standing in front of him, sucking lemon halves. The microphones would have to be turned off and the listeners told that the lengthy interruption of a program was due to static or "unknown interference."

Duane Snodgrass didn't let the pranks bother him. In fact, Ruth's friend and piano partner was quite capable of carrying on his own horseplay, such as playing with his back to the piano and striking the final note of each arpeggio with his heel. Unlike the others, he never picked on Ruth, but he liked to challenge her in a game they called "Perfect Pitch." Both of them had absolute or perfect pitch, so they enjoyed trying to "name that chord."

As Ruth described their musical fun, "Duane would rush madly into the studio and hit a chord, which was most difficult to identify, on the piano. Then I had to rush in and play the same chord in the same key and with all the diminished and augmented notes in their right places. Then it would be my turn to try to stump him."

Through Snodgrass, who left WKRC in 1937 for a job as an actor on WLW, Ruth became friends with Tyrone Power, Jr. Born in Cincinnati, Power had lived in California during the early years of his life with his parents, and appeared on stage from the age of seven. He and his mother, Patia, and younger sister moved back to the Queen City a couple of years after his mother and father divorced in 1920. Patia Power supported her children as a voice and drama coach at the Schuster-Martin Dramatic School. She also coached her son in acting.

When Power graduated from Cincinnati's Purcell High School in 1932, he hoped to become a stage and screen star like his late father, Tyrone Power, Sr., and persuaded Ruth to join him and Cincinnati florist Lee Wilson on a road trip to Hollywood. Ruth noted in an interview that the two-week spring trip to the West Coast and back was "a wonderful time," though she missed Power on her return to Cincinnati. He would be a guest on her WLW show, *The 50-50 Club*, several times before his premature death of a heart attack in 1959, at age 44. Lee Wilson, the florist, whose brother, L.B., was the founder of Cincinnati station WCKY, became one of her closest confidantes.

Aware that a radio show with one person talking could have only so much appeal, Ruth began inviting guests to her WKRC programs. She spoke with college professors, attorneys, professional and collegiate athletes and coaches, authors, politicians, and experts on anything. Local singers and musicians (as long as they weren't under contract to a competing station) were popular guests. This group included members of the Cincinnati Summer Opera company, among whose ranks were several internationally famous stars.

Whenever noteworthy people came through Cincinnati, Ruth tried to book them for her show. Actors and singers were easy to bring in, thanks to her now extensive professional grapevine. When a Jimmy Durante or a famous bandleader like Paul Whiteman was in town for a performance, they stopped by WKRC to chat with Ruth on the air. Guests as diverse as Laurel and Hardy, the governor of Hawaii, and ambassadors from India, China, and Germany also visited with the popular host of *A Woman's Hour*.

WKRC was sold again in 1930, less than a year after Boyd and Pickard bought it. The new buyer was a corporation named WKRC, Inc. The owner of WKRC, Inc. was the Columbia Broadcasting System, but CBS's ownership wasn't publicized because there was a growing movement in the radio business against networks owning stations.

CBS starting cleaning house right away, replacing Eugene Mittendorf with Timothy Goodman. Several other staffers were let go over the next few months. Operations were tightened up and the network announced plans to remodel the studios and offices.

RUTH ENJOYED THE KIND OF FAME afforded by radio. It wasn't like being a stage or cinema star. Strangers didn't bother her at Shillito's or Alms & Doepke or the corner grocery. If she was stopped in a shop or on the sidewalk, it was most often by someone she knew, although she was gratified when people recognized her. She was the station's only woman announcer, so anyone who listened to WKRC knew her voice well. (She sounded a bit like Gracie Allen.)

She normally arrived for work before eight o'clock in the morning. The early-morning announcer and *Sunrise Worship* speaker were there to greet her, along with Chief Engineer John Church and the station's other organist, Gladys Catron. Various singers and other staff members filed in throughout the morning. WKRC carried CBS network programming for most of the morning until 10:15, when it was time for *A Woman's Hour*.

After Ruth's half-hour show, the station aired a mix of network and local programming until 2 p.m. Then it was either the Army Band in concert from the network feed, or Ruth dispensing hints to housewives for forty-five minutes.

At 3:15, Ruth gave a one-hour piano concert, billed in the radio program guides simply as "Ruth Reeves." Half an hour after the concert, at 5:45, either Ruth or Gladys Catron played for twenty minutes. (Some mornings Ruth sat in for Catron, too.) On alternating days, Ruth played accompaniment for Howard Hafford from 4:15 until 5:45. She also handled announcing chores as needed and, throughout the day, slipped into the studio at the top and bottom of the hour for a few bars of musical fill.

Two nights a week, Ruth hosted *The Rubel Hour*. What began as a fifteen-minute program of piano music one evening a week, had become an hour-long program on Tuesdays and Thursdays, starting at 7:15 p.m. Always a newspaper advertiser, Rubel's bakery saw the sales of its products—especially Rubel's Rye Bread—soar with radio advertising. Its newspaper ads promoted *The Rubel Hour*, and the company—itself a Cincinnati tradition of fifty years' standing—would have no one but Ruth host the program.

These were the longest days of the week for Ruth—at least thirteen hours. They also could be the most trying. Some of her co-workers saved their more outrageous practical jokes for the evenings because fewer people were in the offices. It got so bad, Ruth routinely locked the door to the piano studio early in the evening. But the jokesters found a key or picked the lock, and in one memorable practical joke, one of them hid under the piano and waited for Ruth. When she began the show, he grabbed her ankles and didn't let go until the end of the program. Ruth ignored him and played the entire hour, much to the amusement of the board operator and others in the control booth.

Now and then, CBS programming replaced one of her shows, giving her a brief break. But just as often, she filled in for a CBS show when there were technical difficulties. Schedule changes also were dictated by WKRC's program director and by the programming budget. Specific schedules varied, but Ruth found herself in the studio at least ten hours a day, plus Saturday mornings. When she wasn't on the air, she was in her tiny office, researching and planning programs. As time permitted, she helped with cleaning, sorting and filing, and other jobs. The entire day, she had to be ready to play piano or organ, literally on a moment's notice.

Multi-tasking was the usual lot of radio talent, except for the big stars. Announcers, musicians, singers, actors, and writers—all filled a variety of roles so that the audience would think the station had a larger talent pool (it was even suspected that WKRC's second organist, Gladys Catron, was merely another stage name for Ruth Reeves). At WLW, even top acts like Fats Waller and the Mills Brothers were forced to do extra shows, both as themselves and under pseudonyms. Singer Eddie Albert was sometimes pressed into service as an actor.

Ruth's schedule limited her time with the family and Johnny. She was gone two nights a week, doing *The Rubel Hour*. The other three nights often found her too tired to do anything more than go home and put her feet up—unless Johnny could persuade her to go for a walk to Snyder's, a couple of blocks away. What shopping Ruth had to do, for work and herself, she handled on Saturday afternoons. Occasionally she spent Saturday afternoon or evening with Johnny, but she had to carve out time for her parents and her sister Rose, too.

The weekend was the only time she got to see her family. Sundays began with Ruth and Johnny attending Sunday school at his family's church, the Columbia Methodist-Episcopalian Church on Eastern Avenue. Afterwards, they went to services at the Presbyterian Church, where they usually participated in the afternoon and evening activities, with Ruth still committed to singing and playing piano with her father and uncles.

She had no qualms about attending different churches, nor even—as the future would have it—shifting her allegiance to a new faith. She had always attended church, but was not a fervent worshiper like her grandmother Reeves. Having grown up in a time when many Protestant churches—especially those in cities—shifted from fundamentalism to a kind of modernism that focused more on service and brotherhood than on doctrine, Ruth, like her mother, was more spiritual than religious.

When the station hired an assistant, Bernice Foley, to schedule guests for *A Woman's Hour* and lighten Ruth's heavy workload, she just took on other jobs. In November, 1931, for example, H.V. Kaltenborn, a celebrated CBS network news commentator, visited Cincinnati and ended up in the hospital for emergency surgery. Kaltenborn was such a dedicated radio man that he insisted on doing his nightly news program from his hospital bed as he recovered. So, every evening for more than a week, Ruth produced the remote from the hospital, beginning at 7:30.

When WKRC began supplying CBS with Saturday afternoon orchestra concerts from the Cincinnati Conservatory of Music, Ruth was there, too. She produced each broadcast and put out fires during the week, such as a soloist coming down with the flu. (She continued producing the Saturday morning concerts of the Cincinnati Symphony.) What drove her to assume so much responsibility? Clearly, she enjoyed the rewards of the creative process. Since childhood, she had seized any opportunity to perform, seeming to draw even more energy from a show or a job than the extraordinary time and effort she put into it. Radio allowed Ruth to channel her high level of energy into her music and her conversation with the audience.

No matter what else she was doing, though, *A Woman's Hour* was her showcase. She enjoyed playing piano and organ, but the talk show let her communicate directly with an audience—and get things off her chest. A steady stream of telephone calls, letters, and cards attested to Ruth's popularity. In fact, *A Woman's Hour* was more popular than similar shows on other Cincinnati stations. The only program that came close to approaching Ruth's ratings was WLW's *Crosley Woman's Hour and Musicale*, hosted by Marsha Wheeler. It aired in the same time slot as *A Woman's Hour* but even though WLW had ten times the power of WKRC, Ruth still had consistently higher numbers than Marsha Wheeler.

The difference between the two programs was a matter of conventional versus new wave, and new wave won. Wheeler's show focused on Sunday dinner menus, household hints, poetry, and children, while Ruth didn't limit herself to these so-called women's topics. She discussed subjects that women supposedly weren't interested in—like the Cincinnati Reds. (She had been a Reds fan since childhood, following the scores and riding the streetcar to games at Redlands Field as often as she could.)

Ruth conducted *A Woman's Hour* in an almost stream-of-consciousness fashion, often changing subjects abruptly but careful never to leave her audience in the lurch. People who listened to her on the radio in those days remember that she spoke without hesitation, in carefully constructed sentences. Every day she had an agenda. Sometimes she made notes, but she didn't follow a list any closer than she followed a script, preferring to speak extemporaneously, getting to important items in the natural flow of conversation. After greeting her listeners, she usually led off with the first thought that came into her head. It might be about a specific news item or someone in politics (she was Republican, without flaunting it), or it could just as easily be a more general topic, such as public rudeness or careless drivers, or a hot-button issue such as racial prejudice.

Although Ruth could pontificate on subjects, she never talked down to her listeners. "I assume that my listeners are at least as intelligent as I am," she told reporters, "and have as many interests as I have, so I talk to them as equals."

Most of her audience related to her personal life, of which even the smallest detail was grist for the mill. She could do a lengthy monologue, for instance, on her little aches and pains. "Oh, my back!" or "Oh, my neck!" Or, "I have miserable elbows. They give me trouble all the time . . ." Listeners loved it.

She chatted with her guests about whatever came to mind. She might talk with a famous singer about his latest recording, or ask him about his home life or pets. If a bestselling author was touring, she and the author might trade travel stories instead of discussing the writer's latest book. What most hosts would handle as a formal interview, Ruth treated like a café klatch. She was normally relaxed as she spoke, though she projected her voice as if in a room filled with an audience. And she kept a picture of that audience in her mind's eye as she spoke. With or without a guest, her listeners were, figuratively, in the room with her.

And never a script. Sponsors' commercials were always aired as scheduled, sometimes read by the show's announcer, Lin Mason. But Ruth didn't read any scripts she was given. At most, she paraphrased them, turning each commercial into an off-the-cuff ramble that fit in with her normal patter. New sponsors sometimes protested her ad-libs, but kept quiet after reviewing their sales charts. She was reluctant to use catch-phrases or product mottos, especially when phrased in a manner foreign to her pattern of speech. Ruth had her doubts about some products, and knew that others made exaggerated claims. But she couldn't do anything about them—not yet, anyway.

The Depression deepened. Some, however, were unwilling to acknowledge the economic truth. "There's no Depression," said Henry Ford, "but only if you know it." Cincinnati industrialist Powel Crosley, Jr., offered a more complicated theory but said the same thing. Most people could not ignore the evidence of the devastated economy. It was all around them, encroaching upon their lives. They didn't believe in industry or government. They were just fighting to survive.

THROUGHOUT 1930 AND 1931, John Lyons, Sr., fought a losing battle to keep his business. Day after day, he rode the streetcar into the city and dusted and arranged stock as the world drifted past his door. There were many days— too many—when he didn't make a single sale. The only thing he could count on was disappointment. His shoe store had become a liability, costing him more to keep its doors open than closed. Discouraged and depressed, he finally sold out.

His son Johnny, though, remained optimistic. Pearl Insurance had grown and prospered during his seven years with the company and would continue to prosper throughout the Depression. Life insurance was an investment, and many policy owners were reluctant to give up their protection. Those who had owned a policy longer than a year or two could borrow against its cash value, preserving some of the insurance coverage and freeing them from reliance on commercial lenders and higher interest rates. Like other businesses, insurance companies also lowered operating costs by letting go many salaried employees and developing novel compensation plans for those who were retained. The more successful companies lowered premiums and devised easier payment plans for their policyholders and became diversified, revamping their sales strategies for casualty and health insurance as well as life insurance to suit the times.

A diligent employee, Johnny Lyons tried to learn about aspects of the insurance business beyond his job, hoping to make himself indispensable. It paid off as he moved up the management ladder, with corresponding increases in salary. He was able to save money and even buy a car.

Ruth's business was good as well. With little money to spend on entertainment, people stayed home and listened to their radios. Advertisers, seeking to stimulate languishing demand for their products, turned to the air waves as the quickest way to reach the largest number of people. Big-brand companies, in particular, charted a direct relationship between their sales and radio advertising. Some companies who didn't advertise often, faded away as brand recognition was lost. Procter & Gamble, perhaps the savviest advertiser in the world, doubled its advertising every two years during the Great Depression—most notably on its soap operas, which P&G invented. Other companies, small and large, increased their advertising or began advertising for the first time.

Radio stood solid as the third most-popular advertising medium, behind newspapers and magazines. By then, individual broadcasters and the radio networks could charge advertisers $1,200 an hour or more, generating huge cash reserves that they used to build more buildings, increase power, and hire more people. Contractors and suppliers were beneficiaries of radio's surge in popularity. Western Electric sold one hundred 5,000-watt transmitters like the one WKRC bought, and many stations were going to 10,000 watts and even 50,000 watts, like WLW.

WKRC hired more technicians and support staff, and extended its broadcast hours. Ruth was promoted from assistant music director to music director and given a handsome raise. Her predecessor, Eugene Perazzo, had left during the CBS housecleaning. The new responsibility and title sparked personal changes in Ruth. Her lean body filled out a bit, and her flat cheeks grew rounded. Her higher salary allowed her to dress more stylishly. Her outfits—hats and all—were up-to-the-minute in fashion, but she avoided over-dressing. She let her blonde hair grow a couple of inches and began having it styled in permanent waves. Always conscious of her looks, she used minimal makeup to good effect, something she learned from her friend Rose Laird. Laird was the proprietor of Rose Laird Cosmetics of England, a company that specialized in creating cosmetic blends for each customer. She had been a good friend to Ruth since appearing on *A Woman's Hour* a few years earlier.

By the end of 1931, there was more good news as James Reeves was put in charge of both the Foreign and Travel departments at the Provident Bank. John Lyons, Sr. also had found work. Thus, with both of their families back on solid financial ground, Ruth and Johnny at last were free to marry and establish their own household.

Ruth Evelyn Reeves and John Daniel Lyons, Jr., were married on Tuesday, August 2, 1932. It was a low-key event. The ceremony was conducted at Ruth's parents' home on Morris Avenue by the Reverend John V. Stephens, a Presbyterian minister and son of the director of the noted Lane Theological Seminary. The best man was Miller Everson, who worked as a singer at WKRC with Ruth. Ruth's sister, Rose, was her attendant. In addition, a few close friends and family members—as many as could fit in the house—were present.

For their honeymoon, the couple had planned a trip to Toronto—by car. They would first make the two-day drive to Niagara Falls, traveling the 3-C highway from Cincinnati through Columbus and Cleveland. After a day at Niagara Falls, they would motor around Lake Erie to Toronto, where they would enjoy a week of sight-seeing. On the return journey, they would take a side-trip through the Adirondack Mountains. They changed their plans slightly, however, after learning that some male friends had decided to play a practical joke on Johnny and disable his car, thereby postponing the honeymoon. The couple decided to take the train, instead.

Upon their return, Ruth and Johnny moved into a modern flat at 2628 Cleinview Avenue in Walnut Hills. Built in 1928, the stylish brick apartment building was just five blocks from the Hotel Alms and Ruth's job.

heroine of the flood

As Ruth and Johnny settled into marriage and their new apartment, they saw less of one another than before they were married. Most mornings revolved around the rush to get ready for work—somewhat hampered by the apartment's single bathroom. Johnny dropped Ruth off at the Hotel Alms on his way downtown to the Pearl Insurance offices on Garfield Place, unless it was a nice day and Ruth felt like walking. If she had to be at the studio particularly early, there was always the streetcar.

Ruth went out into the flood to see for herself, and her broadcasts reassured an anxious city.

Regular lunch hours were rare for both of them. A radio program schedule was an unbendable and occasionally harsh master. If they did meet for lunch, there was time for little more than a quick "How's-the-day-going?" Supper was a possibility, unless Ruth was stuck with doing someone else's job or had an evening program. On the days she slipped home for a meal before returning to the studio for an evening program, she made her own way to the apartment, often arriving after Johnny. Whatever time she made it home at night, she was usually so tired she went right to bed.

Weekends were impossible. In addition to the Saturday morning concerts, Ruth also produced Saturday afternoon performances for the Cincinnati

Symphony Orchestra and CBS. Sunday was a swirl of families and church from morning through late evening.

Johnny's schedule was sometimes as unpredictable as Ruth's; more than ever, he threw himself into the job, going in early, working late, and bringing work home. He was driven by his duties and self-renewing goals. Every day was one day closer to the next promotion, another raise, and greater security in an uncertain economy.

For Ruth, work was its own reward. She welcomed the money, but she set no goals. Music and communicating with her audience had become her life. Her accomplishments and ideas were spontaneous, just like *A Woman's Hour*. Having devoted listeners was a blessing from God.

Ruth talked to her fans about everything imaginable. But she had nothing to say about her home life on the air. She might let it be known she was married, but there was no banter about life with Johnny because, quite frankly, there was nothing to talk about. Johnny and Ruth were two workaholics who probably should never have gotten married.

THE LYONS AND THE REEVES families still needed financial help. Although their daughters and son were married and out of the house, 64-year-old John Lyons, Sr., and his wife, Louella, once again had money problems, as expenses outstripped income. Louella had last worked as a nurse nearly ten years earlier, but now she couldn't find a job that paid enough to make it worthwhile.

"I don't talk all the time, just mostly."—Ruth Lyons

On Ruth's side, her father's health was deteriorating. Now 63, Samuel Reeves suffered from a series of non-specific ailments that left him weak, in pain, and sometimes disoriented. Disappointment with the various setbacks in his life wore heavily on him, the stock market losses in particular. In light of later developments and considering the stress he was under, it was possible he had suffered one or more small strokes. A sedentary lifestyle probably also contributed to the long-term deterioration of his health.

His wife, Margaret, worried over him, and that affected her health. Ruth's sister, Rose, did what she could to help, but if Rose followed the pattern of other women her age (21), she would be married and out on her own before long.

As if the family trials weren't enough, Ruth had an attack of appendicitis several weeks after she and Johnny moved into their apartment. The ensuing operation kept her in the hospital for several days. To her displeasure, she was forced to spend the early part of the holiday season convalescing at home. All she could do was read or knit. Even more bothersome, recovery kept her away from work. The musical staff at WKRC covered for her, handling her accompanist chores and *The Rubel Hour*, and it was likely Bernice Foley who filled in for Ruth on *A Woman's Hour*.

Friends came to visit Ruth daily, and fans literally lined up in the hallway to the Lyons apartment. The attention his wife received caught Johnny off guard. He had always been the popular one in their crowd, at least since Ruth left college. She had always been a cutup and everyone liked her, but he was not accustomed to her getting all the attention. Realizing he had to share his wife whether he wanted to or not, Johnny accepted her divided attention—and the diminished intimacy that came with it.

Ruth didn't have much time or energy to think about the relationship. Because she never talked about her marriage publicly, and because those who knew them both are gone, we can only speculate about her feelings. With the stigma of divorce lurking in the background, perhaps she didn't want to think about where the marriage was going. But friends always said that the two were in love, so maybe there was reason for Ruth to have hope.

All she could do was take one step at a time. WKRC was enjoying tremendous success with the financial backing and professional management of CBS. Despite the hard times, CBS increased the number of staff from fewer than twenty to more than thirty on-air and off-the-air employees. Dick Nesbitt replaced Lin Mason as Ruth's announcer on *A Woman's Hour.*

Meanwhile, Ruth's responsibilities grew as she got involved with all aspects of her programs, including sponsors. She worked with the sales department, met with potential advertisers, and planned commercial schedules. She persuaded Rubel to expand its advertising from the twice-weekly *Rubel Hour* to include spots on *A Woman's Hour.* New sponsors, like Shillito's department stores, signed on as advertisers as well. Ruth was busy enough that the company hired a personal secretary for her, Vera Tyson, after Ruth had pushed her former assistant Bernice Foley into a more active role on the air.

After their lease expired, Ruth and Johnny moved about eight miles east of Walnut Hills to a new apartment on Grace Avenue. The neighborhood, Madison Place, was not far from her family's former Peabody Avenue home. Sandwiched between Madisonville and the village of Mariemont, Madison Place was a middle-class development with its own neat little shopping district, and located very near Cincinnati's only suburban hospital, Our Lady of Mercy.

The move was ostensibly to place them nearer to their respective parents—and they were closer, by three miles and twenty minutes. The drive from Madison Place to Tusculum was almost a straight shot, mostly on Columbia Parkway. It was an easy ten-minute drive, a third of the time it took to travel from Walnut Hills along a route through crowded neighborhoods.

Another reason for the move may have been their relationship. The period of growing apart was closely associated with their old apartment. Perhaps one or both of them believed the new environment would be a refreshing change and liven up their marriage. Ruth went shopping for her own automobile.

JOHNNY LYONS HAD BECOME an important asset to the Pearl Insurance Company. He was a senior employee with experience in just about every department in the business. So when Pearl sold its Eureka insurance division and decided to move its Cincinnati headquarters in 1934, Johnny was given the opportunity to transfer to another Pearl office. The opportunity included a promotion to underwriter and a healthy pay raise.

For Johnny, there was no question about taking the job. The position of underwriter was a highly responsible one, and one of his career goals. Underwriters calculated risk. They decided whether to issue insurance on certain risks, and often set the cost of insurance. The underwriter's judgment was one of the foundations of an insurance company's success.

There was only one problem: the job would be in Cleveland. Ruth was thrilled that Johnny had advanced this far, but . . . Cleveland? She didn't want to leave Cincinnati for anywhere else. Her family and her job were here, and all of her friends. Cincinnati was home. It was her life. Nor did she want to break up the marriage. How could she—or anyone—decide which was the more important of the two?

In the 1930s, it was still a given that a wife's desires and choices were subordinate to those of her husband. Women were supposed to stay at home, cook and clean, and raise children. Why would a married woman want to work? Her husband was supposed to provide for her, which was often given as the reason why men were paid more than women. Unlike most women, Ruth refused to accept these terms. But her heart was torn. She wanted Johnny to be happy and successful, for his success would benefit her as well. She also wanted to stay married to him. But her job and family were in Cincinnati.

Ruth didn't want to believe that her choices were limited to being married in Cleveland or living solo in Cincinnati. She reviewed every option. Refuse to move to Cleveland? Divorce? No! Try to force Johnny to remain in Cincinnati? She could see the conflict that would bring. There was one other choice: a commuter marriage. Stay married and visit one another on the weekends. This option appealed to Ruth; it seemed as if she could have her cake and eat it, too. Or so she thought.

Johnny agreed to the proposal and moved to Cleveland before the end of 1934. Ruth moved in with her parents for a few weeks, then found an apartment in a building at 3528 Burch Avenue, just a couple of blocks from East High School (now known as Withrow). She took the train to Cleveland some weekends, and on others Johnny came to see her. Eventually Ruth found a car, both for local transportation and as an alternative to the train. She often had a companion when she traveled to Cleveland—a woman named Mildred Uible, whose husband, Frank, had also been transferred to Cleveland by the Pearl Insurance Company.

The weekend reunions continued through 1935. Ruth found the travel wearing. It wore her down to the point where she decided to find a job with a radio station in Cleveland. She decided that she loved her husband enough to leave their hometown, but she would not give up her career for him. Maybe, she rationalized, living in Cleveland wouldn't be as bad as she feared. And certainly a woman with her resume—over ten years in broadcasting—would have no problem finding work.

Ruth took a few days off and stayed with her husband in Cleveland. She applied first to WHK, Cleveland's 5,000-watt CBS affiliate. She discovered that WHK had no openings for a keyboard player, though, and assumed the station had enough women's programming already. There was no interest in a show like she was doing at WKRC. (Ruth didn't inquire about a job as a singer. While she could sing in key, her voice wasn't exactly what you would call professional quality.) The response from other stations was the same. No one at WJAY, WGAR (NBC Red), WTAM (NBC Blue), or any of the smaller stations had a position for her.

The time in Cleveland was frustrating, primarily because Ruth didn't want to be there. The job-hunting was a secondary annoyance, for she was simultaneously seeking a job but secretly hoping she wouldn't find one. After a week of searching, she returned to Cincinnati—relieved.

Over the next two years Johnny would be transferred to New York, then to Chicago. Still, neither he nor his wife could make a decision regarding the marriage, but they gave up commuting and drifted farther apart.

WHILE RUTH PONDERED the news of Johnny's promotion, WLW trumped broadcasters around the world and made history by putting a 500,000-watt transmitter on the air in May, 1934. As the original superstation, WLW adopted the sobriquet, "The Nation's Station," and meant it. It remains the only commercial station in North America ever to transmit with so much power.

At a half-million watts, or ten times the power of the nation's largest commercial stations and one hundred times that of WKRC's transmitter, WLW could easily be heard across North America. At night in New Zealand, South America, and Europe, listeners marveled at the American radio station. The Duchess of Windsor once telegraphed a music request. The signal was so powerful that WLW programming emanated from metal fences and downspouts for miles around the transmitter. Farmers couldn't shut off their barn lights. A motel in the neighboring town of Mason, Ohio, found that its neon sign glowed brightly even when it was turned off.

WLW raised its advertising rates to network level, from $880 to nearly $1,200 per hour. Its new reach had some impact on WKRC's ratings, but Ruth's listeners stayed right where they were. And she continued to attract new advertisers, some of them thanks to the repeal of Prohibition.

Cincinnati's predominantly German citizenry had developed an extensive beer brewing industry in the 19th and early 20th centuries. Before Prohibition, two dozen breweries were producing 1.5 million barrels of beer per year, about half of that for distribution to other states. Given Cincinnati's population of around 500,000, the per capita consumption rate was still over thirty gallons per year.

Prohibition knocked the local economy for a loop. Hundreds of jobs were lost at the beginning of 1920. Fortunately, Cincinnati's growing machine-tool, leather, and other industries absorbed the excess labor force within a few months.

When Prohibition was repealed in 1933, old Cincinnati brands with names like Hudepohl, Bavarian, and Wiedemann pulled out all the stops to get back into production and slake the public's thirst. In addition to the breweries already in business, new brands such as Schoenling (1933) and Burger (1935) emerged.

In the crowded Cincinnati market, Burger had to be a real scrapper to stay alive. It adopted a tongue-in-cheek commercial tagline reflecting the region's German heritage: "Vas you efer in Zinzinnati?" Burger advertised heavily in newspapers, gave many a tavern new indoor and outdoor signs, rented billboards, and participated in festivals and other events, aggressively working to establish itself as a hometown favorite.

Burger also took on sponsorship of Cincinnati Reds broadcasts—the play-by-play called by the legendary Waite Hoyt—over WKRC and two other stations in 1935. Burger beer became almost synonymous with the Reds. Response to the game broadcasts was so positive that the brewery decided to underwrite a weekly evening musical program on WKRC called *Burger Music Time*.

Burger Music Time—"from the maker of Burger Bohemian Beer"—was a variety show that featured an ever-changing roster of singers, each accompanied by Ruth Lyons on organ or piano. With her WCTU background, she must have appreciated the irony. Fortunately for Ruth, it was not a live program, or she would have lost another weeknight to work. The show was "transcribed," or recorded on a thin disc made of a cellulose material known as acetate. The disc was played at the program's scheduled time. Acetate discs were good for very few playings before they became worn, which is why, in those days before tape recording was common, so few of the old radio shows survive.

WKRC had only one studio, which meant that *Burger Music Time* and other material had to be recorded when network programs were on the air. Better facilities were on the way, however. CBS was building new studios in a penthouse suite at the Hotel Alms, but it would be months before the project was finished.

Work on the new studios continued throughout 1936. Always thinking and looking to the future, Ruth developed two new shows that year. One was a half-hour news commentary titled *A Woman Views the News*. To accommodate it, *A Woman's Hour* was moved back to 9:30 a.m. The other new show was a musical talent search, which aired in the afternoon.

A Woman's Hour featured the same blend of chatter, conversations with guests, tips, and Ruth's personal opinion that it always offered listeners. Over at WLW, they still didn't understand why Ruth's show was more popular than their own *Woman's Hour*, and continued focusing on "women's programming" interspersed with music.

At L.B. Wilson's WCKY in Kentucky, the women's director (a title given many a female broadcaster) took a somewhat different approach. Tremette Tully shared recipes and household tips, along with covering selected news "of interest to women," but added another dimension. She promised to answer any question that listeners sent in, no matter what the topic—and if she didn't have the answer, she'd find it.

Wilson tried, on more than one occasion, to hire Ruth away from WKRC, offering to match any salary and give her whatever she wanted at WCKY. Ruth had known him for some time, as she was a good friend of his brother, the florist Lee Wilson. But with her management and production responsibilities, her two daytime programs, plus the evening *Burger Music Time*, Ruth didn't have a lot of time to ponder job offers.

She had plenty of other considerations as well, including her marriage, her in-laws, and of greatest concern, her own family. In 1935, with her father still ailing and retired from Provident Bank, and her mother growing thin and tired from caring for him, Ruth rented a four-bedroom house in Linwood, part of an upscale neighborhood in the hills to the north of Lunken Airport and Tusculum (now known as Mt. Lookout and Lower Hyde Park), and moved her parents and her sister Rose in with her. She feared her mother would get sick, and fretted over her younger sister, hoping, among other things, that Rose would make a good choice in marriage.

Ruth wasn't interested in jumping ship and joining another station. WKRC was her refuge, even during those times she had to fill in for someone else.

Then, the rains came.

WORK ON THE NEW WKRC studios made the old studio impossible to use from time to time, so the station would have to use the facilities at the College Conservatory of Music, which was already wired for remote broadcasts. One such occasion was Friday, January 22, 1937. It had been a week of endless rain and Ruth wrapped it up by producing an afternoon concert at CCM, after which she drove back to WKRC under gloomy, weeping skies.

"I returned to the studio," she recalled, "to find the air filled with bulletins of the imminence of a tremendous flood. It was raining very hard then, and we were all given rooms in the Alms Hotel so that we might be standing by, should we be needed."

Ruth shared a nicely appointed 12th-floor double with another female staffer. The upper story rooms were nice enough, but conditions were going downhill as rain pounded the region without letup. On Saturday, the water works faced contamination from the flooding, so the city shut down the pumps. Ruth and her roommate had prudently filled a bathtub with water, although the fire department would become the main source of potable water, with tankers hauling it in from neighboring counties.

By January 24—forever after remembered as "Black Sunday" in Cincinnati—parts of downtown Cincinnati lay under several feet of water as the rain continued. It was already the worst flood in Cincinnati's history. Thousands of people were evacuated from flooded homes. The Cincinnati Gas & Electric company was forced to shut down its coal-fired generating plant next to the river. Emergency power for hospitals, radio broadcasts, and the telephone system was shunted from the Dayton electric grid, fifty miles north. WKRC still broadcast with battery power part of the time.

Situated on one of Cincinnati's fabled Seven Hills, the Hotel Alms was safe from the floodwaters. But no electricity meant no elevators, so Ruth and others with rooms on upper floors stayed downstairs in the studio. She described the scene to WLW newsman Peter Grant years later: "We slept on desks. We used telephone books for pillows. We realized that this was the greatest crisis that Cincinnati had ever faced. Not only Cincinnati, but New Richmond and Lawrenceburg and Aurora, and all the towns along the Ohio River."

Indeed, the nearby town of Aurora, Indiana, and the region around it was placed under martial law, and the U.S. Army moved in to provide rescue services and maintain order. The river rose more than twenty-five feet above flood stage, cresting just below eighty feet. Then, a different kind of disaster struck. In a heavily industrialized area a few miles north of the Ohio, near the Miami River, was a so-called "tank farm" with huge bulk gasoline and oil storage tanks. Two of these immense containers—one filled with 250,000 gallons of gasoline—broke loose from their foundations and were set adrift on the river. Other tanks started leaking. The floodwaters gleamed with a mixture of oil and gas, estimated to be two inches thick.

CG&E had shut down its generators, but the city's street railway system had its own generators, so the overhead trolley wires were still live. A sparking wire on a suburban street line in Northside—just northeast of downtown Cincinnati—set the floating liquid ablaze, and within minutes two square miles of water were covered with sheets of flame. Hundreds of workers fled as the fire roared toward blocks of factories. Most of them had been laboring to move equipment and office items from flooded first floors. WLW and WSAI employees on the eighth-floor of Crosley's main factory building also left. Several structures were completely engulfed by flames. Firefighters, held at a distance by rising water, could only try to keep the blaze from spreading to other buildings. With untiring effort, they succeeded in limiting the fire to the structures it was already consuming.

FOR TWO DAYS, WKRC was the most powerful station on the air, twenty-four hours a day. It took that long for Crosley engineers to get WLW and WSAI up and running in WSAI's former headquarters—on the third floor of Crosley Corporation's old factory several blocks from the main plant. (Both stations' transmitters were located on high ground in Mason, Ohio, miles from the Ohio River and its flooded tributaries.)

With WLW and WSAI silent, people listened to local stations WCPO and WCKY, but thousands tuned to 550 on the radio dial and heard Ruth Lyons for the first time. Ruth and other WKRC employees remained at the station until Tuesday. "We had a direct line to city hall," she remembered, "and constantly warned everyone to evacuate where the waters were coming up fast, to dispatch workers with sandbags, to boil all drinking water, and to donate to the Red Cross."

Ruth would rather have been home with her family. She knew her parents were listening to news of the flood every waking minute and that they would be worried about their old neighborhood. Stress was not good for her father's health. But she stayed on duty, and it was her voice that people in the Ohio Valley heard, encouraging the public while delivering vital information.

Before the fires were out—even before the water began to recede—the emergency relief efforts began. Ruth played a big part, appealing to her listeners for donations to the local Red Cross. The response was gratifying. In two days, she raised $56,000. One donor, in particular, impressed her. A farmer. "[He] had come forty-eight miles to bring me a mason jar filled with change that he had saved over a long period of time. He felt that 'this was what I must do with this money, this is a real need,' and had driven through all sorts of roads that were under water and everything else to bring that money himself."

The farmer's jar held only about ten dollars, but it was as important as any other donation. "I have never forgotten that," said Ruth later. "It's typical of the big-heartedness of people in this area."

She was able to get close to the devastation two days after the fires. "On Tuesday afternoon a police officer took me downtown to see what I had been talking about for days. We got into a rowboat and rowed into the downtown streets over the tops of streetlights." That evening, she returned home for the first time in five days, to rest and visit with her family.

"These were dark days for Cincinnati, where millions of dollars of loss were incurred in the downtown business section and surrounding localities," Ruth wrote in her memoirs, summing up the natural disaster. The flood and relief efforts were the focus of attention across much of the country. *The New York Times*, *Washington Post*, *Chicago Tribune*, and *Atlanta Journal-Constitution* carried extensive coverage in all editions, and the networks reported on conditions during every newscast. Ruth, however, had to do some damage control of her own after an out-of-town correspondent swaggered into town and went on the air with a report as potentially devastating to WKRC's hard-earned credibility as the Great Flood, itself, was to the city and surrounding region.

His name was Floyd Gibbons, a newsman who had been an early "embedded" war correspondent. Gibbons rode with General John Pershing into Mexico in pursuit of Pancho Villa in 1916. He was aboard a ship that was torpedoed in the Atlantic in 1917—and survived—and lost an eye to German machine-gun fire in Belleau Wood in 1918. He continued covering World War I as it wound down following his recovery in a field hospital.

After all his adventures, Gibbons had a deservedly high opinion of himself that his employers shared. Back in the United States after the war, he delivered his daily network news briefings and commentaries in an omniscient, staccato style. Wearing an eye patch and hip boots, he often made personal appearances and was the subject of frequent newspaper coverage, his opinion sought after.

While the flood waters were still rising, Floyd Gibbons let CBS know that he would deliver an eyewitness report on the great flood in the Ohio Valley. He boarded a train for Cincinnati over the weekend. (Commercial air traffic into the city was suspended, with Lunken Airport under ten feet of water). On Tuesday, January 26, Gibbons strutted into the Hotel Alms lobby in his hip boots, trailing three secretaries, each carrying her own portable typewriter. He commandeered an office and his secretaries set up their typewriters. They worked behind a closed door, a murmur of voices and the tap-tapping of typewriters the only indicators of their presence.

Ruth was a bit mystified by all the commotion over one commentator. Just before she left at five o'clock in the afternoon, Gibbons gave the station manager a script that was supposed to represent his newscast. The manager signed off on the script and went home. But, perhaps not surprisingly for Gibbons, the famed commentator broadcast something quite different that evening. It was more a drama than a newscast, almost a complete fiction. In Ruth's words, "What a shock when we heard Mr. Gibbons telling the nation that the water was rising around his ankles, and the screams of 'telephone operators' were heard as they supposedly leaped from the windows."

APPARENTLY THE OHIO RIVER flood was a bit too tame to a man who had cheated death so many times. He hadn't traveled hundreds of miles to tell the world that the emergency was under control. So, instead of reporting the facts, Gibbons created a script with parts for his helpers.

Ruth and the rest of the city were disgusted. "The next day," she recalled, "the newspapers and radio stations did all they could to refute the broadcast." Gibbons's credibility suffered. He later received a summons to a court in New York that was investigating him for false reporting, but nothing came of it.

Ruth was outraged by Gibbons's lies, and felt that it was an attack on the believability of radio. Reminded of the incident in 1959, she said, "From those dark days in 1937 until the present, I have tried to keep that believability alive. This has been possible because I am employed by a company that sustains the same policy, and because I take this business of radio and television as a serious and happy obligation."

When Cincinnati finally returned to normal, Ruth found herself the woman of the hour. "As the water finally receded and mopping-up jobs were completed, I discovered to my complete surprise that I had become the heroine of the inundation. It seemed that I had gained, through a disaster, the confidence of the public."

Benefiting from the suffering of others was an uncomfortable feeling. Ruth was being completely modest when she said, "I had just done what was necessary in a crisis." But at the height of the crisis, it was her voice everyone heard, heralding the promise of aid and comfort, and telling them where to go for shelter, water, food, and medical help.

Ruth Lyons's efforts during the disaster were recognized with acclaim and awards from the mayor, the fire and police departments, and the Red Cross, as well as citizen organizations. Newspapers carried photos and interviews with her.

WKRC's management raised her pay and promoted her to program director. (Or, as the newspapers referred to her, "program directress.") There had been female program directors at other stations, most notably Eleanor Poehler at WLAG in Minneapolis/St. Paul in the early 1920s. Both WLW and WCKY had women's programming directors, as did other stations. But this was a first for Cincinnati radio. Characteristically, Ruth hung on to her title and duties of music director.

There was some concern at WKRC and CBS about Ruth being lured away by another station. This was entirely possible, given her sudden celebrity. Loyal to a fault, though, Ruth had no desire to leave, and no offers from other stations were forthcoming, other than L.B. Wilson's periodic overtures.

When the waters flowed safely in their channels again, tens of thousands of men, women, and children marched to churches and evangelists' tents up and down the Ohio River Valley. The humble and the fearful stood alongside the doubting and the brave, each in search of hope. They filled services to overflowing, seeking comfort and word of what God might be trying to tell them about the disaster of the Great Depression, the Dust Bowl, and now the Flood of '37, an uncomfortable reminder of Noah and the original Great Flood.

changes in the air

After the flood, Ruth rarely went out without being
recognized. Any reader of Cincinnati-area newspapers, which frequently
published her photo, could spot WKRC's star in an instant. Ruth's fame spread
as radio stations in other cities bragged about one of their own taking charge in a
time of crisis, and national trade journals and fan magazines carried stories about
her. She now had more listeners than any of WLW's or WSAI's programs.

A bigger audience attracted more sponsors—so many that *A Woman's Hour,*
A Woman Views the News, and
Ruth's other programs could not
accommodate all of them unless
she cut her air time in favor of
commercials, and she wasn't about to
do that. Sponsors owned too much
of every hour as it was. Management
asked her to create a one-hour
afternoon program to accommodate
the new advertisers—Kroger, P&G
and other major businesses—who
wanted to back a Ruth Lyons show.
So she got together with announcer

Ruth had never been in a childrens' hospital before,
and she was shocked. So began her Christmas Fund.

Dick Nesbitt and developed an hour-long morning program for housewives
called *Open House.*

Open House was more of a variety show than *A Woman's Hour*. Ruth lined
up daily interviews and developed a host-sidekick relationship with Nesbitt. He

played the beleaguered and confused male to her efficient and in-charge female, with lots of humorous banter between the two of them. Ruth would use this formula the rest of her career.

WKRC FINALLY MOVED into its spacious new facilities in the converted penthouse suite of the Hotel Alms. Each of the two new studios was larger than the old one in the basement, and the offices actually had windows with views of Walnut Hills and several miles beyond. Some cosmetic work remained to be done—painting and adding trim—but the station's new home was wired, soundproofed, and on the air.

One of the studios could accommodate an audience of thirty or so people for *A Woman's Hour* and later, *Open House*. A real audience, not just a couple of guests and people from the station, was important. It put WKRC on par with network radio programs, not to mention WLW, and gave Ruth the kind of immediate feedback performers crave. The format helped her refine the techniques that would make her so popular on television a decade later.

The live audience, which closely mirrored the demographics of her listeners, also helped Ruth and the WKRC marketing and sales staffs gauge response to sponsors' products. Ruth wanted the audience to have product samples before they came to *A Woman's Hour*

> "There comes a time every now and then, when I cannot let the sponsors have the upper hand in the show. At least five days a week I feel that way."

so that she could poll them for their opinions and use the information in future commercials. If a product was well thought of, she would feel more confident about recommending it to her listeners. In turn, she would earn their trust.

CBS and WKRC, however, weren't quite ready to take this next step. Commercials were aired whether the host liked the products or not, and in the manner dictated by the advertiser. As long as the sponsor paid on time and wasn't presenting anything illegal or in poor taste, management's attitude was "the customer is always right."

Ruth's idea, however, was a valid one. Many businesses were already collecting consumer opinions, including the Cincinnati-based Kroger Company, which operated more than 5,000 grocery stores in the Midwest and the South. In the early 1930s, Kroger began to monitor the quality of the products it sold and to introduce new marketing concepts. One element of the program was the Homemakers' Reference Committee, a group of 750 housewives who were regularly sent samples of Kroger and competing brands to test under "field conditions." The homemakers detailed their experiences with the products, and Kroger used the information to make product and marketing decisions.

Ruth would soon have the opportunity to put her version of the Kroger consumer marketing model into practice on the radio.

CHANGES WERE IN THE AIR, so to speak, at WKRC. In the autumn of 1937, CBS sold the station to Taft Broadcasting for $330,000. The sale was the result of a new Federal Communications Commission (FCC) rule, dictating that no group or business entity could own more than seven broadcast stations.

Taft Broadcasting was owned by the Cincinnati Tafts—the family of the late President William Howard Taft and Ohio senator Robert A. Taft. The latter's cousin, Hulbert Taft, Jr. (better-known as "Hub" Taft), was put in charge of the company. His father, Hub, Sr., was editor of the *Cincinnati Times-Star* newspaper and one of the primary investors in Taft Broadcasting. He had his doubts as to whether WKRC could be a consistent moneymaker, but was persuaded to give the medium a try.

After the sale, CBS dropped WKRC and signed Cincinnati station WCKY as its new affiliate. WKRC eventually joined the new Mutual Network, co-founded by rival WLW. At the same time, the American Federation of Radio Artists' union came to town to organize Cincinnati stations. WKRC lost several of its thirty-eight employees who either left to avoid the conflict over unionizing or because they didn't like working for the highly political Taft family.

Once more, Ruth was hurled into the breach. This time, she pulled in the slack with a program called *Sunday Morning Matinee* that aired from 11 a.m. to noon. Each show featured well-known musical guests, including the Andrews Sisters, Benny Goodman, Doris Day, Guy Lombardo, Stan Laurel and Oliver Hardy, Jimmy Durante, Sammy Kaye, and Nelson Eddy. With so many bands and singers touring the nation, it wasn't difficult to find a big name in town willing to come in late Sunday morning to do the show.

One Sunday in 1938, bandleader Paul Whiteman was Ruth's guest. Whiteman was a popular music icon, like Benny Goodman or Glenn Miller. He had been at the top of the game for over twenty years. Jazz greats like Bix Biederbeck performed in his band, and Whiteman had given singers such as Bing Crosby and Morton Downey, Sr. their starts.

Ruth and Whiteman started talking about songwriting after a singer performed a song Ruth had written titled, "Fooled." (In addition to chatting with her guests, Ruth wrote a new song for a guest singer to perform each week. It kept listeners coming back, tuning in each Sunday to hear that week's song.) Before her conversation with Whiteman got too far along, the celebrated bandleader turned things around and began interviewing his host.

"Do you write fifty-two songs as good as this every year?" he asked.

"Well, I don't know about that, Mr. Whiteman," replied Ruth, clearly nervous at all the attention from "The King of Jazz," as Whiteman was known.

"But ever since we started this *Sunday Morning Matinee*," she continued modestly, "we decided that, just as a little novelty, I'd try to write a tune each week."

"Do you write the lyrics, too?"

"Yes," Ruth said timidly.

"You really knock your brains out!" Whiteman declared.

The normally composed Ruth giggled like a schoolgirl; a listener could imagine her blushing bright red. "The worst part," she conceded, "is trying to get an idea."

After a moment's hesitation, she took a chance. "Now, if you have any titles that you think I might write a tune on, I'm always . . ."

"I've got a good title that nobody's ever been able to write," Whiteman interrupted. "I've given it to buddies and they say they can't do it, so maybe you ought to take a chance at it."

"What is it?"

"Oh," he said offhandedly, "it could be a kind of a torch thing: 'You're So Good to Me, and I'm So Tired of It All.'"

Ruth and everyone else in the studio laughed. "Well," she said, tongue in cheek, "I'll see what I can do with that by next week."

After the show, Ruth showed Whiteman more of her songs. He was impressed by her abilities—so impressed, in fact, he asked to buy five of the tunes. She was thrilled, but there was a sticking point. Whiteman said the songs would have to be published under his name. A song credited to Paul Whiteman and recorded by one of his famous friends could easily have been a hit, but Ruth said no. The idea of a person getting credit for creative work done by someone else—especially her creative work—ran counter to her ethics. Moreover, the idea that someone thought she might be susceptible to flattery and charm was almost an insult, even if it came from "The King of Jazz."

RUTH WAS FULLY AWARE of her power as program director, and wasn't shy about using it, especially to help women get into radio. With approximately twenty people reporting to her, she controlled a significant portion of WKRC's $5,000 weekly payroll. All other things being equal, she would hire a woman as easily as a man—though she might be overruled if she tried to hire a woman for a position such as newscaster. The still-young broadcasting industry ruled *that* to be a man's job. Women could comment on the news, but delivering the serious facts required male authority, or so went the thinking at the time.

Ruth also created new jobs for women. Bernice Foley, her former assistant, was promoted to the position of educational director, producing and directing a variety of special programs at WKRC. Twenty-three-year-old Virginia Golden was hired as the feature editor for *A Woman's Hour*. Always brimming with ideas, Ruth had come up with a concept for a show segment titled, "Personalities on Parade." The five-minute spot would acquaint listeners with "celebrities, people with human-interest stories to relate, and characters of general interest."

She assigned Golden to research, write, and deliver the feature. Golden had already gained on-air and writing experience working with WKRC in cooperation with the Federal Radio Workshop, a Works Progress Administration program. The new feature slot was a natural next step, and kicked off a successful career for Golden.

As program director, Ruth made some unpopular decisions and, as a result, some enemies as well. At the top of the list, apparently, was WKRC publicity man Charleton Wallace. Wallace, a bridge fanatic, was sure that a program about the card game would be a success and that as an ardent player and winner of regional bridge tournaments, he should be the one to host the show.

"It's a good idea," Ruth told him. "But if you're going to have a bridge column on radio, you're going to have to start with beginners." Referring to his proposal, she said, "This is for people who already know bridge."

Wallace stormed out of their meeting, taking Ruth's rejection personally. Later, in 1953, while still doing publicity work for WKRC, he was hired as TV/radio editor of the *Cincinnati Times-Star* and informed his competitor at the *Cincinnati Post*, columnist Mary Wood, that the first thing he was going to do in his new job was "destroy Ruth Lyons."

Wood was taken aback. "Why?" she asked. "You don't really know her."

Wallace told Wood about what happened at WKRC. As promised, he took potshots at Ruth as often as possible, hanging the nickname "Queenie Lyons" on her and in general holding her up to ridicule. Ruth ignored his rantings. She certainly never mentioned Wallace's name on the air. But she did praise Mary Wood's column. At least once a week, she would ask her listeners, "Did you read Mary Wood's column in the *Post* last night?"

Wood got lots of calls of support for Ruth, people telling her that they were dropping the *Times-Star* and sticking with the *Post* because it carried Wood's column. The calls continued for over a year, until the *Post* bought the *Times-Star*. For decades, the name on the masthead was *The Cincinnati Post & Times-Star*, but to readers of the evening paper, it was simply known as "the *Post*."

The demise of the *Times-Star* had little to do with Charleton Wallace denigrating Ruth. The paper had been losing circulation before Wallace went to work for it. But Ruth's praise of Mary Wood helped further the career of the *Post's* columnist.

SAMUEL REEVES'S HEALTH was going downhill when the family moved into the Russell Avenue house. His wife served as nurse and took care of all his needs, with whatever assistance their two daughters could provide. Ruth was at work most days and evenings. Rose had been working, off and on, for several years, most recently as a clerk for attorney Benjamin F. Sheatzley. She gave her mother a break in the evenings.

By the end of summer, 1938, Samuel was rallying, helped perhaps by the new surroundings. At the same time, according to Ruth, her mother had completely exhausted herself. Fraught with worry and rarely sleeping, Margaret Reeves became seriously ill. It started with a persistent cough. Then came chills and shortness of breath. Ruth was reminded of the time her father had pneumonia when she was in high school. Now she feared for her mother's life.

Margaret had contracted pleurisy, an inflammation of the cavity surrounding the lungs. As the disease progressed, she suffered excruciating pain with just about any movement. It even hurt to breathe. The disease had been known for centuries, but there was no definitive cure. Treatment ranged from time in a sanitarium to binding the victim's chest. Author John Steinbeck, a pleurisy sufferer, reportedly had a rib removed.

Margaret Henry Reeves died suddenly on November 11, 1938, shortly after suffering two strokes. Ruth was devastated. "This was my first experience with death," she noted in her memoirs, "and I just couldn't quite accept it." She grieved along with her father and sister, but she knew that she couldn't allow her grief to overcome her. Ruth literally worked her way through the sorrow, putting so much time and energy into her job that she scarcely had time to think about her mother. "There was always that little inexplicable box called radio that needed to be fed incessantly," she said, "no matter what personal tragedy struck. And so I went on."

IN APRIL, 1939, Ruth did something she said she never would have done while her mother was living: she filed for divorce.

The end of her marriage to Johnny Lyons was not fueled by anger or spite. Ruth and Johnny had not been close for years. They rarely saw one another, and had officially separated in 1938. Their divorce was just an overdue formality. Johnny, now living in Milwaukee, didn't contest her filing, which specified gross neglect of duty and extreme cruelty only because cause had to be given. The court hearing was set for June 8, and the divorce decree was granted.

Ruth let the newspapers think that financial problems, coupled with the fact that she and Johnny lived in different cities, had caused their breakup. One report stated, in part, "Mrs. Lyons said she had worked all her married life and that [Johnny] Lyons had not provided for her." It was true, although it sounded worse than it was.

She kept her married name because she had built her career as Ruth Lyons. Taking her maiden name again after all the years of marriage would have been a lot of bother, anyway. To avoid referring to the marriage, she began telling the story that she had adopted the name "Ruth Lyons" when she got into show business. No doubt some fans felt sorry for her. Ruth, though, felt a vast sense of relief.

While she struggled to maintain the other aspects of her life during the divorce proceedings, the New York World's Fair was going full tilt. The mammoth international, commercial, governmental, and cultural exhibition often eclipsed the events in Europe, as monumental as they were. Cincinnati was ably represented by the Crosley Corporation and Crosley Broadcasting. WLW broadcast daily from the Crosley Pavilion, an eye-catching art deco structure with twin towers and an outdoor lounge, set on spacious landscaped grounds. A visitor could enjoy a ride in a new Crosley automobile, chauffeured over a miniature parkway by one of the Crosley "Glamor-Tone Girls." But something even more fascinating could be found inside the pavilion. There, in addition to Crosley radios and appliances (including the mysterious Xervac hair-restoring machine), Crosley and the DuMont Company were demonstrating a new medium: television. Crosley had its first TV camera, and DuMont was preparing to manufacture TV receivers.

A short distance away, just on the other side of the AT&T Pavilion across the street, RCA had its own TV demonstration. The hometown company received all the press attention, but Crosley was just as ready as RCA to move ahead, not only with television broadcasting but the manufacturing of TV sets. Both companies awaited only the ironing out of some technical standards and the FCC's permission to proceed with their plans. Like so many other things at the World's Fair, television was a wonderful glimpse into the future, a future that everyone thought was just around the corner. No one had a clue that world events were about to delay TV's debut for another decade.

Ruth Lyons was too busy to make the trip to New York, but had she gone to the World's Fair she would have seen her future in the Crosley Pavilion.

BROADCAST PERFORMERS and show hosts are often asked to donate their talents to a good cause. Ruth Lyons received more requests than most of her peers because of her popularity and high profile. Despite her heavy workload, she emceed several awards dinners, charity events, and other functions every year. In the summer of 1939, WKRC received a different request, this one from Children's Hospital: could some of the staff stop by the hospital, which was just minutes away from the station, and entertain the young patients there?

Ruth organized a small troupe that included a comedian and several singers, whom she would accompany on piano. She was surprised and saddened, however, by what awaited her. "I had never been in a children's hospital before, and although this one was a fine new building, I was shocked at the cold, sad interior, with no toys or pictures for these dear little children who were sick and away from their parents."

For months after the visit, "it kept coming back to my mind," Ruth said. "So a few weeks before Christmas, I told my radio audience what was troubling me, especially after calling the hospital as to what was done at Christmastime for the children." Each child, she was told, received an orange and a share of whatever candy the staff brought in. A small Christmas tree was set up in the lobby, and those children who weren't completely immobilized were brought down to see it.

"I couldn't believe that this was true," Ruth recalled years later. "So I begged my audience to send me a nickel, a dime, or whatever they could spare, and we would really make it Christmas for these little children in the hospital.

"The response was most gratifying," she reported. Most of the donations were small—a dollar or two in hand-addressed envelopes. They totaled just over $1,000. Managing that much cash in small bills was awkward, but every donation was welcome.

"One of our sponsors was Arnold's Fairyland, a toy shop," Ruth remembered. She felt that shopping there would be appropriate. "I asked them if I might buy at a discount. When they said yes, I was overjoyed."

Ruth and her personal secretary, Vera Tyson, turned the donations into toys a few days before Christmas. They had a list of the children who were in the hospital and bought age-appropriate gifts, including dolls, games, books, crayons, and trucks. Ruth did not allow any of the money to be spent on toy soldiers, guns, or other weapons of war. She and Vera brought the toys back to WKRC that afternoon and wrapped them. On Christmas Eve, they took the colorfully wrapped packages to Children's Hospital. One of the men dressed as Santa Claus and handed out the presents, one per child.

"It made Christmas much more meaningful for all of us," Ruth said, "and delighted the children and the hospital staff. Thus, on the eve of Christmas, 1939, the Ruth Lyons Christmas Fund began!"

The Christmas Fund became an annual event, kicking off each year on Ruth's birthday, October 4—a tradition that has continued into the 21st century. Fund-raising topped $10,000 in the second year, and within a few years total donations exceeded $1 million. There was so much money, Ruth and her staff found it impossible to spend it all, so with hospital officials they set up a fund that could be tapped year-round to provide gifts not only at Christmas, but also Easter, Halloween, and on children's birthdays.

With good works like the Christmas Fund, and the power of Ruth's personality, *A Woman's Hour* was rated the most popular program of its kind in a national survey by *Billboard* magazine in 1939. Yet, a few months after Ruth first visited Children's Hospital, federal regulators put the clamps on broadcasters in a decision that would shift the balance of power, so to speak, among Cincinnati radio stations and affect, indirectly, Ruth's own future.

For some time, WLW had been engaged in a battle to retain its 500,000-watt license, which had to be renewed every six months because it was deemed "experimental." Other broadcasters were applying for the same license, but the FCC refused to authorize other stations to broadcast at such high power. The regulators feared that a half-dozen such stations could cause massive interference nationwide, render smaller stations inconsequential, and drive many out of business. As a result, WLW's high-power permit was not renewed.

On March 1, 1939, the so-called "Nation's Station" cut back its transmission power to 50,000 watts. As a consequence, WLW's income dropped and the station no longer could afford many of its grand productions; union scale wages made them too expensive to put on the air. Now a regional broadcaster, WLW saw many of its performers, writers and commentators leave for the network centers of Chicago and New York, where they could gain wider exposure and make more money. Even Red Barber, the famous baseball play-by-play man, left Cincinnati to broadcast the New York Yankees' games over the network.

The exodus of talent from WKRC's rival gave Ruth center stage and her ratings climbed even higher. At the same time, WLW began scrambling in search of new voices.

FOR SOMEONE WITH HER INFLUENCE and popularity, Ruth found it hard to avoid the politics of the day. She was not a political person. She voted her conscience and didn't try to force her mildly conservative views on others, counting among her friends Republicans, Democrats, Independents, Socialists, and doubtless a few Communists.

Samuel Reeves, on the other hand, was vocal about his Republican politics, and though her father didn't insist that she share his convictions, Ruth was happy to attend a rally in 1940 for Republican presidential candidate Wendell Willkie, more or less on her father's behalf. At the behest of Hub Taft, she also attended the event as a member of the press.

She explained the situation this way: "Because of my father's adamant Republicanism, and since I was working for a station that was owned by a cousin of Mr. Republican himself, Robert A. Taft, I went . . . to the big rally and parade in Elwood, Indiana, for Wendell Willkie." (Elwood was Willkie's hometown.)

To balance things out, Ruth was present for Franklin Roosevelt's unprecedented third inauguration in January, 1941. She met scores of people in Washington, the most memorable being Mr. and Mrs. Robert A. Taft and Cincinnatian Charles Sawyer, a Democrat and future Secretary of Commerce in the Truman Administration. Sawyer, a member of the board of the Crosley Corporation, served as Ruth's guide through Washington society dinners, parties, and other events.

On January 27th, Ruth traveled on to New York to meet with a music publisher, who bought two of her songs: "Let's Light the Christmas Tree" and "Fooled." The former, "Let's Light the Christmas Tree," was written to raise money for the Ruth Lyons Christmas Fund and was included on several singers' albums over the next three decades. It can still be heard in Cincinnati during the weeks leading up to Christmas.

The inauguration and New York trip provided Ruth with a gold mine of subjects to talk about on her shows. She returned from the three-week sojourn, however, to find her father seriously ill again. The stress of being responsible for her elderly father, after such a long break, hit her hard. She found it increasingly difficult to do several shows a day. "I considered giving up my work on the air," she later wrote, "and devoting my energy to being program and music director only. But something my mother once said to me when I had mentioned doing this very thing came back to me, and it was this: 'As long as the public accepts you and you bring pleasure to them, stay right where you are. No one can take your good name away from you, but those behind the scenes are often replaced.'"

In those words, Ruth found the strength to soldier on. A few months later, 70-year-old Samuel Reeves had a stroke and was hospitalized. His stay was lengthy. When his doctor released him from the hospital, he showed little improvement. The care he needed was beyond the capability of Ruth and Rose, and he was moved to a rest home.

The sisters gave up the rented house in Linwood and took an apartment at 2715 Eden Avenue, just blocks from the University of Cincinnati and the Hotel Alms. Optimistically, they chose an apartment that would have room for their father if his health improved. Because money was tight, they sold some furnishings they couldn't fit into the new place. Some personal items were disposed of, too, out of necessity. Among other things, Ruth remembered, "We sold all my mother's fine glassware and china, never realizing their true worth."

After scaling back her life, Ruth found new energy as well as enough money for a few extras, even though she was paying her father's hospital and rest home expenses. She was also temporarily supporting Rose, who had lost her job. (Rose soon found a position as a maid in the home of Cincinnati industrialist James H. Heekin, head of the Heekin Can Company.)

Ruth traded in her old car for a newer, more reliable Chrysler convertible. She enrolled in some classes at the University of Cincinnati, where she won a scholarship to study piano at the College Conservatory of Music. She also managed to squeeze in some rest and relaxation, occasionally going to a concert, undertaking various knitting projects, and adding to her doll collection.

Most days, she got up at dawn, and when the weather was nice she tried to get in a round of golf before going to work. The California public links near Eastern Avenue were only a couple of miles from the Eden Avenue apartment. The quiet, wooded area served as a retreat where she could forget the rest of the world for an hour or two.

Ruth wasn't a night person, so she wasn't seen in the Cincinnati or Northern Kentucky nightspots that so many of her jazz and popular musician friends frequented. She stayed in touch with the music scene through WKRC performers, as well as people like pianist Cliff Lash, who would become a good friend and station employee, though not a suitor. Her schedule allowed almost no time for socializing, anyway. Nor did she seek companionship, not while she was still recovering from the demise of her marriage.

high spirits

In 1941, the air crackled with reports and rumors of war. Some Americans wondered if the United States was going to get involved in Europe. Others felt it was only a matter of time.

Contingency plans were already in place for the nation's industries to convert to war production. In Cincinnati, Crosley Corporation would turn out field radios, aircraft canopies, specialized munitions, and other military items. Hearse and ambulance maker Hess & Eisenhardt was on the list to manufacture bicycles

Crosley Square—the old Elks' Lodge—became Ruth's radio home for a quarter of a century.

for airborne troops. Even the Kroger Company was involved, assigned to supply soldiers' field ration kits.

Radio stations were given strict instructions on procedures to follow during national emergencies. Crosley Broadcasting would have special roles to play, among them transmitting propaganda and coded messages directly into Europe and Africa.

Late in the morning of December 7, 1941, Ruth Lyons was driving with Cliff Lash to Music Hall, where they planned to attend a performance of *Swan Lake* by the Ballet Russe de Monte Carlo. Like Ruth, Lash lived in Walnut Hills, and they often traveled together to events in town. Esther Hanlon of WKRC had introduced them a few months earlier.

Muted jazz drifted from the car radio as they motored down Vine Street hill. The wind fluttered the Dodge's canvas top in syncopated rhythm. Just after noon, an announcer broke into the musical program with the news: carrier-borne Japanese dive bombers and fighters had attacked and virtually destroyed the U.S. naval base at Pearl Harbor, Hawaii.

Like most Americans, Ruth didn't know Pearl Harbor existed. It may as well have been a port in India. "I must confess that it didn't mean much to me at first," she later admitted. When she and Lash walked into the lobby of Music Hall, the early performance was just letting out. It was obvious the news had not penetrated the immense brick edifice, so they quickly passed along what they'd heard. Ruth remembered, in particular, the reaction of John W. LaRue, editor of the *Cincinnati Enquirer*. "I could not imagine why [he] rushed wildly out the door when we told him about it in the foyer of Music Hall."

Ruth would not remain uninformed, not in her job. She brought herself up-to-date on world affairs, and learned a lot about places with exotic names. Over the coming months, the guest list for *A Woman's Hour* included politicians, government experts, Army recruiters, naval officers, and representatives from business and industry involved in the war effort. While the other stations in Cincinnati stuck with the news events of the day, Ruth expanded WKRC's war coverage by assigning Bernice Foley to produce and direct a series of features about the armed services. The programs, explaining the functions of various elements of the military, were very popular with listeners of all ages. In part because of Ruth's efforts, WKRC was voted the most progressive station in Cincinnati in a *Variety* magazine poll, and ratings for *A Woman's Hour* climbed higher than ever.

"Engineers I have always found to be a fine breed of humans, and they do stick together."

WEDNESDAY, MAY 6, 1942, was a cool, clear day. Ruth had a ticket to an afternoon benefit concert at Music Hall. The featured soloist was Lily Pons, the Metropolitan Opera's principal soprano, whom Ruth was particularly keen to hear. She quickly found her seat, pulled some knitting from her handbag and sat back to enjoy the performance. Sitting just in front of her, to the right, was a handsome man who looked familiar, but she couldn't place him. She returned to her kitting and forgot about him until the house lights came up for intermission and he spoke to her. He had dark hair, blue eyes, and "a beautiful deep voice," as Ruth described him. "He . . . asked if I would like to walk around a bit. As we started to walk up the aisle, he told me his name was Herman Newman and that we had met before at the University of Cincinnati."

Memories flooded back. Ruth asked Herman what he had been doing since college. "What hadn't he been doing might have been a better question," she recalled. "He had graduated from the University of Cincinnati, spent a year in law school, studied for the Unitarian Ministry in Chicago, won a scholarship to Oxford, England, traveled through Europe, filled a pulpit in Erie, Pennsylvania, for six years, and then had come back to Cincinnati and was at that time doing social work (as a counselor for juveniles in the Hamilton County court system)."

Ruth was impressed by Herman Newman's education and travel abroad. As they strolled the wide, carpeted hallways of Music Hall and admired the neo-Gothic décor, she told him about her work. Before returning to their seats, Herman asked if she would like to go out with him the following Saturday night. She accepted the invitation.

At home that evening, Ruth had second thoughts, imagining where things might go with this man who was so attractive and obviously attracted to her. She had already sacrificed a marriage for her career, and long since decided she would never marry because, as she told her friends, "I'll never find a man who wouldn't hate my success." She wasn't going to give up her career for a man, so why risk getting involved?

She telephoned Newman to cancel the date, claiming she had forgotten a business commitment for Saturday evening. But Herman protested. "I've waited ten years to work up the courage to ask you for a date," he confessed, "and I'm not sure I'll ever find the courage again!" Overwhelmed by his appeal, Ruth gave in and agreed to go out with him Sunday. When Herman arrived at her door, he was carrying a quart of wild strawberries in an old-fashioned wood-slat box. Ruth was charmed.

On their first date, they went to a club in northern Kentucky. In those days, if you wanted to see the "name" acts like the Mills Brothers, Rosemary Clooney, Louis Armstrong, and Sammy Kaye, you went "across the river." In several northern Kentucky towns—most notably Newport—there was also gambling and prostitution, discreetly conducted behind the façades of small bars and classy nightclubs. And during Prohibition, there was booze. After the repeal of the Eighteenth Amendment, you could get liquor anywhere, but Kentucky's tax on alcohol was significantly smaller than Ohio's, another attraction.

The allure of living on the edge, maybe even mingling with the mob—reputed to be behind the girls and the gambling—drew thousands across the Ohio River every weekend. Not everyone, though, partook of forbidden pleasures. Clubs such as The Flamingo, the Lookout House, the Beverly Hills Supper Club, and the Latin Quarter hosted gambling in their back rooms and basements, but up front provided quality dining and headliner entertainment at high prices.

Herman took Ruth to the Beverly Hills Supper Club. He wisely allowed her to order first. She asked for a strawberry shake, he had the same. Neither was a drinker. In honor of their relationship, Ruth soon began collecting strawberry-shaped pin-cushions, dishes and ornaments decorated with strawberries, any strawberry knick-knack she could find.

AS RUTH AND WKRC SURGED ahead in the ratings, WLW, which had been forced by the FCC to cut its power back to 50,000 watts, urgently searched for new talent to replace the singers, actors, and musicians who left the station for Chicago and New York. Though it still reached a big audience, WLW no longer could match the coverage, salaries, and prestige of the networks.

In the past, sensational acts like the Mills Brothers and the Ink Spots had shown up out of nowhere. WLW hoped it would happen again. It did in 1942, when Doris Day and the Williams Brothers (with Andy Williams) joined the station. Like the other star-quality talent, however, Doris Day and Andy Williams eventually left Cincinnati for more money (often joking that WLW stood for "World's Lowest Wages"), but not before they gave WLW a much-needed boost.

WLW program director, George Biggar, was too impatient to wait for the next Doris Day to walk in the door. Biggar, an import himself from Chicago's WLS, had raided stations in Chicago, St. Louis, and other regional markets for artists. (One of the St. Louis recruits was "Sally Carson," who changed her name to Bonnie Lou, recorded several hits, and was a regular on *The 50-50 Club* and *The Paul Dixon Show* in the 1960s.) But the well soon dried up. So he turned to WLW's backyard.

General manager Robert Dunville had noticed how much Ruth Lyons was cutting into Marsha Wheeler's audience for The WLW *Consumer's Foundation*, not to mention the station's afternoon programming. Every day, more people were talking about Ruth Lyons, in the newspapers and on the street, and the ratings confirmed her growing popularity. More than one advertiser had dropped WLW and moved to WKRC to sell to Ruth's listeners.

One day in the middle of May, Ruth found a message waiting in her office: would she please telephone George Biggar at WLW? She assumed the call had to do with a cooperative fund-raising program for the Community Chest, so she put the message on her list of calls to return and went on to a meeting. Late that afternoon, Biggar called again. This time she picked up the phone.

The program director wanted Ruth to meet with Crosley Broadcasting's top executives, Dunville and James Shouse, but Biggar couldn't say what the meeting was about. He had simply been told to invite her to sit down with Shouse, the company's vice-president of broadcasting, and Dunville, general manager of WLW and WSAI. Ruth, though, had some idea of what might happen, so when she met with the two men a week later she was only mildly surprised when they offered her a job working at WSAI and WLW—with a $10 per week raise. That would put her over $60 a week, good money at the time.

The plan was for Ruth to host an afternoon show on WSAI, similar to WKRC's *Open House*. It would air three days a week. As Dunville described it, the show would have its own orchestra, headed by local bandleader Burt Farber, as well as staff singers and guest entertainers. Plus, each day would feature a different interview guest—a celebrity, a politician, an expert in some field, people with interesting stories to tell. Dunville also assured Ruth that she would have free rein with commercials on the show.

On WLW, she would take over Marsha Wheeler's morning program, *Consumer's Foundation*. It was exactly the type of show she wanted to do at WKRC: a panel of 200 women volunteers tested advertisers' products and reported their experiences. Ruth could share the information with listeners as she wished on the program, which aired three days a week. She did not have veto power, however, over what was advertised.

It was an attractive offer. WSAI and WLW had a listener base second only to network radio. WSAI was "Cincinnati's own" station, entertaining listeners with a blend of local news and personalities (Powel Crosley had announced that WSAI would concentrate on Cincinnati when he bought the station.) WLW covered a greater territory and was heard throughout Ohio, Indiana, and Kentucky, and into Michigan, West Virginia, and beyond—in 465 cities and towns throughout the Midwest. At night, the station was picked up by radio listeners in fourteen states. It was particularly popular in the South at night because of its "hillbilly music" shows, such as *Boone County Jamboree*.

Ruth liked the plan laid out for her by the Crosley executives, although she had some reservation about displacing Marsha Wheeler, the founding host of *Consumer's Foundation*. Marsha Wheeler Moelloring (her married name) had been producing programming for children on WLW since 1927. She was also the station's director of women's activities. Wheeler would retain both positions when Ruth was hired, and be given responsibility for managing the *Consumer's Foundation* panelists. Still, Ruth couldn't help but feel some guilt over the situation.

Crosley offered her more money than she was making at WKRC, an important consideration for Ruth with her sister, Rose, again out of work, and her father's mounting medical bills. Five hundred dollars more a year would go far in meeting her debts. Even though she had been in a terrible money crunch since her father had been placed in a nursing home, Ruth had not requested a raise at WKRC, for several reasons. She knew the Tafts were tight with a dollar. Her upbringing also told her it would be presumptuous to ask for a salary increase when she was already making more money than her co-workers.

Ruth asked Dunville and Shouse for a few days to make a decision. She confided in her sister and her new friend, Herman Newman. Herman, in particular, was encouraging, displaying an enthusiasm for her career that gave her the courage to decide move forward. She accepted the job on the condition that she be allowed to give WKRC the opportunity to meet the Crosley offer. Dunville and Shouse told her they would wait while she worked out whatever notice was necessary. Although she probably didn't know it at the time, they were prepared to get down on their knees and beg her to sign a deal. They felt Ruth Lyons was that important to the future of WLW, and they were right.

Now came the difficult part: giving notice to WKRC, or more specifically, to Hub Taft. Ruth admired Taft and considered him a friend and a true gentleman. He had always been more than fair with her. "I had to tell Mr. Taft that after thirteen years I was leaving to work for the opposition," she said, "and, to make it worse, I had to go to his home, where he was recovering from a broken leg."

She felt like a traitor.

"Mr. Taft was his usual kindly self," Ruth reported, "and said he understood perfectly." But he would not match the salary offer from Crosley Broadcasting. Ruth was not surprised; the Tafts were bastions of conservatism, and not just politically.

It was a decision Hub Taft would regret. A decade later, he told *Cincinnati Post* TV/radio columnist Mary Wood, "That ten dollar raise has cost me millions over the years!"

Ruth granted WKRC a generous six-week notice, during which she continued working as she always had, putting in long hours and lots of energy. She never bragged about it, but it took two men to replace Ruth Lyons at WKRC. When she left, staffer Syd Cornell was promoted to program director and the station hired a new music director.

WLW AND WSAI HAD MOVED from their longtime home on the eighth floor of the Crosley Corporation factory—on orders of the U.S. Navy, for whom Crosley was a prime contractor. No one knew it at the time, but Crosley already had started pilot production of a top secret weapon that would be a deciding factor in winning the war in the Pacific: the proximity fuze.

America's enemies knew nothing of the fuze, an electronic device that used radio to detonate a bombshell when its sensor detected the target. What they did know was that gunners on American warships showed a terrifying new accuracy, knocking their aircraft out of the sky at an unprecedented rate.

A proximity fuze was about the size of a quart of milk, which inspired the clever idea of shipping them in milk containers. Each fuze was packed with fifteen others in a milk case. Thus disguised, the "dairy shipments" were picked up by regular milk delivery trucks that drove inside the Crosley plant for loading. They were then delivered to Cincinnati's Lunken Airport and flown to their final destinations.

The Navy, though, was nervous about the civilians coming and going at all hours of the day in the building across the street from the Crosley factory. These singers, writers, musicians, and other bohemians were considered unreliable at best. Thus, Crosley's radio studios and offices would have to be relocated to eliminate what the Navy deemed a security risk.

Initially, the plan was to build a new complex overlooking the city on Mt. Adams. But Crosley dropped that project in favor of buying a building recently placed on the market, the historic Elks Lodge at Ninth and Elm in downtown Cincinnati. The massive, block-long structure had some unusual features, among them a cavernous two-story high room with no windows on the third floor—perfect for a radio or television studio. "Crosley Square," as the building was called, would become Ruth Lyons's home for the next twenty-five years.

RUTH CONTINUED WORKING at WKRC through the July Fourth holiday. Her first day on the Crosley airwaves was July 6, 1942, and the whole city knew about it. Newspaper announcements and promotions on WSAI and WLW hyped Ruth Lyons's debut for a week. A special remote broadcast of *Consumer's Foundation* originated from the gilded, mirror-lined dining hall at Cincinnati's posh Netherland Plaza Hotel, an art deco palace completed in 1931. The event included a breakfast for Crosley and community luminaries, as well as representatives from several women's organizations and stars from Cincinnati's Summer Opera. WLW's George Biggar and WSAI program director James Leonard were on hand to welcome Ruth formally to their respective staffs.

The fifteen-minute broadcast began promptly at 8:45 a.m. and was announced by George Skinner, who went on to become a CBS executive in New York. After organ music by Arthur Chandler, Jr., it was left to the outgoing host of *Consumer's Foundation*, Marsha Wheeler, to introduce her highly-publicized replacement. Following the Netherland festivities, Ruth drove the few blocks to Crosley Square to begin her new job. There were two studios—one on the third floor and one on the fifth floor—and both were large enough to accommodate audiences. The third-floor studio had an elevated gallery for additional seating.

One of the studios was prepared for Ruth's new WSAI show, yet to be named. Cincinnati's mayor, James Garfield Stewart, was to be the special guest that afternoon, and a half-dozen singers were on hand, backed by Burt Farber's ensemble. After a musical introduction, Ruth greeted listeners with the trademark phrase she had chosen for the new program, a merry "Hello, hello—how's living today?" She made sure to remind them about the contest to name the show, which also had been publicized over the preceding week. The remainder of the unscripted hour flew by as Ruth interacted with the studio audience and chatted with Mayor Stewart about the city and his family.

Another host might have conducted a conventional "Q and A" with the mayor, plodding along with serious questions about the city's problems and its future. But this was a friendly conversation, cued by audience reaction and the show's schedule. There were commercials, but they weren't read from a script. Music and song filled out Cincinnati's new favorite radio program.

Ruth was thrilled with the studio, the crew, the band, with everything about her new shows. She loved the name for the WSAI show, chosen from among listener entries: *Petticoat Partyline*, submitted by a Mrs. Margaret Johnston. It perfectly described the mix of talk, entertainment, and interaction with the mostly female audience. As for the name of the show, readers may recall that telephone subscribers once had the option of sharing a line with several others in their area. When one person was on a call, the others could listen in and talk if they wished. Referred to as a "party line," it cost less than a private line. For her apt designation, Mrs. Johnston received a $25 war bond.

It took Ruth some time to learn her way around the company, with its more than 200 employees. "At WLW," she noted, "things were not as uncomplicated as they were at WKRC. It was a much larger organization. It was a much larger organization in every way. And it took me a few months to learn who all the people were and what their jobs were."

At least she hadn't walked into a group of complete strangers. Ruth already knew some of the staff professionally. Several had migrated from WKRC, including her good friend, Duane Snodgrass, who now worked as an actor. The engineers at WLW and WSAI were impressed when Ruth told them that their counterparts at WKRC had sent her a basket of flowers for her first broadcast. "Engineers," she said, "I have always found to be a fine breed of humans, and they do stick together."

Not everyone was friendly, though. Ruth remembered her reception at WLW as "anything but cordial by many of the staff, especially the girls." A few days into the new job, she took the stairs down to the employee cafeteria and found several of the "girls" seated around a table, including Mary Wood. "We were . . . drinking coffee and dissecting Ruth—pro and con—when she breezed in and sat down with the astonished group," recalled Wood, then a soap opera scriptwriter at WLW. Ruth knew they were talking about her and that it wasn't all good. After all, her arrival at WLW meant the demotion of Marsha Wheeler, who counted more than a few of these women among her friends.

"There was a brief, stricken silence, which Ruth broke almost at once," said Wood. "'Well,' she asked, 'have you decided whether or not you like me?' From that moment she was in like Flynn. Who could resist such an honest approach?"

Ruth Lyons was "in like Flynn" with the management at WLW and WSAI, too. Ratings for *Consumer's Foundation* shot up from her very first day, and fourteen sponsors followed her from WKRC, just as Crosley's executives, Dunville and Shouse, had expected would be the case. WLW raked in more from these advertisers in a single day than the monthly salary of its new star. Ruth was well aware of her drawing power, using it as leverage in future salary negotiations and to gain more control over her shows.

IN A CONFLICTING but not unusual arrangement in those days, WLW provided the *Cincinnati Enquirer* with a daily radio column that—no surprise— reported only on WLW. It appeared under the byline of a man on Crosley's publicity staff. The *Enquirer's* editor had planned to free up a reporter for other duties by running the column contributed by the radio station, but instead complained that he had to get one of his staffers to rewrite the publicity man's copy every day.

Not wanting to ruin the cozy arrangement, WLW's publicity director turned to the station's soap opera crew. Surely there was one capable writer among them. At least they were paid to be writers. The job was given to Ruth Lyons's new friend, Mary Wood, whose father was a *Times-Star* columnist. The *Enquirer* continued to carry the radio column, now written by Wood, under the byline of Crosley's publicity man, and WLW paid Wood what they paid her when she was hired by the station—$17.50 a week. When she asked for a raise to $25 per week, she got a pink slip. It was a typical Crosley response. Dozens of former WLW employees—actors to engineers—suffered the same fate after requesting a raise or complaining about policies or conditions at the station.

Wood, though, quickly landed a job at the *Cincinnati Post*, writing obituaries. In her autobiography, *Just Lucky, I Guess*, she noted that she received a large number of letters from people who appreciated how considerate she was in writing about their departed loved ones. In 1946, she was chosen to take over the *Post's* radio column when the radio editor was drafted. In her new position, Wood's friendship with Ruth Lyons would serve her well over the next thirty-two years.

love at first sight

Ruth's new suitor, Herman Andrew Newman, was born to Andrew H. Newman and Elizabeth Randley Newman on November 11, 1906. Elizabeth Newman died of an infection within weeks following the birth of her son. Andrew Newman's widowed aunt, Francis Poth, volunteered to take both

On their first date, Herman asked Ruth to marry him. She gently turned him down.

him and baby Herman into her home, a two-story shotgun house at 423 Warner Avenue. Raising children was nothing new to "Fannie" Poth; she and her late husband had raised Andrew in this same house, and the arrangement worked out well. Father and son had a home, Herman had a doting "mother," and with her new family, Aunt Fannie was never lonely. Without complaint, Andrew Newman supported the household in his position as a warehouse clerk for a grocery wholesaler, a job he had held since the 1890s and where he would eventually become warehouse manager.

Aunt Fannie's house was in a hillside neighborhood called Fairview, a mile north of downtown Cincinnati. Clifton and the University of Cincinnati were perched at the hill's summit, over 200 feet above the city. Fairview was draped across the treacherously steep hillside below them. The slope was so precipitous that an inclined plane railway had to be built to carry the Cincinnati Street Railway's trolleys serving the University area.

The neighborhood at the foot of the hill was called "Over the Rhine" because of the preponderance of German immigrants who settled there and the canal that separated it from Cincinnati proper. The waterway, once the terminus of the Miami-Erie Canal, spanned the width of the city, but went nowhere and was abandoned in 1878. People moved up the hill to escape its stagnant waters, leaving Over the Rhine to the poor, and avoided the canal except when they had to cross one of its bridges located every few blocks. Not until 1920 would the waterway be drained and covered over as part of a post-war subway project.

To get to the Newman house on Warner Avenue from the bottom of the hill, you had to struggle for 1,000 feet along the aptly-named Ravine Street—itself a canyon into which side streets flowed like tributaries. A lengthy trudge put you at the top of the hill. The alternative was to take the trolley up and walk down to where you were going. No one kept horses; the lots didn't provide enough room. Houses and their tiny lots lined every street in Fairview, clinging to the impossibly sharp slopes. Some yards went uphill in two directions. Slip in icy weather, and you'd find yourself at the next cross-street, and probably slide downhill from there. If nothing else, the challenging geography was good for young Herman's constitution.

Andrew Newman remarried on June 2, 1917, to a woman named Olga Hauth. Like half the neighborhood, Olga was of sturdy German stock. The other half were Irish. Most people knew her as "Ollie." Anyone close to her also knew Ollie was a stubborn sort who almost never gave up a position once she'd set her mind to it. She was the only woman Ruth Lyons ever found intimidating.

> "I knew that all I was doing was trying to be honest with my audience."

Nevertheless, Ollie was a good stepmother to Herman, whose life changed little following his father's remarriage. He and his father did go to church more often after Ollie joined the family. Herman, in fact, enjoyed meetings at the Unitarian church on Macmillan Avenue, though not as much as he enjoyed school.

After attending Fairview Elementary School, Herman entered Hughes High School in the fall of 1921. Hughes was a vast, citadel-like building, with a tower and a crenellated façade, half a block from the University of Cincinnati's McMicken Hall. It was a fifteen-minute walk (or climb) from the Newman home. Herman's interests and activities were wide-ranging, from the school's Art League to the Athletic Association. The Cincinnati public school system placed a special emphasis on music education, so he took up an instrument like many of his classmates, playing the violin in the Senior Orchestra. He was talented enough that he eventually organized and conducted a dance orchestra to earn extra cash, but never seriously considered music as a vocation.

In his four years at Hughes, Herman established a reputation as a likable person with "a cheerful and optimistic spirit." His senior photo shows a handsome young man with dark, wavy hair, serious eyes, and a quiet, engaging smile. His school nickname was "Herm," and his motto was, "I smile in the face of trouble."

Herman began an uneventful four years at the University of Cincinnati in the fall of 1925. He maintained a high grade point average, served as a class officer, and graduated in 1929 with a bachelor of arts degree. Still living with his father and Ollie, he attended law school for a year, but gave it up in favor of what he felt to be a calling to the ministry.

Because it was his calling, Herman decided he should pay his own way. He went to work as a salesman for a wholesale flour company for a year, saving as much money as he could. During the year's hiatus, he applied to and was accepted by Meadville Theological School in Chicago.

While Herman was away at the seminary, his surrogate mother Aunt Fannie died. She willed her house to Andrew Newman. No doubt weary after years of fighting their way up and down the Fairview inclines, Andrew and Ollie Newman sold the Warner Street house and bought another residence at 3640 Penrose Avenue in Westwood, one of the city's less hilly neighborhoods. The move met with Herman's approval. He had gradually adapted to the flat landscape of the Chicago area and the Fairview hillsides seemed to grow a little steeper each time he had returned home.

After three years at Meadville, working through the summers and serving an appropriate period of internship, Herman Newman was ordained a Universalist minister. He had no pulpit, but he did have a destination: Oxford University. After applying for and winning a scholarship for a term at one of the world's leading universities, Herman left for England in 1933. He returned to the United

States on August 8, 1934, aboard the S.S. *Olympic*, having spent the summer following his academic term at Oxford exploring Europe. An affable and talkative person, he made several friends overseas and vowed to return.

Back home in Cincinnati, Herman received word that the Universalist church in Erie, Pennsylvania, was seeking someone to fill its pulpit. The members of the church's search committee were impressed with Herman's training and experience, and hired him to be their minister. In addition to serving the Erie church, he was a frequent speaker at other churches, as well as rallies and youth meetings. In sum, Herman's tenure at the Erie Universalist Church was one of dedication and service.

But after six years of leading the flock, something changed his mind about religion. He never spoke of it publicly, but in 1940 he resigned from the ministry and returned to Cincinnati. Why give up the pulpit? In light of later developments, it seems he was beginning to doubt his faith.

Herman returned to Cincinnati and temporarily moved back in with his father and Ollie. He found a job with the local Hamilton County juvenile justice system as a youth counselor and juvenile parole officer, visiting offenders and helping them work out problems at home.

ON THEIR FIRST DATE, Herman asked Ruth to marry him. Maybe it was the excitement of wartime, with so many other people getting carried away with romance. Perhaps it was prompted by whatever made him decide to give up the ministry. Although it pleased Ruth to think of his proposal as "love at first sight," she gently turned him down, citing her father's lengthy illness and the medical bills she was obligated to pay. Plus, she barely knew Herman. "I could not ask him to share that financial burden," she explained years later. "And I was sole support at that time of my father and younger sister Rose."

They continued dating through the summer. As new couples do, they cautiously exchanged the stories about their lives. Ruth learned of Herman's education, his ministry, the early death of his mother, and the remarriage of his father, who had passed away two months before they met. At the time, Ruth's sister was beginning to get her life together, at last. Rose was working again, and she was seeing a lot of a Kroger advertising copywriter named Herb Lupton. With the military draft looming, Lupton joined the U.S. Coast Guard and apparently was posted to duty in Cincinnati.

With her new job and the new man in her life, Ruth hardly had time to take notice of what her younger sister was doing. Since late July, she had been engaged in a project dreamt up by WSAI's publicity department. To promote the sale of war bonds and garner publicity for the station, Ruth would compete with "Colonel Cumquatt," the star of a WSAI comedy show, to see who could sell the most war bonds. The winner would be named "Mayor for a Day," with Cincinnati Mayor Garfield's blessing.

Bond sales ran neck and neck until the first week of September—the final week of the contest.

RUTH AND ROSE VISITED THEIR FATHER as often as they could, though nearly every time Ruth saw him she felt heartsick. He had suffered another stroke in the rest home and sometimes didn't recognize his daughters. Other times he was asleep or just somewhere else in his elderly mind.

Samuel Spencer Reeves died on September 1, 1942. He was 71. His death was not unexpected, but it was no less a trauma for Ruth than her mother's death. Once again she threw herself into her work as therapy. In the bond sale contest, she had lost several days and fell hopelessly behind Colonel Cumquatt. But she rallied and spent most of the final Saturday soliciting friends and business acquaintances.

The following Monday, Ruth presented $40,000 in sales to the station's publicity director. Colonel Cumquatt had sold $37,000 in war bonds, so Ruth won the honor of Mayor for a Day. It was a much-needed moment of lightness in an otherwise trying time. Ruth was particularly impressed by the head of Shillito's department store, who bought $10,000 in bonds, and even though Shillito's wasn't currently advertising on her show, she mentioned the long-time Cincinnati institution when appropriate.

Having recently experienced the loss of his own father, Herman gave Ruth a strong, caring, and understanding shoulder to lean on during this period. And so in September, when he asked her a second time to marry him, she agreed. He was 36, she was 37. Grooms were usually older than brides, so Ruth gave in to the temptation of shaving three years off her age when she and Herman applied for their marriage license, claiming she was born in 1908.

They were wed on October 3, 1942, in the home of one of Herman's friends, a Presbyterian minister. Herman wore a three-piece herringbone suit, and Ruth wore a new chiffon dress with a square neck and velvet bow. She topped off an elaborately curled hairdo with a fashionable new hat. He placed a topaz-studded gold wedding band on her left ring finger.

The newlyweds traveled to the historic Beaumont Inn in Harrodsburg, Kentucky, on their honeymoon. The Inn's main building was a former women's college dating back to 1845, and replicated a classic southern plantation house, complete with Doric columns on the front porch. Beaumont College was operated as a female or mixed school until 1917. Two years later, the Beaumont opened as a hotel-resort with thirty-three rooms and suites. In keeping with its genteel history, semi-formal dress was required in the evenings.

The drive from Cincinnati into the picturesque Bluegrass Region of central Kentucky in 1942 was something of an adventure. Their 100-mile route took Ruth and Herman through thinly-populated areas that varied from rural to outright wilderness. The hilly, wooded land made for poor farming. Tobacco and corn, the main crops, had already been harvested. The tobacco leaves hung in drying sheds, while the corn was shipped north. They traveled most of the way on U.S. 127, a narrow but well-paved highway, but a few of the roads were gravel. Nevertheless, Ruth and Herman enjoyed the brilliant autumn displays.

At the Beaumont, walking trails beckoned every morning. Some led to hillside glens where the waters splashed across rocks on their way to somewhere far away. In the early evenings, the couple watched deer feeding. Brave squirrels and raccoons sought handouts from their human cohabitants. The Beaumont warned about black bears, though none had been spotted that year.

Days were pleasant, but nights were cool. Tired guests found the inn's porch and patio inviting when it wasn't outright chilly. The dining room and tavern were pleasant venues for late-evening chat. The more active played shuffleboard or other games.

Local distilleries offered tours for visitors. Most were small operations that differed little from their predecessors two centuries earlier. Although Herman and Ruth had no interest in the distilleries' end product, they had the opportunity to learn everything there was to know about bourbon.

The week was refreshing—as pleasant a honeymoon as the couple could have hoped for.

The trip home yielded a legend they would share with friends and family for decades. Ruth spotted a roadside stand selling, among other things, bittersweet.

She knew the herb was used to treat skin allergies or rashes, and she asked Herman to buy some of it. By the time he stopped the car, they were a few dozen feet past the stand, so Herman walked back to purchase the bittersweet. In the meantime, Ruth decided to help her husband by backing the car nearer to him. She slid across the seat, started the vehicle, put it into reverse, and was rolling toward the roadside stand just as Herman turned to walk back. The rear bumper brushed his leg, and thereafter Herman joked about his new bride trying to get rid of him on their honeymoon.

THEIR FIRST HOME was a tidy little house at 3138 Penrose Place, right next door to Herman's stepmother, Ollie, in Westwood. Built of brick in the style known as "Chicago Bungalow," the house was one-and-a-half stories with a basement. Herman and Ruth paid around $5,000 for the home.

The next spring, Herman caught scarlet fever while making his rounds for Hamilton County Juvenile Court. The Newman house was quarantined by the Cincinnati Board of Health, which meant neither Herman nor his wife could leave. Ruth wrote a song titled "Quarantine Blues."

Can't take a walk to the corner,
Can't ask my neighbor the news,
I'm not as free as I once used to be,
I've got the quarantine blues . . .

Crosley Broadcasting was loathe to allow Ruth to miss even one scheduled day of her show, let alone a week or two under official detention. Fortunately WSAI and WLW were well-practiced in doing remote broadcasts. There's no record of whose idea it was, but it was determined that Ruth would broadcast her show from home as long as the quarantine was in effect.

The Cincinnati & Suburban Bell Telephone Company ran a special line to the house that connected directly with the studio. An engineer had to be on hand for each broadcast, and one in particular was terrified of catching scarlet fever. When he was on duty, he stood outside at the house and handed the microphone in through the open dining room window. No one else came down with scarlet fever. Some even found humor in the situation.

Elsa Heisel, Ruth's new assistant, gave Herman the nickname "Scarlet

O'Herman," a takeoff on the film *Gone with the Wind*, released five years earlier. Elsa was a pretty young woman who came to work for Ruth immediately after graduating from the University of Cincinnati in 1942. She was part of an entire WLW department devoted to Ruth Lyons. Vera Tyson, Ruth's personal secretary, came with her from WKRC, and two girls named Ethyl and Carol worked with Elsa Heisel under Vera's supervision. There were also three music directors, plus the show's director, producer, and engineer, Bert Farber's band, five page girls, and two "setup" girls. And that was just staff for *Petticoat Partyline*.

Ruth emphasized the human interest story on her new show. During the first year, a blind teenager named George Corey played "Skater's Waltz." A two-year-old kid sang Bing Crosby tunes. A four-year-old crooner serenaded the audience. Models, movie stars and political notables made appearances on *Petticoat Partyline*. A frequent guest was James Stewart, Cincinnati's six-term mayor, whose son grew up to be U.S. Supreme Court Justice Potter Stewart. Guy Lombardo and Jimmy Durante also visited the program that first year.

Perhaps the most fascinating guest of 1943 was Margaret Kathryn Irion (Mrs. Charles P. Irion), a wheelchair-bound young woman. President of WSAI's "Bluebird" fan club and an occasional guest broadcaster, Kay Irion walked for the very first time when she was in the audience of *Petticoat Partyline*. WLW highlighted Irion's dramatic appearance on Ruth's show in the station's promotional yearbook, but didn't specify whether her problem was congenital or the result of an accident.

Petticoat Partyline became known for its stunts involving the audience. Once, when Ruth hadn't had time to iron Herman's shirts, she brought them to work. Several of the ladies in the audience volunteered to help and took turns pressing the shirts, right there in the studio. Several times a year, Ruth would designate an upcoming day as "Ye Old Swapper Shop." Women in the audience could bring in items and swap them. (Husbands, of course, were out of bounds.) If one of the show's staff members had a birthday coming up, she would let listeners know and invite them to bring in gifts. Ruth never asked for gifts on her birthday, but when fans brought them anyway, she donated the presents to the needy.

For the two days each week that *Petticoat Partyline* wasn't on the air, Ruth created a mini-game show called *Collect Calls* from Lowenthal's, sponsored by Lowenthal Furrier. On the show, she made random telephone calls, and if the person who answered the phone was a regular *Petticoat Partyline* listener and responded appropriately, he or she would "collect" a cash prize. Those who hadn't previously tuned in to Ruth's shows probably became listeners.

WLW DIDN'T GET CAUGHT NAPPING when the United States entered the war. The week before the bombing of Pearl Harbor, George Biggar created the position of War Program Director for Crosley Broadcasting. Katherine "Kit" Fox filled the post at both WLW and WSAI. She coordinated the war bond sales contest and also arranged for the stations' on-air personalities, singers, and musicians to participate at events related to the war effort, including USO benefits and scrap drives to collect steel and iron, cooking grease (to make explosives), and rags.

Ruth made her share of appearances, especially at the USO Club Room in downtown Cincinnati. At one USO event, she and her fellow "Partyliners" collected 2,000 cartons of cigarettes and $475 for "smokes for service folks." Programs on WLW and WSAI with names like *Your Son at War* and *Camp Wolters Calling* put a face to the conflict and buoyed up patriotism.

In the fall of 1942, WLW and the British Broadcasting Corporation (BBC) arranged for a unique exchange of programs, transmitted across the Atlantic by shortwave radio. BBC and WLW hostesses and listeners swapped information on gardening and home life through *Petticoat Partyline*. Midwesterners listened to details of the hardships of farm life in wartime England on *Everybody's Farm*. (WLW itself owned a large working farm, just across the road from its transmitter and tower in Mason, Ohio.) And *Consumer's Foundation* examined the roles of British women in the war. On several programs, BBC listeners responded to questions submitted by the WLW listening audience, and vice versa.

As the war dragged into its second year, Americans learned about rationing. The obvious consumer goods were rationed—sugar, coffee, and gasoline, anything used by the military. These and other commodities were in short supply due to enemy forces controlling sources of raw materials. Not-so-obvious items were also rationed—shoes, for example, and tires. Eventually, just about everything seemed to be rationed, limited to a certain quantity per person, per week, or per month. People were issued commodity-specific ration books or coupons, without which they could not buy the rationed item.

The well-to-do generally found ways around the rationing, through influence, intimidation, or outright bribery, while a lively black market trade in ration coupons and rationed goods arose in quite an egalitarian manner, encompassing, at one time or another, almost everyone. Apparently Ruth didn't know about such things, or chose not to deal with black marketers. One day she complained to her listeners about how difficult rationing made it to keep her wardrobe updated, especially when it came to shoes. Within days, fans had sent her dozens of their own shoe coupons—more than enough to last out the war.

Beyond the war programming and rationing, the conflict barely touched Herman and Ruth. The toughest part was seeing the draft take away friends and co-workers.

RUTH WAS SUPPOSED to write a script for *Petticoat Partyline* and read it on the air, which she did for one week. "I . . . was never more miserable," she said, emphasizing how difficult the task was for her. "Then I just started to ad-lib it with the announcer, thereby breaking one of the cardinal rules of 'The Nation's Station.'"

Apparently nobody noticed, for nothing was said for a long time. But in the event someone *did* raise an objection, Ruth had Elsa Heisel prepare a script for each morning's show. She never used them, of course, but she put a letter-grade on each one and Elsa filed them. The system worked well, according to Ruth, until one day immediately after the show she received a call from the WLW vice president Robert Dunville, asking her to come to his office and bring the script from that morning's program.

"My knees quaking, I went to his office and confessed that I had not been writing the show for months, but had been ad-libbing it. I fully expected a real blow-up," she said later, "but Mr. Dunville laughed and said he knew that I had been working without a script, and he thought it was time to let me work in my own way on WLW, as I had been doing all along on WSAI."

To Ruth's further surprise, Dunville proposed that she do a noontime show on WLW in addition to *Petticoat Partyline* on WSAI. The name of the half-hour show, later expanded to an hour, was *Your Morning Matinee*. Meanwhile, *Consumer's Foundation* was marked for retirement. Ruth asked for a big band, and the request was granted. She chose WLW announcer Frazier Thomas to be her sidekick. Thomas, a jovial, heavy-set young man, was the perfect foil for Ruth's humor.

Your Morning Matinee would be ad-lib all the way, including the commercials, which were the main reason for the new show. As was the case at WKRC, this new hour-long program could not accommodate all the sponsors who wanted Ruth Lyons to represent them. Dunville, though, was planning for the future. He said nothing to Ruth, but he knew plans were brewing in Washington that could force Crosley to sell WSAI.

The rest of 1943 was busy. The new show was a smash hit. "The Crosley Broadcasting Corporation presents Ruth Lyons, America's most glamorous blonde, in *Your Morning Matinee*," signaled to thousands of women that it was time for Ruth Lyons.

The Ruth Lyons Children's Christmas Fund had its WLW debut on *Your Morning Matinee* in October of '43. Her staff kept a tally of donations, which Ruth announced each day during the campaign. A total of $54,000 was raised that year, thanks to the extensive exposure the Christmas Fund received on WSAI and WLW. Some of the money went to Cincinnati Children's Hospital, as well as hospitals in Louisville and Indianapolis, while Ruth and the station received a lot of good publicity.

Ruth's sister, Rose, became officially engaged to Herb Lupton. After much debate, they decided on a November wedding. Herman, still licensed to solemnize marriage, conducted the matrimonial service for Rose Jayne Reeves and Herbert Lupton.

Your Morning Matinee had plenty of room for an audience, and every day it played to a packed house. The studio could accommodate more than 150 patrons on two levels, and was always filled with women, men, and children—but mostly women.

"Every morning, busloads of people arrived at the studio, coming from all over our listening area, to 'see' our radio show," recalled Ruth. "One morning there were ten busloads and the people had to be seated in our two studios, one on the second floor, and one on the fifth. We did the show racing up and down by grace of the kindly elevator." And a crowd of 11,000 women and children showed up for a weekday Partyliners' Picnic at Coney Island.

The success of *Your Morning Matinee* created a few conflicts between Ruth and the sales department. Many sponsors wanted to buy short-term contracts, which the station's ad men liked because they could charge the top rate and get a higher commission than with six- or twelve-month contracts, which came with a discount. The sales department also liked selling to as many different sponsors as possible. This way, there would never be a shortage of sponsors if a slot opened, and the demand for commercials would always be heavy, keeping the price up. At times, a salesman might play one advertiser against another, seeing who would offer the most for a time slot on a particular show.

Ruth, though, wanted to keep her advertising honest, and felt that establishing a strong relationship with the sponsor was the best approach. She didn't want pit to one brand against another, nor did she want an advertiser to disappear when she was just getting started with a product. The sales manager thought otherwise. "He tried to persuade me to sell one brand of coffee one week, and another the next," Ruth said. But there was no way she was going to agree to such a sales strategy. Switching loyalties, she felt, would reduce the effectiveness of her recommendations.

Ruth won that battle, although she would have to take her case all the way to the top, getting Dunville's approval. She also pressed for the right to reject a product—something unheard of in the broadcast business, as long as a product was legal and not in bad taste. The first time she ran into a problem was with a sponsor who wanted to give away pins described as "exact replicas of an old Victorian broche." When Ruth examined one of the pins, however, she noted that it was nothing more than stamped and painted tin.

"I refused, point-blank, to describe them in glowing terms or to offer them to my listeners," she said. "I was accused of insubordination, of embarrassing the station, and affronting the sponsor. But I knew that all I was doing was trying to be honest with my audience."

Ruth decided to solicit the help of the *Consumer's Foundation* panel of 200 women volunteers. Each was sent one of the pins with the sponsor's description and asked to consider whether the product lived up to the advertising.

"The answer," said Ruth, "was an overwhelming 'No!'"

Thus, she won the first of a long list of confrontations with both management and sponsors. And from that point forward, if Ruth Lyons thought a sponsor was doing itself a disservice with a particular advertising approach, she intervened and offered alternatives.

The new year, 1944, saw America deeper into the war and yet closer than ever to winning the conflict. In February, Ruth learned she was pregnant and due in November.

a gift of love

At the age of 39, Ruth knew her pregnancy came with risks, but she desperately wanted a complete family. Without a child from her first marriage, she knew this was probably her last chance.

Her sister Rose gave birth to a girl, Linda Jayne Lupton, late in the summer. As godmother, Ruth held the baby the day she was born, and the experience gave her a much-needed boost of confidence and strengthened her resolve to

They named her Candace Laird, because Ruth thought *Candace* was beautiful and because Rose Laird was her long-time friend.

have a child of her own. She and Herman began looking for a larger house. It seemed as if everything in her life was coming together.

Meanwhile, *Your Morning Matinee* and *Petticoat Partyline* continued to hold top spots in the ratings. But almost without notice, *Petticoat Partyline* on WSAI was gone, the victim of a new FCC rule dictating that no single entity could own more than one radio station in a given broadcast area. Crosley Broadcasting sold WSAI to Marshall Field, III, an heir to the famous Chicago department store, Marshall Field's. The deal was official on June 3, 1944, and Ruth and her listeners said goodbye to *Petticoat Partyline*.

Something had to be done to take care of sponsors, so a Saturday broadcast of *Your Morning Matinee* was added to WLW's program schedule. Its popularity dwarfed that of any of the station's other shows. The number of listeners in Ohio, Kentucky, Indiana, Michigan, and West Virginia approached one million. Sponsors paid prime-time rates and felt fortunate for the chance to do so.

Busloads of women arrived at Crosley Square every morning to fill the studio seats on the main floor and the balcony. More than 80,000 children under the age of 12 were enrolled in the show's birthday club. Each received a card the week of his or her birthday. Because so many young children accompanied their mothers, Ruth came up with another feature to entertain the kids: the "Peppermint Horse." At her request, WLW obtained an old merry-go-round horse, painted it in red and white stripes, and mounted it on a stand. Before the show, each child was allowed to sit on the horse for a make-believe ride, drawing enthusiastic applause from their mothers and others in the audience.

"THE YEAR 1944 WAS ONE NEVER to be forgotten," Ruth wrote, twenty-five years later. "On August 27, 1944, at 7:34 in the morning, our dearly beloved Candace Laird Newman was born. We called her Candy. [For] several weeks after Candy's birth I broadcast from home, and daughter made her debut at the mike at the age of six weeks. Our house was filled once more with the comings and goings of engineers, and that Christmas the Ruth Lyons Christmas Fund swelled to one hundred thousand dollars."

The sentiments were authentic. But a different, sad reality lay behind Ruth's story. On August 29, she was rushed to Cincinnati's Jewish Hospital in labor. (In her will, Ruth would leave the rights to her songs to Jewish Hospital.) She was just six months into her pregnancy. Her baby, a girl, was stillborn.

The experience was too terrible to contemplate. After waiting so many years—how could such a tragedy occur? Ruth was beyond heartbroken. She remembered how her older brother died when he was

"No child was ever more wanted or cherished."

just a few days old, and wondered if that family tragedy was somehow related, if there was a problem that was carried from one generation to another. She blamed herself for wanting a child. She blamed herself for things she had never done. On the baby's death certificate, Ruth's occupation was listed as "housewife."

Herman did his best to chase away such thoughts and reassure his wife that she had done nothing wrong. But he was angry—angry with God or fate or whatever agency had brought this on Ruth. How was it that he, who had always done the right thing, who had served God—a God he was doubting more and more—how was it that he and his wife were handed this cruel blow? And the most innocent of all, the baby. Why?

In the midst of their grief, Ruth's doctor came to the couple with a proposal. A girl had been born in the same hospital two days earlier. Ironically, Ruth and Herman knew the mother. The doctor encouraged them to adopt the baby and raise it as their own. Some sources maintained that the child was an orphan; others stated that the baby's mother gave her up. Regardless, Herman and Ruth embraced the decision to adopt the healthy baby girl.

They named her Candace Laird Newman, the name Ruth had settled on months earlier. She chose "Candace" because she thought it was beautiful. "Laird" was in honor of her long-time friend, Rose Laird, an internationally famous cosmetologist whose cosmetics were sold by upscale stores across the country. Laird was a frequent guest on Ruth's WKRC shows. They hit it off from the beginning, and had gotten to know one another well. She was often a guest at the Newmans' home when she was in Cincinnati. Ruth chose Rose Laird to be Candy's godmother, much to Rose's delight.

Ruth and Herman were committed to treating Candy as their own natural child. "No child was ever more wanted or cherished," said one of Ruth's closest friends. Candy was bright-eyed and plump, just as Ruth had been as a baby. Like Ruth, she also had red-gold hair with a slight curl. The Newmans maintained the fiction of Candy's origins for all but a very few close friends. Some listeners, co-workers, or other acquaintances may have done the math, but none broached the question. Yes, the baby was a bit premature. But, miraculously, she had no health problems.

The family secret was closely held for years. When Mickey Fisher went to work for Ruth in 1957 after being a fan for years, she didn't know Candy was adopted. "All I knew is she went to the hospital, had the baby, and came home with the baby." Mickey learned what really happened some months later when she and Elsa Heisel, Ruth's assistant, were answering Ruth's fan mail. A letter writer wanted to know if Ruth's baby had died in delivery and if Candy had been adopted.

"I went to Elsa," Mickey related, "because we were answering the mail on our own. I said, 'What do I say?' and Elsa said, 'Just for your information, Candy is adopted. We don't acknowledge that, we don't write back to people who ask about that. We put the letters in the round file.' So into the round file the letter went."

Mickey and everyone else on the staff strictly adhered to that policy. "I never answered any letter that brought that subject up," she said, although she did wonder what curious fans thought about the lack of a reply.

Candy's introduction to Ruth's radio audience consisted of a few baby vocalizations that Ruth coaxed out of her at six weeks of age. Thereafter, her life at home—her first tooth, first words, first steps, and all the other milestones of a toddler's life—was detailed on Ruth's shows. Life at home, in general, became a more frequent topic of conversation—Herman's habits and irritations, shopping, appliances going on the blink, the traffic getting to work, anything Ruth thought her audience would identify with. There was a world of difference between this marriage and her first, and she reveled in it.

Ruth and Herman bought a larger house, and Ruth hired two full-time housekeepers to do the cleaning, cooking, and caring for their daughter on weekdays. Candy, though, was not neglected by either of her working parents. Her mother and father doted on her, cherishing and teaching her. They gave her just about anything she wanted, somehow without spoiling her. She was, as Ruth maintained, a unique child—unique in more ways than one.

EARLY IN 1945, Crosley Broadcasting was sold to AVCO, the Aviation Corporation. With the war winding down, many companies retooled to manufacture consumer goods. The Crosley Corporation was among them, but the company's president, Powel Crosley, Jr., had his mind set on being an automaker.

Crosley became a radio pioneer when he introduced the first affordable radio receivers in 1921. A few months later, he founded WLW so people would have a reason to buy radios. Over the next two decades, he created one of America's major corporations, a company whose products—ranging from radios to refrigerators—were sold on every continent. He also built aircraft and ventured into other fields, and along the way became a multi-millionaire.

But his lifelong dream had been to make automobiles. (His brother, Lewis, once said that the only reason Powel became wealthy was so he could be an automaker.) He built a few thousand Crosley cars between 1939 and 1942, but was interrupted by war before he really got started.

Powel Crosley hadn't originally intended to include the broadcast operation in the sale of his corporation to AVCO, but his financial advisors told him that he would take an enormous hit in taxes if he retained WLW. During the war, AVCO built aircraft, ships, and a host of other items for the military. Cash-rich with its war profits, AVCO became a multi-tentacled conglomerate, buying up a variety of manufacturing concerns. Already the owner of two major aviation companies, it bought Lockheed, then swooped up a diverse, unrelated group of properties, among them Crosley, the New Idea farm implement company, American Standard, and Bendix electrical products. (An article in the October 7, 1946, issue of *Time* magazine labeled AVCO "Everything, Inc.")

AVCO enlarged Crosley's appliance line and made WLW its flagship station. WLW's management, programming, and financial operations were left unchanged at first. Gradually, however, AVCO's corporate leaders tightened budgets, cut expenses, and delayed pay raises within its Crosley Broadcasting division, trying to increase its profit margin. On the revenue side of the ledger, the simplest way for WLW to improve its bottom line was to raise its ad rates. But an arbitrary rate hike might drive away business. Rates varied from show to show and by how much advertising was purchased at any one time. Certain sponsors also paid more or less than the set rates, depending on their relationship with the station. One strategy for increasing revenue was to replace a low-rated show with one that drew more listeners and thus commanded higher ad rates.

WLW had one asset that was all but guaranteed to bring in the advertiser dollars: Ruth Lyons. With the sale of WSAI and demise of *Petticoat Partyline*, Ruth had some free time. Now that she had a family, she refused to work morning, noon, and night the way she did in the 1930s when she was a career-building single woman, but she could still do a morning show AND an afternoon show. Herman was at work all day, anyway. There would have to be a raise, though. By this time she was earning over $100 a week. A new half-hour show would add another ten hours or more to her weekly schedule. Ruth already brought in thousands of dollars a week for WLW and, with sponsors waiting, a new show would bring in thousands more. Thus she had no qualms about demanding higher pay.

Ruth knew her listeners' likes and dislikes, and how they responded to various segments of her shows. This would be another opportunity to tailor a program to their needs and interests. She considered how limited daily life was for many women—cleaning, laundry, ironing, washing dishes, and all the other chores that marked most of their days. It occurred to her that there were thousands of women from nearby small towns who had never had lunch in a big hotel. A broadcast from a nice dining room in a hotel, like she had done with the first *Consumer's Foundation* show—that would be the ticket.

She pitched her idea to WLW vice president Robert Dunville, who liked the concept. Any show by Ruth Lyons was bound to be a moneymaker. They determined that fifty was a good number for an active, engaged audience. Dunville told her to work out the details and that he would put the resources of the station behind her. He had in mind shaking up the early afternoon lineup—a time when lots of housewives were listening. (The noon to 1 p.m. time slot featured the news, *Everybody's Farm*, and a Procter & Gamble soap opera, *Linda's First Love*. Unknown to WLW, P&G was making plans to fill the entire hour with its soap operas, thus giving P&G products maximum exposure during the most listened-to daytime hour.)

Ruth decided on the Gibson Hotel, located downtown on Walnut Street, as the site for the broadcasts. It was older than the Netherland, but a true landmark that was still one of Cincinnati's best. (She may have felt that the Netherland was too posh and sophisticated for her audience.)

Ruth negotiated with Gibson management what is termed today as a "win-win." To accommodate WLW's new show and its audience, the hotel converted some formerly wasted space on its mezzanine level into a radio studio. Crosley Broadcasting may have helped fund construction of the room, and the company's engineers assisted in its design. It partially overlooked the main ballroom, giving the Gibson extra space for banquets and other functions on the weekends.

With tables for fifty people, Ruth wanted to call the show *The 50 Club*. Management thought it should be the *Ruth Lyons' Luncheon Show*. "I have never used my name in connection with any show that I have done," Ruth said, "for I always felt that, should I leave the show, it might well continue without my name." So it was called *The 50 Club*. Lunch was served at noon, after which tables were cleared and the broadcast started at one o'clock. *The 50 Club* only ran for half an hour. Another P&G soap opera, *Big Sister*, came on at 1:30 p.m.

Ruth's *Your Morning Matinee* still ran for an hour, six days a week; neither P&G nor NBC had anything it wanted to push before 9 a.m., so WLW could do what it wanted with the early morning. With "great fear and trepidation," said Ruth, she broke the news of her new afternoon show on *Your Morning Matinee*. "I told my audience about the new show we had in mind, and invited them to send in for tickets. The tickets cost one dollar per person. (Ruth didn't think WLW management would underwrite the cost of the daily luncheon.) The next morning we were deluged with mail, and we had sold enough tickets for the next three years." The total came to more than 37,000 guests, many of whom arrived early to join the audience for *Your Morning Matinee*, guaranteeing an audience of enthusiastic fans for *The 50 Club*.

THE PROGRAM MADE ITS DEBUT on Tuesday, February 5, 1946. To save space, there was no band. Instead, Ruth played the theme song on a small piano. The first show starred Ruth and her announcer, Paul Jones, and the fifty ladies in the audience. Ruth awarded prizes during every show, a signature of *Your Morning Matinee*. Local merchants and manufacturers donated prizes. To give *The 50 Club* a touch of class, a stylish and expensive lady's hat was given away every day. As a comedic touch, Paul Jones, a former Marine, modeled each day's hat.

"We gave household hints and played musical chairs," Ruth remembered, "with a prize to the woman who finally wound up on the magic chair. What a scramble! We had guests from the theater, writers, and others of note who came to town, and the women loved it."

The 50 Club was billed as an "audience participation show," and Ruth made sure the audience participated. She selected women to come to the microphone and talk about their pet peeves in a segment called "Get it Off Your Chest." Another segment, "Here's Your Chance," gave an audience member the opportunity to do something she had never done but always wanted to do. Ladies were encouraged to share their own household hints in a bit called "Help Paul with His Housework." Some of the tips were tongue-in-cheek, such as burning wool pants to keep away mosquitoes and washing chickens with Oxydol laundry detergent.

Ruth interviewed individuals in the audience, but the interviews were not the conventional Q&A style. They might begin with, "Where are you from?" and "How many children do you have?" But Ruth would draw them into a casual conversation on the topic of the day or about their everyday lives. Her interviews were galvanizing, not unlike reality TV, and drew listeners to the show.

Several WLW staffers also participated in the program. There was always at least one engineer and several setup boys who doubled as ushers and gophers and whatever else was needed. One of the setup boys, Gene Walz, would be appointed as the director of *The 50 Club* when it moved to television. He didn't have any on-the-job experience, but Ruth said he was going to be the director, so he was.

Ruth was always willing to do someone a favor. If she thought a co-worker, such as Walz, was capable to doing more than he was already doing, she arranged for his advancement. She was also a willing listener when people had problems, and usually offered surprisingly practical advice. Thus she was given the nickname "Mother," and it stuck, spreading beyond WLW's staff and into the public. From the mid-1950s on, her fans casually referred to her as Mother, as did the local press from time to time.

Those who worked for Ruth Lyons respected her. Like Elsa Sule, they also found her intimidating. Elsa, just out of college, said she was "scared to death" when she met Ruth in 1943. Singer Marian Spelman remembered Ruth as "captivating," "warm and nice" in their first meeting in 1951. "But she was intimidating in a way, not meaning to be," added Spelman. "She was just such an enormous power."

THE DAYS FELL into a pleasant rhythm. Ruth and her cast did the morning show at the studio, and then rode the few blocks to the Gibson Hotel. Ruth, Elsa Heisel, and another staffer went on an outing once a week to pick out the hats to be given away.

The 50 Club's first sponsor was Procter & Gamble. The early shows began with announcer Paul Jones reading a lead-in that directly identified P&G's products with the show and Ruth: "From the Hotel Gibson in Cincinnati, Oxydol, the soap that gets your whole wash sparkling white, sparkling bright, sparkling clean, and Crisco, the pure, all vegetable shortening—it's digestible— presents a daily luncheon meeting with the famous *50 Club*."

With P&G headquartered in Cincinnati, it was appropriate that the company sponsor the region's most popular radio program. Ruth's relationship with P&G would not always be so harmonious, however.

a star is born

Procter & Gamble had three soap operas running on WLW in the coveted noon hour, filling all of its minutes but the fifteen occupied by Ernie Lee, a country music singer with a large following. The company, however, wanted the entire noon hour for broadcast of its soap operas and advertising of its products. Following a format reshuffling, part of it to accommodate NBC and the Mutual Broadcasting System, which pressured the station to carry more of their shows, Ernie Lee was pushed later into the day, replaced from noon to 12:15 by P&G's homespun Ma Perkins, the most famous

Ruth's Christmas Fund shows were demanding, but there was still her own family Christmas as well.

widow in America and one of the few to own her own lumberyard. Perpetually in her 60s, she was well on her way to an ageless twenty-seven-year radio career. Needless to say, P&G had, at last, exactly what it wanted— the entire noon hour. For the moment, anyway.

P&G continued to sponsor *The 50 Club*, which had been moved to 11 a.m., but the schedule was turned upside down again in the spring of 1949. A few months earlier, Ruth began lobbying for a noontime start for *The 50 Club*. She knew what P&G already knew: more women would be sitting down to lunch or on break at noon than at 11 in the morning. With a five-year-old child of her own, she knew that thousands of women would be busy with welcoming their children home or preparing them for kindergarten in the late mornings and early afternoons. (Candy did not attend kindergarten. Her socialization was probably limited to her parents, the household help, and her cousin, Linda, who was a regular playmate.)

James Shouse, Robert Dunville, and the rest of the WLW management team knew better than to argue with the station's ratings star. Besides, a noon start for *The 50 Club* could be sold to advertisers as an advantage. So, on Monday, April 4, 1949, Ruth's show moved to the top of the day and was followed by a fifteen-minute news segment and a fifteen-minute program called *Everybody's Farm*.

P&G, as anyone could have guessed, was not happy about the new schedule changes. *Guiding Light, Linda's First Romance,* and the company's other soaps were not broadcast at noon on every station that carried them.

But Procter & Gamble wanted the midday time slot in its hometown, and threatened to pull its advertising from *The 50 Club* if it didn't get its way. Forced to choose between a major sponsor and its most popular performer, WLW went with Ruth Lyons. P&G stopped advertising on Ruth's show. Other sponsors, however, lined up to replace the consumer giant. P&G

"I woke up about four o'clock and discovered my entire body was broken out in immense hives."

continued advertising on other WLW programs—the company could not afford to *not* advertise on WLW—but ads for its products would not be heard or seen on *The 50 Club* for years. In fact, the dispute would turn into a private war.

WLW HAD A TRADITION of taking its acts on the road. This tradition began in the 1920s, when radio stations discovered that their performers could draw big crowds and attract new advertisers with live shows. The shows were cheap to put on, and station promotion guaranteed a packed house. Expenses were covered by a small admission fee.

The touring continued in earnest in the 1930s when WLW's half-million-watt signal blanketed regions that few other stations could reach. It was primarily the country and western stars who went on the road, plus the occasional comedian.

Popular singers, dance bands, and jazz groups did their own booking, but most didn't have the drawing-power of the so-called "hillbilly" performers—at least not among the majority of WLW's listeners.

Putting musicians and singers (and everything that went with them) on the road in four or five states was not easy. To get the job done, WLW hired George Biggar and Bill McCluskey away from WLS, where they had been fielding acts for the Chicago station. McCluskey was responsible for the heavy lifting, making all the arrangements for appearances and ensuring that everyone got where they were supposed to be. With Biggar at the helm, the road shows grew in frequency, as well as the number of towns visited. WLW talent played at civic and corporate auditoriums, theaters, county fairs, and beginning in 1939, the Ohio State Fair.

The idea to scale up the road shows originated with Shouse. Always promotion-conscious, the WLW executive saw the station's shows and its performers as "goodwill ambassadors." Doris Day, Bonnie Lou, Merle Travis, Red Foley, and Whitey Ford often played to standing-room-only crowds. At any one time, half of the cast members of *Boone County Jamboree*, a Saturday night country music and square-dance show (later called *Midwestern Hayride*), might be performing in other towns and venues, along with several WLW solo acts. Frazier Thomas, an announcer for the shows, also doubled as a comedian and stage magician.

In November of 1945, WLW took *The 50 Club* on the road for the first time, broadcasting from Muncie, Indiana, sixty-five miles northwest of Cincinnati. "It was a long trip," Ruth recalled, "and it snowed very hard that Friday morning. But the crowd that turned out to greet us filled the theatre with standing room only." WLW put the show on in Muncie with only a couple of weeks' notice, confident in the drawing power of Ruth Lyons and *The 50 Club*.

Right away, Ruth decided to do Saturday shows for hospitalized children in Louisville and Indianapolis in addition to Children's Hospital in Cincinnati as part of the annual Christmas Fund drive. The preparations for these shows, along with the travel and the actual broadcast itself, demanded a lot of time and energy. Ruth drove herself through the long days, robbing herself of sleep when necessary to meet all of her commitments while still doing her daily shows, too.

The hard work and long hours foreshadowed the future. Indianapolis was the final hospital show, just a week before Christmas. "The morning of our visit to Indianapolis," Ruth remembered, "I woke up about four o'clock and discovered my entire body was broken out in immense hives. The doctor came and gave me a shot of adrenalin, and very shaken and scared, I caught the train to Indiana. But at the Riley Memorial Hospital I forgot temporarily my own discomfort when a little blind boy, just four years old, insisted that I—and I alone—give him a tool chest and let him feel each tool."

This was not an isolated event.

"At all the Christmas parties," said Ruth, "we had a crying room where we would go before the parties and weep as they brought the little stricken ones in wheelchairs and carts to the various playrooms."

She had to ask Herman to cut her girdle off her when she got home after the long day in Indianapolis. Ruth more or less dismissed the case of hives, once the doctor took care of them. But it would not be the last time her body reacted violently to overwork, worry, and stress.

The 50 Club was becoming a phenomenon. After a second round of ticket sales in 1945, WLW received enough ticket requests for ten years of sellouts, but sales were limited to three years. Ruth's staff spent quite a bit of time returning the cash and checks sent with requests that couldn't be honored. Elsa Sule, in charge of tickets at the time, noted that some ladies wrote to tell her that they had included their *50 Club* tickets in their wills.

Being part of the studio audience of a Ruth Lyons program was important enough that small-town newspapers in three states devoted coverage to groups of women attending *Your Morning Matinee* and *The 50 Club*. Some groups chartered buses to take them to Cincinnati from Zanesville, Indianapolis, and other distant towns. A mother and daughter attending Ruth Lyons' show might merit a paragraph in their hometown paper, while a local group rated a headline, like this 14-pointer from *The National Road Traveler*, of Richmond, Indiana: "Posey Home Demonstration Club Enjoys Cincinnati Trip."

According to the Richmond newspaper story, the thirty-two Home Demonstration Club members and seventeen guests boarded two chartered buses at 6 a.m. to depart for Cincinnati. They arrived two hours later at WLW's studios, joining the audience for *Your Morning Matinee*, followed by a luncheon and *The 50 Club*. The newspaper listed the names of the women who "got on the air," as well as the prizes won by each of the ladies. (No one ever left a Ruth Lyons show empty-handed; companies that couldn't buy air time because it was all sold out got at least a mention when Ruth gave away their products.)

Even as the newspapers competed with WLW and the other radio stations for the same advertising dollars, they gave Ruth and her show a lot of publicity, which attracted more listeners and advertisers. The celebrities on her guest list often were big enough to get the papers' attention, and the Ruth Lyons Children's Christmas Fund was a favorite of local editors.

The fund drive lasted for nearly three months every year, with the press cheering it on the whole time. Total annual donations had quickly grown to six figures, and the money went for far more than toys. It often paid for specialized medical equipment. In addition to the Children's Hospital, the Christmas Fund was shared with Cincinnati General Hospital, Riley Memorial Hospital in Indianapolis, and the Children's Hospital in Louisville. When Ruth and other *50 Club* cast members visited the hospitals, around Christmas and often during Easter, there were always stories and photos in the local papers. If she sought coverage of such events, it was to bring in donations, though WLW's publicity department customarily sent out advance notice of her visits.

Ruth Lyons expanded beyond the Midwest in 1947. Crosley Broadcasting bought radio station WINS in New York City that year, and *Your Morning Matinee* was added to the WINS program schedule. Ruth was now in seven states, including New York and New Jersey. Ohio, Indiana, and Kentucky constituted the main broadcast zone, but WLW also had listeners in southern Michigan and West Virginia. There were loyal listeners in Illinois and Pennsylvania as well, sometimes battling static to tune in.

Most of the crew from *Your Morning Matinee* did the show from the WINS studios for a week during the Christmas Fund drive. Listeners were generous with donations, so Ruth added New York's Hospital for Special Surgery to the Fund's beneficiaries. *Your Morning Matinee* was carried by WINS for the next two years, while *The 50 Club* stayed home, regarded as too Midwest-oriented for New York listeners.

The medium of the future—television—arrived in Cincinnati in 1947, though few were aware of it. Transmitting under the call sign W8XCT (the X in a call sign meant it was experimental), Crosley Broadcasting beamed out TV pictures and sound for exactly one hour a week. It was one of only eight stations in the United States.

next stop, the future

On April 4, 1939, under the call sign W8XCT, Crosley Broadcasting held its first television demonstration for the press. It wasn't a broadcast—that would come a few years later. Instead, the signal was carried by a coaxial cable, running from WLWT's forty-eighth-floor studio in the Carew Tower

The studios and tower, on a cliff overlooking Fairview Heights, was called "Mt. Olympus."

to a conference room in the H&S Pogue department store on the ground floor. This first closed-circuit TV program featured performers from WLW and WSAI talking and singing under incredibly bright lights. The picture was tiny, gray, and blurry around the edges, but it was television—a moving picture with sound.

Inventors and experimenters had been saying that television was "just around the corner" for twenty years, going back to the early days when radio stations like WRNY in New York used mechanical scanning systems to transmit pictures to home-built sets. Magazines and newspapers carried announcements that this broadcaster or that manufacturer was just months away from bringing TV to the masses. Few, however, were ever heard from again. None fulfilled the promises made. Neither the Carew Tower demonstration nor the Crosley/DuMont and RCA demos at the 1939 New York World's Fair sent people rushing out to buy TV sets, not that there were any to buy. Technical standards had yet to be established, and without them the manufacturers couldn't begin to design sets for the public.

Powel Crosley, Jr. didn't mind his engineers tinkering with television, but the Crosley Broadcasting founder never really got behind the effort to develop the technology. He was highly critical of TV's commercial potential and unwilling to bear the huge development costs, as his company and other manufacturers had done with radio. Instead, advertisers and consumers would have to pay for television's development—and they would, with sky-high prices.

World War II put television on hold, as it did just about everything non-military. Technical resources and brainpower, as well as manufacturing capability, were diverted to the war effort. But after the war, RCA and other manufacturers quickly developed the necessary standards. Crosley Broadcasting had already received permission from the FCC to build a television station in Cincinnati, barring an unforeseen continuation of the war.

In June, 1946, AVCO/Crosley made its first experimental broadcast, beaming a silent test pattern image from the Carew Tower to WLW's building at Ninth and Elm. Two days later, the same setup transmitted the image of a box of Borax soap, a precursor of television advertising.

Television in Cincinnati went to a regular schedule in July, 1947, when W8XCT began broadcasting one hour per week. By year's end, the station was broadcasting twenty hours a week, much to the delight of the several dozen TV set owners in the Cincinnati area.

"I was too fat! And television added at least ten pounds to one's appearance."

After these tentative steps, Crosley Broadcasting made its commercial television debut as WLWT on February 9, 1948—the "T" standing for television, thus distinguishing it from WLW radio. Crosley soon began operating stations in Dayton, Columbus, Indianapolis, and Atlanta, called WLW-D, WLW-C, WLW-I, and WLW-A, respectively.

Engineers at WLWT usually got the broadcast day started by transmitting the test pattern—a still image with a number of calibrating marks—for a few hours. This warmed up the equipment and served as a tool for checking signal quality. It was also a source of mystery and awe to many folks who enjoyed looking at the strange image on the little boxes in their living rooms. Some newspaper program schedules for Cincinnati and other cities listed "Test Pattern" with the rest of the programming.

Talent was another of Powel Crosley, Jr.'s reservations about television. "There won't be enough good talent to fill the broadcast schedule," he predicted. Crosley, of course, turned out to be wrong, although no one knew who or what would click with viewers. The *Cincinnati Times-Star's* book reviewer was given a fifteen-minute segment to talk about books. A circus that came to town was televised. News was a staple. Soap operas were converted from radio, with a quick change of actors in some instances. Boxing, wrestling and other sports were hits. The first local baseball telecast took place on September 21, 1941, when the Cincinnati Reds beat the Pittsburgh Pirates 3-1, but no one paid for its broadcast. The first commercial broadcast in Cincinnati was not baseball but a Golden Gloves title bout, sponsored by hometown Weidemann Beer—held a week before WLWT's official opening in 1948. On the station's opening day, the first sponsored programming was a broadcast from Cincinnati's Sinton hotel, titled *Luncheon at the Sinton.*

PRODUCING ABOUT FOUR HOURS of its own daily programming, WLWT signed up as the first affiliate of the newly-organized television network, NBC, in April, 1948. NBC filled the evening hours with variety shows starring nationally-known performers, as well as sporting events and plays, both original and adapted.

The Newmans had a rocking chair in every room—and one television set in the house. Herman and Candy spent quite a bit of time in front of its seven-inch screen. Ruth feigned a lack of interest, but enjoyed watching a number of programs, including basketball games.

People who couldn't afford sets often haunted shops that sold TVs during the afternoon hours, when broadcasts started. Bar and restaurant owners capitalized on the demand for television by installing receivers for their patrons to watch. The average neighborhood bar saw its business increase by a third after adding a TV set. Newspapers carried ads for establishments with TVs, especially when a sporting event was scheduled to be televised.

In 1948, the price for a table-model Philco with a seven-inch screen was $395. That was large sum of money for most folks. A console or floor-model Philco with a built-in AM/FM radio receiver and record player went for $595. Other brands carried similar price tags. Deluxe sets with fine veneer and woodworking could cost much more. (Television screens were often described not in corner-to-corner diagonal measurement, but in the number of square inches of screen surface. Thus, a television with a seven-inch diagonal screen could be touted as having over fifty square inches of screen.)

Television was an expensive proposition for broadcasters as well. Crosley made a huge investment with no guarantee of income. Its first TV camera cost $15,000, enough to buy a couple of houses and a trio of Crosley automobiles. The company also poured several hundred thousand dollars into a brand-new facility to house WLWT's studios, transmitter, and offices, with the antenna tower alongside it. The site was nicknamed "Mt. Olympus," because it overlooked the city from a cliff above Fairview Heights, where Herman Newman grew up.

FOR SEVERAL YEARS AFTER THE WAR, Herman and Ruth took Candy to New York City to celebrate New Year's Eve. Herman joined the hundreds of thousands of people crowding Times Square, while Ruth and Candy watched on television in their hotel room as the big lighted ball dropped. Afterwards, Herman returned with a surprise selection of snacks he picked up at delis on his way.

Ruth always hurried back to her shows within a day or two, even though January was normally a quiet month with people and businesses still recovering from the lengthy holiday season. January of 1949 was no different from any other January until Wednesday, January 17. As the *Associated Press* reported the next day, "Ruth Lyons' *50 Club* program over radio station WLW, went off the air at noon yesterday after eight minutes when a guest became ill. A physician was summoned and gave the unidentified guest first aid." The woman had suffered a heart attack, but survived. Ruth, on the other hand, was so shaken she couldn't go on with the show. The remaining twenty-two minutes were filled with music.

A few weeks after this frightening event, Ruth was surprised to be handed the job of program director at WLWT. She hadn't asked for it, but her experience made her a logical choice. Besides, nobody knew what this new medium was supposed to be. Like everyone else in television, Ruth made it up as she went along, with the help of Vera Tyson. She put together a full daytime schedule, in addition to *The 50 Club*. Bill Nimmo, who would go on to fame as a network performer, and Betty Clooney, Rosemary's sister, were among the first staff additions.

Ruth gave special attention to developing shows that focused on sponsors, like *The Pogue Style Show*. (Broadcast on November 13, 1947, this was the first television show produced at Crosley Square.) She continued hosting *Your Morning Matinee* and *The 50 Club* on radio, driving between Crosley Square and Mt. Olympus as necessary. The WLWT program director job was supposed to last six months, but it was nine months before she was freed of the responsibility. It was a difficult nine months, as Ruth was hosting *The 50 Club* five days a week and *Your Morning Matinee* six days a week. (The local newspapers often referred to her as "femcee" of these shows.)

To educate herself and get fresh viewpoints, she visited other TV stations in Chicago and New York. One new idea came to her as she sat in the audience for a rehearsal of *The Perry Como Show*. The cameras blocked her view, which she considered a handicap for performers as well as the audience. "I saw nothing of what was happening onstage," she later reported. "I made up my mind right then and there that I would never work with cameras between me and my studio audience." She knew, too, that it worked both ways; those onstage saw nothing but cameras and lights, so they couldn't respond to the spectators.

Initially, Ruth argued against moving *The 50 Club* to the TV studio on Mt. Olympus, eliminating the sound-only broadcast on WLW altogether. Her first reaction was right to the point: "I was too fat! And television added at least ten pounds to one's appearance." She was five-foot, three inches tall and weighed over 160 pounds, and she had been gaining weight slowly but steadily for the past five years, which she blamed on the fine food and desserts served at the Hotel Gibson for *The 50 Club*. Reluctantly, she finally agreed to give TV a try —for one week.

When she stepped into WLWT's makeshift studio for the first time in May of 1949, the heat from the lights was intolerable. She found it difficult to see in certain directions, and worried that she would look terrible, squinting into the lights. As she walked across the studio to the stage, a voice came over a PA system: "Miss Lyons, the first rule of television is never cross in front of a camera."

"I hadn't even seen a camera," she said years later, recalling that first day on the set. "Then the boys began to tell me where I must stand, sit, where I should be when talking to the women in the audience, and that I must always face the camera."

Ruth Lyons was accustomed to giving directions and orders, not taking them. In all her years on radio with a studio audience, she moved wherever she wanted, even walked among the audience. She wasn't about to take a back seat now, and immediately ordered that the lights in the studio be changed, against the wishes of some of the engineers. The next day the hot lights had been replaced by what she described as "cool incandescent" lights.

Ruth was discouraged at the end of the trial week after viewing kinescopes of her show. (Before videotape came into use in 1956, television programs were captured and copied by filming them directly from TV screens with a high-quality sixteen-millimeter camera. These films were called kinescopes.) Ruth thought she looked awful. The more she thought about the move to television, the more she was against it. A week after the trial run, she told Dunville she wanted no more to do with TV.

"Well," the general manager replied, "it's here to stay, and it will be around for a long time after you're gone."

Ruth realized she was protesting the inevitable.

"I pray," she wrote, "there is a place in television, that there is a place for me, who in no way looks like a starlet, and doesn't sing like Doris Day, a place for a housewife who was born in Lincoln's time, who is comfortably padded and who is more interested in children and farmers and good food than in glamour."

Ruth didn't return to television until September, after WLWT moved from the Crosley Square studios to Mt. Olympus. In the interim, she lost forty pounds and regained her former slender figure. Her weight-loss over the summer fueled speculation as to what sort of diet or other regimen she followed. *Cincinnati Post* columnist Mary Wood, as a part of a lifelong campaign to render the mundane intriguing, fabricated a story about Ruth living on grapefruit for a couple of days, then fruit juice and nothing else for month. Wood claimed Ruth lost "fifty or sixty pounds" in just four weeks—a health-threatening proposition. But there was no secret diet or magical formula. Just fourteen-hour days for four months, according to Ruth. And small meals.

SHE GOT WHAT SHE WANTED for the studio setup of *The 50 Club*. With the new RCA video cameras positioned so as to not get between Ruth and her audience, the show's director, producer, and camera men had to be very creative and ready for anything. There was no telling which way the host might turn or where she might go next. Ruth roamed the stage like a tiny tornado at times, and mingled with the audience at will. Gene Walz, the first director of *The 50 Club* on television, learned to follow her gaze. "I could always tell what she was going to do next," he said, "by watching her eyes."

Ruth gratefully gave up the job of program director in October when John T. Murphy was brought in from Dayton. Murphy, who had served as general manager of Crosley Broadcasting's relatively new TV station, WLWD, got started in the business as a page at NBC while he was in college and later worked in sales and management. He was known as the executive who discovered and signed Buffalo Bob and Howdy Doody at NBC.

In his job with the network, Muphy traveled to affiliates around the country, watching their operations, fixing problems, and advising station management, so he was in close touch with dozens of broadcasters. When he learned that WLWD was going on the air and needed a general manager, he asked Crosley Broadcasting for the job and was hired in 1948. The station was housed in an enormous old skating rink—a giant Quonset hut that gave WLWD room for two massive studios on one floor, plus a wrestling rink for televised bouts. (WLWD, now WDTN, still works out of the skating rink and remains an NBC affiliate.)

After Murphy took over her programming duties, Ruth could concentrate on *The 50 Club* and *Your Morning Matinee* (still a WLW radio program). At first, the telecast of *The 50 Club* felt just like a radio broadcast, as long as she ignored the cameras. She might have been a little more aware of her clothes and makeup—and especially conscious of details like runs in her hosiery—but so were the other women in the cast. After a few shows, the camera ceased to be intimidating.

As always, though, Ruth played mainly to the audience. In order to see what the viewers saw, she persuaded engineers to set up a TV monitor within view of the stage so she could keep an eye on the live broadcast. It took some getting used to, but during rehearsals she found that she could glance at the screen while she was performing and not distract the audience or herself from what she was doing.

When *The 50 Club* returned to television in September, Ruth asked for a new monitor. The one she was looking at didn't have a tuner nor did it have an antenna, and it was designed to accept the television signals through a cable. She described it as "decrepit" and noted that "the picture was fuzzy and kept rolling constantly." It was an ironic request, given that Crosley Broadcasting's sister company, the Crosley Corporation, manufactured television sets, including the first portable TV in America. After trying "in vain," Ruth said, to get Crosley to send her a new model, she took her appeal to the airwaves.

"One day on the show I said that if any dealer who sold TV sets would send one to me, I would have it set up and would mention his name. The next morning as I drove up the hill to the TV studios, I almost didn't make the show. There was a long line of trucks, lined up to the very door, and inside were nineteen television sets being installed." The monitors sat in front of the stage, tabletop and console models alike. The dealers who weren't busy with the installations were explaining the features of their sets to the audience and staff. For that day, at least, the WLWT studio was the biggest television showroom in town, with more than a dozen brands on display—Zenith, Philco, Emerson, Muntz, RCA, Sylvania, Stromberg-Carlson, DuMont, and others.

"I was so delighted," Ruth chuckled, "that I gave each one of them a plug. The next day they were moved out by order of the management, and a brand new Crosley set was finally installed. Sometimes you have to resort to drastic means in order to achieve a very simple thing."

The 50 Club did well. By 1950, the show had twenty sponsors. Conspicuous by their absence, though, was Proctor & Gamble. P&G remained unhappy with Ruth for not yielding the noon hour to them on radio—and for tying up the coveted time slot on television. P&G and their advertising agency requested that Lyons' show at least be moved from a noon start to 12:30. But Ruth refused, and there was nothing that Murphy or Dunville, her nominal bosses at WLW, could do.

HERMAN AND CANDY seemed to take Ruth's fame in stride, but it did have its effects on the family. Rather than attend public or private school, Candy was tutored at home. Ruth feared that other children might taunt her out of jealousy, or expose her to bad habits. She and Herman also wanted to control the quality of their daughter's teachers, so accredited tutors were brought in for various subjects.

Candy was very intelligent, and turned out to be more left-brained than right. She had no ability in music, but she was fascinated by science and nature. For most of her childhood, it was her ambition to become a veterinarian.

Herman had joined the University of Cincinnati faculty as an English instructor and everyone on the Clifton campus was aware that Professor Newman was married to the famous Ruth Lyons. His courses were easy to pass, but he

warned students that he would flunk anyone who called him "Mr. Lyons."
(The name "Lyons" held more meaning for him and for Ruth than anyone else.
Ruth had long ago began telling members of the press and other people that
Lyons was merely a stage name she had selected when she began working
in radio.)

Otherwise Herman was pleasant, intelligent and almost always good for a
laugh. Ruth's co-workers talked about how he always had a joke to tell. One or
two said he was a real ladies' man, though always polite. Herman also was quite
the grammarian. While watching Ruth on television, he would sometimes call
and chide his wife for using imprecise grammar—such as saying "different from"
instead of "different than." Ruth would put him on the air and argue with him.

In September, 1950, he was quoted nationally by the *Associated Press*,
critiquing a speech and subsequent apology made by President Harry
Truman that had stirred public comment. Herman cited Truman's use of the
phrase "Stalin-like propaganda" and the president's subsequent apology as a
demonstration of the power of words.

"The importance of language as a basic factor in social and personal
problems," he said in the *AP* article, "isn't given the prominence in everyday life
it deserves."

The year 1950 also was marked by *The 50 Club's* television debut in Dayton
and Columbus. Thousands of faithful radio listeners were overjoyed to be able
to watch the show, now that it was no longer being broadcast by WLW radio.
(WLW radio stuck with news and farm programming, including *Everybody's
Farm*, during the noon hour.)

Ruth was still doing her half-hour morning radio show, *Your Morning
Matinee*, when, later in the year, *The 50 Club* was moved from Mt. Olympus to
Crosley Square downtown. It simplified her daily routine a bit, with both shows
in the same building.

With the new emphasis on television, WLW's radio studios were moved to
the basement, along with the newsroom. The sub-basement held music storage
and a bowling alley. The TV studios were on the second and fifth floors, in what
had been ballrooms (one of which served as the Elks' formal lodge for meetings
and initiations.) Production rooms, offices, and other elements were scattered
throughout the building.

Not long after the move, WLWT management brought in a consultant to redo the make-up worn by Ruth and other cast members. In those days, because of the lighting and the rather primitive cameras, the make-up had to be mostly dark. (Even today, television requires a different approach to make-up, though not as drastic as early television.) Ruth hated the look. The consultant "insisted on a very heavy dark brown make-up," she said, "with dark brown lipstick that looked as if I had just eaten a handful of chocolates, the kind that melt in your hand. All this was made more ridiculous by covering with white make-up any laugh lines or wrinkles in the face. I simply refused to submit. I could not appear before a live audience made up to look like Minnehaha, but the other girls found something exciting about all this and ran about looking like a band of squaws for weeks."

The consultant kept insisting that everyone wear the make-up, but Ruth resisted. Once again, she used her audience as leverage.

"I finally . . . insisted [that the person] doing the make-up come on the show and make me up in front of the camera. The howls of laughter proved that this [the make-up] was not for me."

In the wake of that incident, *The 50 Club* continued to grow in popularity, and more sponsors wanted the opportunity to advertise. What happened next, according to Ruth, was out of her control. "Despite my bare face showing," she said, "the sponsors began to take over the show, and the show was lengthened to an hour and a half. I worked very hard to try to keep it interesting."

Two major changes were made in *The 50 Club* staff. First, Cliff Lash, the pianist from Ruth's WKRC days, became the show's bandleader. Burt Farber was bumped up to musical director and later would move to New York to work as the orchestra leader for Arthur Godfrey's talent scout show. Then, on-air personality Frazier Thomas went to do another show, so WLW veteran Willie Thall joined *The 50 Club*.

Since 1942, Thall had been a bit-actor (usually in television skits that required a bumpkin), as well as producer, occasional singer, and host of his own variety show. He also had produced, played in, and hosted the very popular *Midwestern Hayride*, wearing bib overalls and a straw hat. He was known for the many costumes he put together on short notice, to suit the occasion. From the beginning, Willie Thall was a hit with Ruth's fans. A comical, slightly rotund character with round glasses, Thall was losing his hair—a fact Ruth exploited mercilessly. He took the kidding good-naturedly and sometimes slyly set himself up for jokes. Occasionally he would take a shot at Ruth about her age, but Ruth always had the perfect comeback. *The 50 Club* director Gene Walz said of Thall, "He was the perfect foil." Twenty years later, he would still be playing second-fiddle, co-hosting old horror films on Cincinnati's Channel 9 (WCPO) for a discount department store chain called Rink's.

NBC HAD BEEN KEEPING an eye on *The 50 Club's* popularity and in 1951 offered Ruth a seven-year contract. Apparently no one gave much thought to how she might meet the expectations of East Coast audiences or others outside the Midwest. NBC's management was fixated on her ability to draw advertiser dollars.

The plan was for the network to carry the first half hour of *The 50 Club*, Monday through Friday. Ruth would not have to work in New York City, something she wouldn't have done in any case. The program would be carried over special telephone lines from WLWT's Cincinnati studio to New York, just as NBC programs were transmitted to WLWT and other affiliates.

Crosley Broadcasting was currently paying Ruth close to $100,000 per year. It's likely that NBC's offer was close to that figure. In announcing the show's addition to NBC's schedule, the network billed *The 50 Club* as an audience participation show and noted that "Mrs. Lyons conducts a folksy-chatter type of program, with music and singing, and is said to draw enough daily mail to keep four secretaries busy." (Mail for Ruth Lyons numbered over 200,000 pieces a year.)

The announcement further stated, "Threading her way dexterously through the labyrinth of conversation, adding spice to the ad-lib proceedings and turning what might be a dull matter into a laugh-filled period, comes seemingly without effort to Ruth Lyons, whose nimble mind switches from a commercial to family happenings or the play she saw the night before with swiftness and a logicalness amazing to the uninitiated."

The schedule was a bit mixed up, depending on which region the viewers were in. When Ruth sang "Let Me Entertain You" to open *The 50 Club*, it was 1 p.m. in New York, where Daylight Savings Time was in effect (Cincinnati was still on Eastern Standard Time). In Chicago, it was 11 a.m (Central Time). Inexplicably, the show's starting time on WFAA television in Dallas, Texas, was 10:45 a.m., on Thursdays only.

The NBC network center in New York always wanted to know what Ruth had planned for every day, which she found stressful because she never knew what she would be doing. She could tell them the name of her guest, and maybe plans for a song or two, but she didn't want to be locked into anything. "I felt that much of the spontaneity of the show was being lost," she remembered.

Ruth also had difficulty dealing with the timing of the show's segments. NBC scheduled commercials every quarter hour, and Ruth figured she would at least follow that rule, in consideration of the money and exposure she was receiving. But she was less free to blend in the commercials with songs and other elements of her show. She preferred to segue into a commercial from a conversation or song that suggested the product, but NBC wasn't having any of that ad-libbing, not with their timing requirements.

With all of her extra tasks for the network, Ruth found that hosting two shows was more than she wanted to do in a day. Late in 1951, she suggested a replacement as host of *Your Morning Matinee*: Judy Perkins. An import from Indianapolis, Perkins sang on *Midwestern Hayride* over WLW and WLWT on Saturday evenings. On weekdays, she was a singer on the WLW's *Top O' the Morning* program, starting at 6:15 a.m.

Perkins took over as host of the radio show, along with singer and co-host Ernie Lee. The duo also stepped in to promote the Christmas Fund that fall, with Ruth appearing on the program once a week or so to appeal for donations. Because *The 50 Club* was being aired nationally, she could not do any fund-raising on her TV show, not with the Christmas Fund's proceeds going only to hospitals in the Midwest.

Ruth received a largely positive reception in the new markets. But a New York newspaper columnist excoriated her as a Midwest bumpkin and portrayed her audience as a bunch of old ladies gossiping over the back fence. The columnist presented various elements of the show out of context, for comedic effect—Ruth leading the singing of "The Marching Song," for example—and he held her up to ridicule for chatting with a woman in the audience about her sister. Such segments were silly, and they were fun—that was the point.

On the other side, Ruth received literally tens of thousands of fan letters from New York, Georgia, Massachusetts, Texas, Washington D.C., and everywhere else NBC aired *The 50 Club*. "Most of the mail we received," she said, "came from Atlanta, Georgia and Boston, Massachusetts. I began to realize that everywhere people were the same in their response to the show."

She might have fulfilled the seven years of her contract, and NBC eventually might have carried the full hour of her show, had Ruth not learned something the network didn't want her to know. A friend at a New York advertising agency told her that NBC's New York salespeople had been ordered to sell *The Kate Smith Show* before *The 50 Club*. Or, as Ruth put it, "The order was given to sell her show in preference to mine." Kate Smith didn't necessarily pull in more money; Ruth's time spots were always sold. But someone—or several people—in the NBC organization wanted the prime sponsors to advertise on Smith's show.

RUTH WAS ON VACATION when she learned that *The 50 Club* had lost several network sponsors.

"Well, that did it!" she recalled. "I came back to the studio before my vacation was over and told our local salesmen that I was not going to continue with the network and that I wanted them to sell out the show locally by the time I returned to work."

In an interview in the 1960s, Ruth said she had "fired" NBC. "If a performer is cancelled by the network, he is told he is being dropped. But I told NBC that I was dropping them. It was probably the first time someone had fired the network."

The WLWT salesmen sold every spot to advertisers in the Cincinnati area—even those who had been dropped to make room for network advertisers. NBC found themselves locked out of selling any ads for Ruth's show. The local sales force, in fact, sold more ads than time allowed, so WLWT management, who were backing Ruth, asked her to extend *The 50 Club* to two hours, which she did. (The reason management backed Ruth was because WLWT got only a percentage of network ad revenue, while the station pocketed all the proceeds from local advertising.)

The lengthy show, without a break, was strenuous even for Ruth. "The two-hour stint was just too much for me to continue," she explained "and we cut back to an hour and a half." Cutting that half hour made no difference in the show's popularity. Tickets were more in demand than ever, and space was made for a larger audience. The exposure also made it easier than ever to book guests. Any prominent person who happened to be in town, and any singers and musicians who were touring, made appearances on *The 50 Club*. The overwhelming majority, however, weren't paid for their appearances. The most anyone was ever paid was one dollar. Ruth had only one requirement: if the guest was a performing artist, he or she had to perform. This went for everyone, from Arthur Godfrey to Bob Hope. Politicians didn't have to sing or dance a jig (though some did), but anyone who was a performer had to agree to sing, dance, or play before Ruth would invite them on the show.

Word spread from New York to Hollywood that, if you were anywhere near Cincinnati, appearing on Ruth's show would be well worth your while. Just about every guest saw a sharp increase in record or ticket sales after a *50 Club* appearance. If a guest crossed Ruth, though, there were likely to be repercussions. Comedian Jerry Lester made that mistake when he was in Cincinnati to do several shows in February, 1951. Lester, host of an immensely popular weekly show on NBC called *Broadway Open House*, was scheduled to be a guest on *The 50 Club*, but showed up late. When Ruth chided him for his tardiness, he shrugged, saying in effect she must not be very experienced in television if she found fault with his being late. Later on the same show, he actually took the microphone away from her.

Ruth kept her cool. Then, the next day, she told her audience she would never have Lester as a guest again. Ticket sales for his Cincinnati shows suddenly dropped off, and women who saw him downtown derided him for treating Ruth so badly. Eventually, he apologized to her on his network television show.

Ruth also could take responsibility if she was wrong. Television personality and newsman Nick Clooney recalled hearing her on his car radio once, apologizing for having advertised some rose bushes the year before. "I planted some of those rose bushes, and they didn't grow," she said. "If I had the money, I would send everyone who bought one their money back. But I don't, so I'll just tell you, don't ever buy those rose bushes."

talk of the town

Mary Wood, like her good friend Ruth Lyons, had a large and loyal following as the TV and radio critic for the *Cincinnati Post*. Wood used her newspaper column to spin tales—some, shall we say, on the tall side—just as she had done in her days writing soap operas for radio. The

Candy and Ruth visited London; on one trip, Ruth saw the Queen.

columnist claimed, for instance, that the poem "Moon River," which was the opener for a late-night WLW radio program of the same name, was written in a speakeasy and was so touching it made the prostitutes who worked there cry. She wrote that the great Fats Waller was fired from WLW for playing jazz on the station's organ and stashing empty gin bottles behind it, when, in fact, the composer of "Ain't Misbehavin'" had been dismissed because he was spending too much time flirting with a secretary—a situation exacerbated by the fact that Fats was African-American and the secretary was white. (Waller, it turned out, was better off for being fired, for he went on to do three films in Hollywood and then toured Europe.)

One of Wood's most entertaining yarns involved Penny Pruden, hostess of a local cooking show called *Penny's Pantry*. According to Wood, *Penny's Pantry* was hurting the ratings of *The 50 Club* because Pruden had "rather large bosoms" and many thousands of viewers tuned in daily to watch them sway and bounce as she beat eggs. So

Crosley executive Robert Dunville offered her $50,000 to leave town, and Pruden had taken the payoff and gone off to live on the Caribbean island of St. Thomas.

Aside from the absurdity of the tale—the majority of Ruth's viewers would have had absolutely no interest in seeing another woman jiggle—Penny Pruden never appeared opposite Ruth Lyons on television or radio. The real story—related by Pruden herself—is that she was advised by her doctor to move to a warmer climate to ease a recurring bronchitis problem, and after visiting St. Thomas, decided the Caribbean isle was just what the doctor ordered. Pruden owned a string of delicatessens in Cincinnati,

"One woman wrote that I had degraded American womanhood by my actions."

Dayton, and Columbus, which is one of the reasons she ended up with a cooking show, and realized a handsome sum from the sale of her stores. She used the sale proceeds to buy land and build a house on St. Thomas, and later bought another house for rental income. Not as exciting, perhaps, as threatening Ruth Lyons's popularity, but certainly more realistic.

Despite her propensity for invention, Mary Wood remained in Ruth's good graces for the rest of her life. Ruth gave the columnist a lot of exclusive information, and Wood was one of the select few who visited Ruth after her retirement. Ruth gave her final interview to Wood, who turned it into a lengthy article for the *Cincinnati Enquirer's* Sunday magazine in 1982.

RUTH HERSELF RELATED several interesting stories about *The 50 Club* and unlike Wood's, they happened to be true.

Once, she was standing among the television audience talking with several women on the air when she clearly heard someone say "Ruth Lyons." She turned and asked who had called her. No one responded, so she went back to talking with her fans. Almost immediately after the show, she received a phone call from New York. In those days, "long-distance" meant business or something important.

The caller was a man she'd known as the manager of one of Cincinnati's theaters, and he told Ruth a remarkable story. His wife, he said, had been ill for many months and hadn't spoken a word in nearly a year. Although she didn't seem to respond to any stimulus, he bought a TV set and put it in her bedroom. He had just turned on the TV and tuned it to Ruth's show when his wife sat up in bed and said, "Ruth Lyons." She had been a regular listener in Cincinnati before the days of television, and recognized Ruth's voice.

On another occasion, which Ruth described as a "dreadful experience," she noticed a woman slumped over in her seat on the front row during one of *The 50-50 Club* shows. Ruth moved to the other side of the studio so the cameras would not show the "dear woman" being carried out on a stretcher—dead.

There was controversy as well. Ruth always—always—spoke her mind, no matter what the subject. In 1952, she had an African-American singer named Arthur Lee Simpkins as a guest on her show. Simpkins was performing at the Beverly Hills Supper Club in Northern Kentucky for a week. Ruth and Herman had gone across the river to listen to him sing the night before he was to appear on *The 50 Club*, and she was enchanted by his pure tenor voice. The next day when Simpkins stepped onto the stage at Crosley Square, he seemed to Ruth to be a bit nervous. He grew even more nervous as he sang his first song. To put him at ease, Ruth took his hand and suggested that he sing what she called his "rhythm arrangement" of a popular song titled "Marie." Then, the two of them danced for a few minutes.

RUTH OFTEN DANCED WITH HER GUESTS, including Milton Berle, Bob Hope, and Arthur Godfrey—but never with an African-American man. Ohio did not have Jim Crow segregation laws, and there were no lynchings as there had been (and would be) in the South. But what Ruth had done was still an unwritten taboo in most of American society—and certainly on TV. She wasn't ready for the uproar—all the hateful letters and phone calls—though Simpkins could have told her what to expect.

"One woman wrote that I had degraded American womanhood by my actions," Ruth said on her show the next day. "I am happy to say that not all reacted in this way!" Then she read a telegraph from a listener: "Dear Ruth, Your open heart made me cry tears of gratitude Tuesday when you so unreservedly demonstrate your heartfelt love for another human being, without being hampered one bit by the color of his skin. Such a spontaneous demonstration is sure to contribute more to racial harmony and good will than you have any idea. God Bless you, A viewer (white)."

Ruth would put the authors of the hate letters in their place by inviting Simpkins to appear several more times on her program—and each time boosting the singer's sales.

The year 1953 was the year of the Coronation of Her Majesty Queen Elizabeth II and, by lucky circumstance, Ruth Lyons was in attendance. She had not been invited as a member of the media, but received an invitation entirely by chance. It happened that WLWT program director John T. Murphy was in New York early in 1953, when a drawing was made for six seats at the Queen's Coronation. Murphy won one of the tickets and gave it to Ruth. She was thrilled, and immediately started making plans for the event.

First, she arranged for a six-week vacation; Willie Thall nervously hosted *The 50 Club* in her absence. Before she left for England, she also made arrangements to send tape-recorded reports to the *Cincinnati Enquirer* by air express. Then, of course, there was the question of what to wear. "One had to wear to the [Westminster] Abbey for the Coronation service, an evening dress, any color but black, and our heads had to be covered," Ruth wrote, recalling her preparations for the grand ceremony. "I chose a gray faille dress, the first and only Christian Dior original I ever owned."

On June 2, the day of the Queen's Coronation, Ruth rose at 4:30 a.m. and skipped breakfast. "I had to be at the Abbey before 6 a.m.," she wrote. "It was a cold, rainy morning, and Westminster Abbey is anything but a cozy place on such a day...." She sat just to the left of the throne, and directly across the aisle were the Queen Mother and her two grandchildren (Prince Charles and Princess Anne), plus attendants. "I shall never forget the thrill of the trumpets sounding, the long procession of peers and peeresses in their scarlet ermine-trimmed robes, and the sound of the magnificent Abbey organ," began Ruth's description. "The new Queen was more beautiful than I had ever dreamed her to be, and Prince Charles looked like all the princes I ever read about in fairy tales. . . ."

The service dragged on for more than six hours. Ruth, however, had prepared herself. "I was the envy of everyone sitting close to me," she wrote, "because I had provided myself with two chocolate bars tucked into the top of my dress."

Candy and Herman made the trip, but they had no tickets, so they waited for Ruth at the reviewing stands. She took a taxi and joined them after the Coronation. Along the way, she saw thousands of people waiting for the royal procession. Many had spent the night along the street. Eventually the royal coach and its retinue passed under sunny skies. Ruth detailed her impressions of the coach, the British Commonwealth dignitaries, and the royal platoons for the *Enquirer*. She and Herman attended one of the several Coronation balls, including one at the Savoy Hotel. Prime Minister Winston Churchill was present, and Ruth presumably managed a few words with the great statesman.

The Newmans remained in London for three weeks following the Coronation, visiting Candy's godmother, Rose Laird, who resided there. They also traveled to Oxford to meet Herman's instructor from his time there in 1933 and 1934. Using her NBC connections, Ruth got to meet British journalist Malcolm Muggeridge, NBC correspondent Edwin Newman, and Walter Cronkite of CBS. And at the BBC, she also met Mrs. Rose Bruckner, the woman with whom she had exchanged broadcasts during the war.

IN HER MEMOIRS, Ruth described a tense scene at a press conference held for General George C. Marshall, who, along with Chief Justice Earl Warren and noted journalist Fleur Cowles, attended the Queen's Coronation in President Eisenhower's absence. Ruth went to the press gathering, hoping to meet the great American field general. She noticed that only representatives of the British press were there, and that they seemed to make General Marshall ill-at-ease after he entered the room. When he announced that he was ready to answer any questions, the reporters were silent. Many Britons were displeased by Ike's decision to send dignitaries in his place.

More than a minute went by, and still no one spoke up. Ruth, ready to lose her temper over the affront to Marshall, remembered something about his wife. She stood up and asked, "General Marshall, how is your wife's back?" Looking relieved at this break in the silence, the general explained that his wife was doing better, and thanked Ruth for asking. Suddenly, the press broke in to take over the conference before this American blonde showed them up.

Ruth, Herman, and Candy later met Marshall, Warren and Cowles at their hotel, the Grosvenor. Ms. Cowles had lost the key to her room, which was on the same floor as the Newmans' room, and Ruth invited them in to call the desk. While there, they raised a toast to the Queen with Harvey's Cream.

For Ruth and her daughter, Candy, this was their first trip overseas. After three weeks in England, they traveled to Holland, Belgium, Luxembourg, and

Germany. Herman proved to be an able guide, drawing upon his time on the European continent after Oxford. While in Germany, Ruth went to the trouble of looking up soldiers from the Cincinnati area in Heidelberg and Cologne. On a tour of Dachau, she persuaded two American soldiers to turn off their transistor radio that was blaring rock 'n roll from the Armed Forces Radio Network, demanding that the soldiers show respect for those who were murdered in the infamous Nazi concentration camp.

After Germany, there was Switzerland and then Paris, which proved to be Ruth's all-time favorite place. She shared her experiences, in detail, with her viewers over a period of weeks after returning to Cincinnati.

The six-week vacation in Europe was a grand education for Candy, who had not yet reached her ninth birthday when the family took a cruise liner across the Atlantic. It was, in some ways, an extension of her tutoring back home. Herman and Ruth had decided to keep Candy at home even before she became old enough to attend school. It was probably Ruth's decision more than Herman's. As Ruth's assistant Mickey Fisher said, "Herman was masculine, but I think Ruth ruled the roost."

Ruth feared for Candy and wanted to protect her from the world. She had already lost a child, and felt there was a connection between her stillborn baby and Candy. They were born less than two days apart, and in the same hospital. For these reasons, she felt Candy was more vulnerable than most children, as if the baby's fate awaited Candy if Ruth did not do everything she could to shield her daughter from threats and hurtful experiences.

Ruth's job and the home-schooling made it possible for her to spend hours with her daughter every day. She saw Candy in the morning before she went to work. Most days she returned home before the afternoon was over, and spent the hours until bedtime talking with Candy, teaching her how to knit, cook, and do other domestic tasks. Some days, she took Candy to work with her, and she more or less grew up on radio, then television. (Herman shared his daughter's interests in science and nature, and also encouraged her as a writer. He was always available to answer questions, or to simply be a father. He was perhaps less protective of Candy than Ruth, but he would shelter his daughter if necessary.)

Most of Candy's socialization was through her cousin, Linda (Rose's daughter), and the many adults of Ruth's acquaintance. Ruth and Herman entertained friends a couple of times a month. There was always live music, and charades was a favorite game for Ruth. The parties were opportunities for her friends to meet Candy and Herman and get to know them better. Candy became a polite, precocious, quiet child who, mostly thanks to her father's influence, spoke proper English.

Ruth's fans sent many gifts to her daughter. She donated most of the presents to needy children, but kept a few of the more interesting toys and games in a closet she called "Candy's Magic Cupboard." On days when Candy was ill or when bad weather precluded outdoor activities, she was allowed to select one item from her "Magic Cupboard."

There were several changes on tap for *The 50 Club* in 1953. Because of advertiser demand, the one-hour show was sometimes extended to ninety minutes, airing from noon to 1:30 p.m. Several times, it went to two hours. *The 50 Club* would continue to bounce around in its time slot through late 1955, when it was finally locked in at ninety minutes. (P&G's soap operas were now televised on CBS.)

The additional half hour gave Ruth time to showcase more of the singers who appeared on her show, including Bonnie Lou, Marian Spelman, Ruby Wright, and Betty Clooney. The studio audience swelled to a hundred (or more) because of the constant demand, prompting a suggestion that the show's name be changed to *The 50-50 Club*. In a few years, the daily audience would grow to 150, but it was generally agreed that calling the show *The 50-50-50 Club* or *The 150 Club* would be a bit much. About this time, WLW raised the ticket price from $1 to $1.25.

RUTH'S STAFF GREW AS WELL. In addition to the producer and director, there were two cameramen, a floor producer, and several prop and setup boys. The prop movers and setup boys wore coats and ties, and also served as ushers. Mickey Fisher, Elsa Sule, Vera Tyson, and two other women worked behind the scenes to make sure everything went smoothly. A Crosley carpenter and electrician modified the stage as necessary, and the luncheon guests were served by a team of three waitresses. Two women were assigned to be official greeters for *Your Morning Matinee* and *The 50-50 Club* in Crosley Square's lobby. They welcomed the audience members and guided them to the elevators when the time came. Handling all the prizes donated by sponsors became a full-time job for yet another employee.

With the half-dozen regular singers and a band that had no fewer than eight members, Ruth's crew numbered three dozen (four women were hired to handle mail and donations for the Christmas Fund for the three months preceding Christmas). WLW had a deep talent pool: three full-size orchestras, a couple of trios, a dozen fulltime singers—male and female—and fifteen country and western performers for *Midwestern Hayride*, one of three shows that WLWT fed to NBC. Not to be forgotten was Ruth's sidekick and foil, Willie Thall. Bill Myers, Ruth's announcer, described how Willie would set up a situation, then let Ruth take it to its conclusion. "Willie knew just how far to go to get under her skin," Myers remembered. "And [Ruth] had a real sense of showmanship and timing. She could see the humor in something and she could play it."

Weather reports became an extra feature on the show during this time. Jim Fidler, WLWT's meteorologist, delivered several reports a day, one always in the middle of *The 50-50 Club*. Fidler had been a radio announcer for nearly twenty years, and in 1939 he gave the first television weather report over Crosley's W8XCT (the first weather forecast on national TV was given by Clint Youle, over NBC in 1949).

Two more famous features of *The 50-50 Club* were the white gloves and the microphone corsage. One day on the show, Ruth wore a dressy ensemble that included white gloves, and she remarked, "I don't think a woman is fully dressed unless she has white gloves." From that day forward, nearly every woman who was in the studio audience wore white gloves. Ruth was so impressed, she wrote "The Waving Song," which was played during every show while a camera panned across the audience to show the women in their white gloves waving to those at home.

The microphone corsage grew out of a complaint. Ruth thought it was bad enough that she had to pull around a microphone cord that she kept tripping over, and that the microphone was so heavy. But did it have to be so ugly? The next day, her producer George Resing arranged to have the mike covered with a bouquet of fresh flowers. It became an everyday thing—and Ruth's trademark.

The women in the audience began asking Ruth for the flowers as souvenirs. With so many requests, Ruth and the staff decided that artificial flowers would be better because they were less costly and reusable. Elsa Sule, the show's assistant producer, made a different arrangement each day, sometimes with ribbons and bows. Before long, Cincinnati florists were sending in artificial arrangements.

There were so many, Elsa had to store them in their own cupboard, and Ruth tried to use several during each show. In addition to the artificial arrangements, live arrangements were delivered to the studio for each show and displayed around the set.

For several years, Ruth's on-stage base was an oversized desk built by the prop department. It had a trap-door in its top, through which a setup boy could hand up products as Ruth talked about them. To entertain the audience, the setup boys cut a hole in the front of the desk and put in a large window so Ruth's fans could watch the person under the desk with the products. Sometimes he would make faces or hold up signs or photos. There were times Ruth didn't know at whom the audience was laughing—her and Willie, or the setup boy.

Later, as she began to entertain more famous guests, Ruth had a rocking love seat and two chairs installed on the set. A coffee table was usually placed in front of the love seat. The background was whatever contemporary design seemed interesting at the time. Ruth loved rocking chairs—there was one in every room of her house—and she decorated her own home with Early American-style furniture. "You can never go wrong with Early American," she liked to say. The cameramen, though, were unhappy with the rocking love seat. The more intense the subject, the faster Ruth rocked and more difficult it became to keep the camera feed steady. Some guests clowned around with her about it, pretending to be seasick. But Ruth held to what she wanted, and everybody else adjusted.

The number and variety of guests was almost overwhelming. Viewers saw stars on *The 50-50 Club* that they would only expect to see on network television. Ted Mack was a guest (and the first to claim seasickness on the rocking seat), as were Sammy Davis, Jr., Tommy and Jimmy Dorsey, Guy Lombardo, Steve Lawrence, Edyie Gorme, Xavier Cugat, Shelley Berman, Dick Noel, Doris Day, the McGuire Sisters, Charles Goren (the bridge expert), Gene Krupa, Sal Mineo, and a pantheon of the famous from the 1940s through the mid-1960s. Roy Rogers and Dale Evans made an appearance, too, with Trigger, who had to be brought up in the elevator. Ruth quipped, "Willie was dressed in his street-cleaner's uniform that day, and luckily so."

WLW RADIO WENT ALONG without *The 50-50 Club* until someone (probably Ruth) realized that there were hundreds of thousands of people from the old WLW audience who were outside the broadcast area of Crosley's television network. WLW still reached throughout Ohio, Indiana, Kentucky, and West Virginia, and could be picked up by listeners in Michigan, Illinois, and elsewhere on a good day. Plus, there were those in the viewing area who couldn't get to a television at midday.

After much argument and technical finagling, *The 50-50 Club* was beamed out to radio and television audiences simultaneously. It was called "simulcasting," and Crosley was one of a very few broadcasters who did it regularly. With simulcasting, a television advertiser could get extra coverage on radio. Not every TV advertiser wanted to pay extra for the radio coverage, but there were plenty ready to sponsor Ruth Lyons on radio again, at premium rates.

There was some concern about how a television show might go over on radio. If someone wore a funny hat or stumbled or gestured, the radio audience might miss the gag. So Ruth tried to include the radio audience in visual gags by describing what was going on without being too obvious. She let as little as possible depend on visuals. A sign at the studio entrance reminded the cast to "REMEMBER RADIO." WLW listeners really didn't care; they were delighted to have Ruth back, even if they did miss a stunt or didn't get the studio audience's laughter now and then.

TV and radio simulcasting was an off and on proposition for a while. There were technical problems, and now and then Ruth had to give up the radio broadcast for another program or an important sponsor. But the simulcast was eventually locked in. As WLW General Manager Walter K. Murdock later joked, "*The 50-50 Club* was the only radio program you could watch on TV."

Ruth's old show, *Your Morning Matinee*, didn't do as well without her. In 1955, it was shortened to fifteen minutes and moved to another time slot in favor of a new show, the hour-long *Breakfast Club*, hosted by Mel Taylor. *Your Morning Matinee* finally went off the air in 1956.

a woman apart

In many ways, Ruth Lyons was more like a woman of the 21st century than the early 20th century. She remained unmarried and self-supporting throughout the 1920s and into the 1930s because she wanted to cultivate her career—and because she did not want to be known as an extension of someone else. Even after marrying for the first time in 1932, she continued to work, though Johnny Lyons made enough money that there was no need for his wife to take a job.

Not overtly political herself, politicians still visited, including Henry Cabot Lodge, Nixon's running mate.

When their marriage threatened her career, Ruth chose the career. She didn't reject marriage as much as she rejected limits. When Johnny accepted the promotion and transferred to Cleveland, Ruth remained in Cincinnati because she failed to find a job in Cleveland and living there would have stunted her career and most likely restricted her to the role of housewife.

She lived apart from her husband for eight years, too busy working to sit down with Johnny and finalize the details of their divorce. She was concerned by the impact that divorce might have on her career (Mary Tyler Moore was portrayed as divorced on network TV in the 1970s, and many thought it scandalous). But there was none. Even though her split with Johnny was written up in the Cincinnati newspapers, the matter quickly faded from the minds of those who took notice of it. In fact, when she married 36-year-old Herman Newman, most people thought it was her first marriage. She claimed to be 34, but was actually 37 years old, not that Ruth's age mattered to her adoring female audience.

Women connected with Ruth Lyons, not just because she was married or had a child, or because she pushed them to use the vote, or because she served as their role-model to step outside the traditional roles assigned them by society. Ruth respected their intelligence and shared their interests, which went beyond the traditional household chores and child-rearing. As she once told an interviewer, "Women have brains, you know, and they're usually pleased when someone takes cognizance of the fact." After noting in an interview with *The Saturday Evening Post* that housewives like shoptalk as much as anyone else, Ruth added, "But I don't believe that the average woman's only concern is with a dust cloth and getting Junior off to school on time. She cares what is happening in her city and in the rest of the world. Well, I get around a bit and I read a lot and I tell my listeners about the things that interest me."

Her audience also appreciated the fact that she was open and honest about her family life. Ruth's candid chit-chat covered the cast members' families, too. When she went to Europe for the Queen's Coronation, her fans took the trip with her—vicariously, of course. She shared every detail of her experiences—and in such a way that it didn't come across as boastful. "When she bought a mink coat," Elsa Sule said, "we all died over what she paid for it." One fan letter read,

"I want you to help me clip her wings."

"I loved your new fur coat that you showed us on television. Though I can't afford one, I'm happy that someone I like and feel I know has such a beautiful coat." On the same subject, Ruth said, "I get a big kick out of buying and doing things that I couldn't afford at one time, and I share that kick with my audience."

A correspondent for the *Ladies' Home Journal* in 1960 surmised that Ruth Lyons must have been empowering for many women, and quoted an unnamed "former associate" as saying, "Ruth Lyons is a very dominating kind of woman. She's successful and powerful and free to say exactly what's on her mind.

She needles and browbeats the men on her program, and this delights the housewives." The magazine correspondent added, "They love to hear someone push men around, though they wouldn't dare try it themselves."

Veteran TV newsman and host Nick Clooney, who worked on *The 50-50 Club*, has a slightly different viewpoint. "She might have been a dictator," Clooney said, "but she was a benign dictator." It may be that Ruth Lyons was simply a strong, intelligent woman who knew how to get what she wanted without resorting to the traditional so-called "feminine wiles." As anyone who ever argued with her would say, she won her battles with a stubbornness tempered by truth and logic. Crosley executive Robert Dunville had many arguments with his star, but won few. His take on Ruth was, "How can you argue with someone who is so right?"

Procter & Gamble did not advertise on *The 50-50 Club* because Ruth refused to surrender the noon hour to P&G for its soap operas. She was well aware of the conflict, of course, but in public her only comment was, "I just couldn't figure out why they refused to advertise."

"IT GOT TO BE A THORN IN P&G'S SIDE," recalled Jerry Imsicke, a former ad salesman for WLWT. "Of course, they could exert a lot of pressure, but Ruth stood firm. She had the ability to go into AVCO president John Murphy's office and if she didn't want something, he'd listen to her. This built up for years, to the point where P&G had a little mini-feud with Ruth. It was a private thing, but it came to a head when the sales department tried to get P&G to sponsor her show with Tide. P&G's reply was along the lines of, 'You gotta be kidding! Why would we want to go on Ruth Lyons's show when she's the one causing us the big problem of not being number one in Cincinnati, our home market?' It got back to her that P&G turned her down," Imsicke remembered. "She got hold of our reps in New York and said, 'I want a soap sponsor. I'm going to make P&G rue the day that they didn't advertise on my show.'"

The ad reps made their pitch to the Fels Company, a small soap-maker in Philadelphia. Fels signed a one-year deal for a minimum of three commercials per week on *The 50-50 Club*. To jump into a fifty-two-week contract, the company either must have done some quick research or already knew how well Ruth could sell products. Fels was a *50-50 Club* sponsor for several years and, as a result, its Naptha brand became the number one-selling soap in Cincinnati.

"To this day, P&G hates to hear it," chuckled Imsicke, "because not only did

Ruth block their soap [operas] in Cincinnati, she also built Fels Naptha to be the biggest soap in P&G's home market. Years later, all was forgiven and she finally did get Folgers coffee [a Procter & Gamble product]. P&G tried to get other products on the show in the hopes that she would kick Fels Naptha off, but she wouldn't do it. She was too loyal."

How did management feel about a female employee in 1950's America making in excess of $100,000 per year and wielding so much power that she literally was able to tell her bosses what to do? Nick Clooney posed the question to five of Ruth's former co-workers and friends in an interview for Cincinnati public television station WCET. The group included Elsa Sule, Cliff Lash, Gene Walz, Marian Spelman, and Mary Wood.

"There is a time," Clooney told the group, "when a personality becomes very strong. That is to say, very popular on the air . . . and managers and general managers begin to have problems with [the person]. They seem to, over a period of time, start thinking, 'Wait a minute, I'd better take this person down a peg or a notch, because no personality is going to be bigger than I am because I am the general manager.' Here is the biggest personality this town, the Midwest, and perhaps any single community has ever seen in the history of television. That must have happened with Ruth."

Indeed, it did happen. By the late 1950's, John Murphy had been promoted from program director to general manager of WLWT. Gene Walz recalls being called into Murphy's office one day, along with Willie Thall, and Murphy announced, "I want you to help me clip her wings."

"We looked at each other," Walz remembered, "and said, 'Not me.'"

This was not the response the GM had hoped for. On another occasion, according to Walz, "[Murphy] was raising hell with us directors, pounding the table, and I finally couldn't take it anymore, so I walked over and opened the door and yelled down the hall in the direction of Ruth's office, 'Mother, he's pickin' on us!' I thought he was going to have a fit."

Murphy didn't try to hide his feelings about Ruth when he signed singer Marian Spelman and Bill Nimmo to a contract to do a show called *Be Our Guest*. "Everything was spelled out," Spelman declared. "John Murphy told me, 'We don't want another Ruth Lyons.'"

Nick Clooney recalled attending a gathering a few years later at John Murphy's house, where he overheard WLWT's general manager and five other executives talking about Ruth. The point of the discussion, Clooney noted, was that "there will never be another Ruth Lyons." There would never be another employee, in other words, with that much power.

THE REFUSAL OF WALZ AND THALL TO TURN against Ruth was just one example of the loyalty Ruth inspired in her co-workers—and she was loyal in return. No one in management could fire or discipline anyone who worked for her. "From my perspective, when you're directing her show," Walz said, "no one's going to touch you. Murphy tried a couple of times, and Ruth said, 'No way!'"

Singer Bonnie Lou remembered when Ruth stepped forward to protect the women on *Midwestern Hayride* from sexual harassment—conduct which had yet to be legally defined in the workplace. "We were having problems with an emcee on *Midwestern Hayride*, and we all marched into Miss Lyons's office and told her our story, and that guy was gone within a month—fired."

Elsa Sule wrote, "Ruth Lyons played parent to all co-workers, as well as to listeners and viewers. When anyone was in a scrape of any variety, 'Mother' Lyons came to the rescue—whether it required patching up a lovers' quarrel or saving a job. She could always be counted on to make the old college try when the cause was just. Justice has always been her fetish." Elsa even asked Ruth whether she and her boyfriend should get married. Marian Spelman asked if it was okay if she got divorced.

Bill Myers, a prop boy, was impressed by Ruth's kindness. "When you hear her referred to as 'Mother,' it's because she cared so much about each [person] in the building," Myers said. When Bill Myers married Crosley employee Marianne Boyd and Marianne gave birth to twins a year later, Ruth sent the Myerses a gift from one of her sponsors—two complete layette sets in cradles with a retail price of $100. When the musicians' union in Cincinnati threatened to strike, Robert Dunville had decided to let the members walk before Ruth walked into his office and informed him that she, too, was a member of the union and would walk the picket line with the musicians. Dunville subsequently worked out a settlement with the group and a strike was averted.

Jerry Imsicke had been a prop boy before joining the WLWT's sales force. Imsicke, who worked at the station for fifty years, said at one point he considered applying for an on-air job at WCKY and leaving WLWT. "When Ruth found out I was interested in going to work with WCKY, she said she would be glad to make a phone call [on his behalf] to Tremette Tully, general manager at WCKY." Imsicke decided to stay put. Working on *The 50-50 Club* carried its own prestige, even for a prop boy. "It was the only show for which you had to wear a coat and tie. There were sixteen or seventeen prop and floor guys at [WLWT], and the prime job was to be on [Ruth's] show. You really thought you were at the top of your little profession if you were on her show."

Ruth kept staffers on their toes with her practical jokes and quirky sense of humor. As one of the prop boys, Imsicke was responsible for putting a sponsor's product on a "hod," or display stand, as Ruth did the commercial for it. Occasionally, though, she would start with Folgers, for example, then in the middle of talking about the coffee brand, switch to another product, leaving Imsicke and the others scrambling for the right display. Sometimes the prop boys would put the wrong product on the hod when Ruth started a commercial, which, depending upon her mood, she either ignored or switched her pitch.

No one was immune from Ruth's potshots. "Herman has terrible taste in clothes!" she disclosed to her TV audience and listeners. "How about your husbands?" Taking a ribbing from the host of *The 50-50 Club* was part of Willie Thall's job description. Ruth once asked Bonnie Lou, apropos of nothing, if she was pregnant, letting the delicate subject hang in the air for several seconds before Bonnie finally joined in the joke and stood up so viewers could see the lack of maternal evidence for themselves.

On occasion, Ruth would pull a prank on the orchestra, which she often referred to as "Cliff Lash and the Uncertain Seven." They might rehearse a piece all morning before the show, for instance, only to be told Ruth had nixed the song in favor of another, which the musicians and singers would have to practice and perform on short notice. Lash and another of Ruth's sidekicks, Peter Grant, were the objects of special teasing. Both were bachelors—confirmed bachelors, as each liked to say—and Ruth was forever trying to marry them off. If a female guest was single, Ruth would make a pitch for Cliff or Peter. She also delighted in playing matchmaker between them and single women of the appropriate age in the studio audience.

The ladies in the audience were not exempt from Ruth's good-natured prodding, either. In one famous incident, she began the show with a song, then said, "You old gals look terrible this morning." After chuckling, Ruth relented, "Really, you look fine!" Then she spun around toward a lady in an aisle seat. "But not you," she added. "Your hair is awful. I have a mop at home that looks better." The woman giggled and blushed. Ruth borrowed her comb and carefully coiffed the woman's hairdo. "There!" she announced when she finished. "Doesn't that look better?" The audience applauded, and Ruth's new friend beamed.

She was known to call in Herman's barber when she thought a man on the show needed a haircut, and from time to time would plop down on the lap of one of the few males in the audience to embarrass him. She might ask, "What are you doing here—can't find a job?"

Whenever she went into the city on an errand by car, she usually took Gene Walz and Mickey Fisher. "We used to ride downtown to return something to a store," Fisher recalled, "and she always parked in a no parking zone—always—leaving us to contend with any police officers who might come by. So Gene would put the hood up on the car and when the police arrived, he would say, 'We'll get this fixed in a few minutes.' Meanwhile, I was thinking, 'Please let her come out, Lord, please let her come out!'"

Ruth could take kidding as easily as dishing it out. Walz recalled the day she telephoned him to pick her up at the hairdresser's. "I went down to pick her up, and I drove up and she started coming out of the door when I noticed some women on the street looking at her like they recognized her. She looked great, and then I got out and walked around and opened up the door and said real loud, 'What's the matter, Mom—couldn't they take you?' She just looked at me and said, 'Oh, hell—get in the car!' She liked that kind of humor."

IN 1955, WLWT HIRED PAUL DIXON to host a mid-morning show for housewives. Dixon had previously worked in Cincinnati as a disk jockey for WCPO radio and WCPO-TV, as well as in his home state of Iowa and in the Chicago and New York markets. It was his job, essentially, to keep *The 50-50 Club* audience occupied until noon.

The Paul Dixon Show began as a half-hour program but was soon expanded to ninety minutes, just like Ruth's show. And just like Ruth's show, Dixon's had a studio audience, prizes, and all sorts of stunts. A male Ruth Lyons, however, Paul Dixon was not. He was bawdy in a benevolent way, but beloved. Dixon developed a trademark routine in which he scanned the legs of the women in the front row with a pair of binoculars, examining, he said, the village of "Kneesville." On every show, he awarded a garter he called the "knee-tickler" to the female in the front row with nicest-looking knees—and the stunts went on from there. Dixon captivated many of Ruth's listeners during his 9 to 10:30 a.m. show. His fast pace and sense of humor also won him an audience of his own. Often there was a cross-pollination of humor between his show and Ruth's. The two hosts also shared the singers in their respective casts. Despite rumors to the contrary, Paul Dixon and Ruth Lyons were good friends and partners in entertainment, ushering in the new medium of television and pioneering what we know today as the TV talk show genre.

million dollar woman

After immigrating to the United States, the grandfather of Robert Earl "Bob" Braun, Jr., settled across the river from Cincinnati in Ludlow, Kentucky. Grandpa Braun allowed only English to be spoken in his home and told people he wanted to be "every inch an American"—

Fans remembered Bob Braun's early career as a lifeguard at old Coney Island.

an apt description, it turns out, for grandson Bob.

Born in 1929, young Bob Braun was truly an All-American boy. Growing up during the Great Depression, he began honing his entrepreneurship skills at an early age. Braun had a paper route, earned tips performing comedy bits, stocked grocery shelves, delivered meat and dry cleaning, in addition to serving as a school crossing guard and playing in the Ludlow Junior High School band. At 14, he landed a job with Cincinnati's WSAI radio, hosting a weekly knothole baseball program. Every Saturday morning, he tested the sports knowledge of two knothole teams, and during the same show, delivered reports on the Cincinnati Reds. He also helped on one of the station's other sports programs.

In his autobiography, *Here's Bob*, Braun described how his budding radio career was cut short just months after it began because his voice changed. "I lost the show and I was shattered," he wrote. Shattered, but not defeated. After delivering candy from a local manufacturer to stores—a job he inherited from his older brother, Jack, who joined the U.S. Merchant Marine when WWII broke out—Braun was intent on a career in show business and with a friend formed a vaudeville act. A former song-plugger, who allowed the boys to perform in his saloon, coached Braun on projecting his voice and on other elements of singing.

Just before he turned 16, Braun and his singing partner joined the local American Guild of Variety Artists and found a local agent. Soon they were busy performing at home shows, theaters, and conventions, and winning talent contests. Braun won one contest, hosted in a local theater, ten times in a row—so frequently that emcee Paul Dixon asked him to retire as champion. Many professional singers and musicians got their starts in the 1930s and '40s just as Braun did, performing live acts in glittering venues.

College and the family business eventually occupied most of his partner's time, so Braun was forced to start over as a solo act. While still in high school, he took a summer job as a lifeguard at the Cincinnati amusement park, Coney Island, which proudly advertised its Sunlight Pool as "the world's largest recirclating swimming pool." With a body type that matched his name, his good looks,

"How carried away can you get over a mop?"

and friendly nature, Braun became a Coney Island favorite. In 1949, after high school, he auditioned for the Cincinnati Conservatory of Music, which awarded him a scholarship. But it was a modeling job that led to his first big break in show business. Braun posed atop the marquee of a Cincinnati movie theater, a film promotion stunt that got the attention of the program director at WCPO-TV. The fledgling station hired him as a singer, cameraman, setup boy, and janitor for twenty hours a week.

Thus began a half-century television career that would be briefly interrupted, and enhanced, by Braun's two years of service in the Army. He ended up with the Army's Signal Corps—working out of Washington, D.C.—and was able to sing with a local band, participate in talent contests over the Armed Forces Radio Network and the Mutual radio network. The Army gave him an education in communication, including newspapers, magazines, television, radio, writing, and speaking. He attended classes five days a week, with weekends off. It was almost as if the government had decided to prep Braun for a future in television. He would share the stage as Ruth Lyons's primary sidekick on *The 50-50 Club* for ten years, and continued the show after Ruth retired.

Ruth Lyons's selling power was legendary on radio long before she went on television. TV merely amplified it. One reason her commercials were so effective was that she brought the same openness and honesty to them as she did everything else she talked about; Ruth never accepted a sponsor until she had tried and approved what the company was selling. The product had to work, or she refused to advertise it. She knew that if she misrepresented poor products, she would lose her audience's trust.

"She refused to do commercials for a sponsor whose product she hadn't tried and liked," said Don Dahlman, who worked in sales and management at WLWT. "It didn't make any difference who manufactured it. And I suppose that kind of integrity eventually was the bottom line that made it work. I suspect that drove advertising agencies wild, but it moved product."

Ruth "moved product" even when she wasn't advertising it. Just before WLWT went to color broadcasting in 1957, a *50-50 Club* guest complimented her on the perfume she was wearing.

"Chantilly," Ruth replied.

In three days, every store in Cincinnati, Dayton, and Columbus that stocked Chantilly, sold out.

WHEN SHE PROMOTED A BRAND, it zoomed up the sales charts. This was especially true of new products. Royal Gelatin and a line of canned foods that Ruth introduced in the late 1950s are often cited as examples of the power of her imprimatur, jumping to first place in their respective consumer categories in just a few weeks in the metropolitan markets that Ruth reached. In its sales literature, WLW summed up Ruth's appeal as "always live and always ad-lib, a warm, meaningful personal recommendation from one woman to another."

Despite her refusal to induce the public to buy products she didn't approve of, salesmen were perpetually pressuring her to take on a new product without trying it. As WLWT salesman Jerry Imsicke explained, "Getting a product on Ruth Lyons's show was like an annuity for a salesman." Sponsors who signed on nearly always stayed on because they saw an increase in profits several times over what they had spent to advertise. Each contract renewal was credited to the original salesman, who received another commission.

Whenever possible, Ruth got personally involved with the products on her show. When her housekeeper, Callie Borham, was ill and the ironing didn't get done, she brought her ironing into the studio as she had done several years earlier. This time, though, she had six ironing boards set up and the ladies in the audience took turns ironing with Easy-On Spray Starch, one of *The 50-50 Club's* twenty sponsors. On a subsequent show, an Easy-On representative demonstrated the most efficient way to press shirts.

Ruth rejected most commercial scripts supplied by ad agencies. "Nine times out of ten, the stuff's written by some kid a few years out of college," she told a writer. "How can he know what interests a housewife, or what makes her buy? The results are a lot of silly, irrelevant overstatements which would insult the intelligence of a child. All I try to do on my show is tell why I like a product and why I think the listener will." Nevertheless, agencies and sponsors continued to submit scripts—at their peril. More than once, Ruth read them on the air, for laughs, without stating brand names. Scripts with visual descriptions—"man's hand picks up glass"—were easy targets for her jibes.

She preferred to say something special, obviously, about each product on her show. Yet despite her facility for making up commercials as she went along, Ruth occasionally found herself at a loss for words. A few minutes of a 1951 show, preserved in a kinescope, demonstrate how she worked around such impasses, as well as how she transitioned from one subject to another.

EARLY IN THE SHOW, Ruth made a lengthy pitch for hand cream, then segued into a commercial for a sponge mop called Minmop.

"Speaking of hands," she said, "let's talk about mopping." After a few sentences, however, it became painfully obvious that Ruth couldn't find anything to say about Minmop. So, with characteristic honesty, she bought time by sharing her frustration with the audience.

"We've talked for nearly a year about Minmop. Did you ever stop to think how difficult it is to say anything new about a mop?"

Willie Thall, seated next to Ruth, acknowledged her question by simply shaking his head.

"How carried away can you get over a mop?" she continued.

Willie mumbled in agreement.

"You just can't," Ruth plunged on, now speaking faster.

Willie gave her an Amen.

"You can state facts. You can say this is why we think this is the best mop on the market, and so forth, but you can't just go into the affirmatives all the time. However, with your Minmop..."

Interrupting herself, Ruth changed tack, trying to find a way around the wall of words she had built. "You do have something I think you don't realize—and that is this." She paused and gestured as if trying to summon a thought. "It has so many other uses other than just mopping floors."

Willie nervously flexed and curled his fingers.

"Yes it does!" he chimed in, clueless as to where the show's host was taking this commercial.

At that moment, Ruth found inspiration.

". . . And today we shall discuss washing automobiles!" she said, making a joke about the weather and how Minmop could be used not only to wash cars but, because the mop was easy to wring out, dry them as well.

If nothing else worked, Ruth could create a jingle for a product. She enjoyed making up simple commercial rhymes. The same kinescope shows Ruth and Willie Thall writing a commercial for one of the show's sponsors, Temtee Pretzels. Ruth sits down at her pink piano and the two try out rhymes for pretzel, but can only come up with "trestle" and "wrestle." Willie then hits upon the idea of spelling out the product's name, as in "T-E-M-T-double-E," with Ruth adding, "How good can a pretzel be?" Several minutes later, they have composed a six-line jingle and melody.

Ruth also did the occasional outside endorsement. In the mid-1950s, she could be found in newspaper and magazine ads, with a product usually carrying the tagline, "As seen on *The 50-50 Club*." She made a memorable endorsement for the improbably-named "Ironwear Insured Nylons." Ironwear ads in eastern newspapers featured the header, "TV star tells why 'I wear and recommend Ironwear Insured Nylons,'" accompanied by a photo of Ruth. She probably wrote the ad copy, which began, "The last thing a busy gal wants to worry about are hosiery runs. . . . That's why my first choice in nylons is Ironwear!" In conjunction with another advertising campaign, a soap manufacturer offered dish towels carrying the image of a very youthful-looking Ruth Lyons.

The national and local endorsements boosted Ruth's income to over $100,000 a year, while her husband earned under $10,000 a year at the University of Cincinnati. Herman was on the faculty of the College of Engineering, where he taught English and sometimes philosophy or semantics, in the interest of helping students in highly technical disciplines broaden their perspectives.

Despite their substantial household income, the Newmans did not see any reason, however, to move to a larger or grander home. They lived in a nice, middle-class neighborhood in a 1,200-square-foot bungalow with plenty of room for them and their daughter Candy. They didn't consider moving until an old farmhouse on Colerain Avenue—along the route both Ruth and Herman took to work—caught Ruth's eye. It was a beautiful home built of masonry and brick, enhanced with gingerbread woodwork. The interior—over three times the size of their bungalow—had ten rooms and several fireplaces. Herman looked at the property from the street and agreed that it would be a fine place to live. There was only one problem: it wasn't for sale. Herman and Ruth decided to keep an eye on the house, so they could be the first ones in line if and when it went on the market.

WHEN SHE WASN'T WINGING a commercial or writing a jingle on the air, Ruth would talk about anything: her husband, her daughter, the household help, shopping, the military, baseball, basketball, racial issues, medical matters, teenagers, traffic, gardening, cooking, vacations, department store customer service, books, politics (though never making a stand for one party or the other), show business, her health, the audience's health, acquaintances, relatives, strangers. There were a few subjects, however, that never came up. Ruth, for example, could not have been blind to the fact that some of her acquaintances and guests were gay. Johnny Mathis, who recorded several of her songs on his albums, was a close friend.

But in the 1950s, homosexuality—and sex, in general—was regarded as an individual's private business, certainly not a topic for discussion on a television show. Drug abuse wasn't yet in the forefront either. Had these subjects been a part of her conversation, though, Ruth would not have given them the sensational treatment they receive on a show like Jerry Springer's. Ruth would have been more like Oprah.

She didn't attack anyone's religion, and was offended when attacks were made on religion, but Ruth railed against injustice. Her blow-up over a radio news report about Hungarian women who were fired on by soldiers when they tried to place wreaths on that country's Tomb of the Unknown Soldier made

The Saturday Evening Post. "What kind of world are we living in when that can happen after so many years of so-called civilization?" Ruth was quoted in the national magazine. "But you and I have no right to be smug. On the same newscast I heard about a minister being beaten up by a mob in Tennessee because he was taking six Negroes to a newly integrated high school!"

After denouncing the attitudes and actions behind various acts of wrongdoing, Ruth would thank the audience for listening—"I just had to blow my stack!"—then move on to a lighter subject.

THROUGHOUT THE MID-1950s, *The 50-50 Club* continued to grow in popularity. Four times a year, Ruth took her show on the road, playing to a packed house in a theater or auditorium in the cities on the Crosley network. A typical venue seated approximately 4,000 people, but there would be 40,000 or more requests for tickets. Each remote broadcast featured at least one celebrity guest—Andy Williams, Liberace and others—plus the local mayor and often the governor of the state.

Even with the road dates, Ruth managed to take a number of vacation weeks every year. Willie Thall hosted the show in her absence. In 1953, the Newmans (with Candy) sailed from New York to Cherbourg, France, aboard the *Queen Elizabeth*. In 1954, the destination was England, as it was in 1955. Once across the Atlantic—Ruth still refused to fly—the family made the most of land and water transport to take in as much of the British Isles and the European continent as possible. From 1953 to 1955, they managed to see something of every country in western Europe.

Ruth shared the almost endless details of each trip with her audience, and there was always a sendoff at Cincinnati's Union Terminal when she, Candy, and Herman boarded a train for New York. No matter what the time of departure, several hundred fans were there to bid them goodbye.

the show goes on

It was a tale of two advertisers that began in 1929 when William H. Albers, president of the Kroger food stores, resigned after a disagreement with the company's directors. Four years later, Albers started his own grocery chain, Albers Super Markets, which by the mid-1950s had sixty-six stores in Cincinnati and Northern Kentucky. Even though Kroger predated Albers by fifty years, the upstart threatened to equal or surpass the Cincinnati institution within a few years.

Ruth did not hide her daughter from the world. Candy appeared on her mother's show hundreds of times, and eventually joined the cast.

The growth of Albers Super Markets could be attributed, in large part, to the company's long-time sponsorship of *The 50-50 Club*. But after Albers merged with the Atlanta, Georgia-based Colonial Stores in 1955, Colonial began questioning the huge amount of money its northern partner was spending every year on TV advertising and sent a marketing representative to Cincinnati to check out Ruth Lyons's show. Reporting back to his bosses, the marketing rep said there wasn't anything special about *The 50-50 Club*—certainly nothing that justified spending tens of thousands of advertising and promotion dollars per year as a sponsor.

So Colonial decided to pull the Albers ads from the program and use the money elsewhere. It was just the opening Cincinnati's other grocery chain had been looking for, even if Kroger had to wait a year before it could advertise on *The 50-50 Club* because of Crosley's contractual obligations to Albers. So highly regarded was Ruth as a marketing force, the Cincinnati newspapers reported the change in *The 50-50 Club* sponsorship lineup and speculated about its impact on both food store chains.

Albers would experience a long, slow decline as thousands and thousands of shoppers switched to Kroger, which built one new store after another and remodeled many existing stores. By the early 1970s, Albers Super Markets had gone out of business.

FAMILY WAS THE MOST IMPORTANT ELEMENT of Ruth Lyons's life, so after learning her sister, Rose Reeves Lupton, had cancer, she found it difficult to maintain an emotional balance. "[Rose] was full of life and had a wonderful sense of humor," Ruth wrote. "But there were many trying days, watching my sister grow thinner . . . and doing all I could to keep my spirits up as well as hers. But the show must go on. At least that is what they say. I do not subscribe entirely to this belief, but I suppose I had an innate sense of trying to do all that I could to keep *The 50-50 Club* going to the best of my ability."

Ruth's anxiety was understandable. Cancer was the most dreaded illness; a diagnosis was regarded as an automatic death sentence. The word itself was rarely uttered outside the medical community. People were conditioned by the fact that cancer usually was, indeed, fatal. The notion that it could not be defeated had

After Willie left the show, she would never again depend on just one man.

been carried over from earlier times when medical researchers and practitioners knew next to nothing about the disease.

Divorced and caring for a teenage daughter, Rose was barely getting by, so Ruth gave her a job to help take her mind off her troubles. Rose managed *50-50 Club* ticket sales from her home and also assisted with the Ruth Lyons Christmas Fund. Later, she worked as one of Ruth's secretaries.

Ruth called upon her friend Gloria Rush to help Rose with the backlog of ticket requests, and sales subsequently were moved in-house to Crosley Square. Three other people—including one of Ruth's neighbors—helped out with tickets and the Christmas Fund distribution during the holiday season.

Herman and Ruth enrolled Candy in public school in 1956 so she could experience a more normal childhood, but there were problems. Other children made fun of her, sometimes because of her famous mother. They taunted her for controversial things Ruth said or did on the air, which they heard about from their parents. It wasn't long before the Newmans called a halt to their social experiment and Candy was back to being tutored at home.

Although she received a fine basic education, she had more contact with Ruth's co-workers than anyone else outside her small family. Her demeanor might be best described as calm, but she wasn't shy or withdrawn. Former newspaper reporter Randy McNutt, who was then a few years younger than Ruth's daughter and whose mother was one of Ruth's friends, recalled Candy as "a sweet girl and rather quiet." Even at 14 years of age, she had "lots of common sense," noted Ruth's friend Gloria Rush.

In their time together, Ruth encouraged Candy to focus on cooking and other domestic activities. No doubt the housekeeper and cook were helpful in her domestic education. While Ruth, herself, didn't have much time for the concerns of home, she liked to boast about her daughter's cooking and how helpful she was around the house. It was obvious to anyone who knew them that Ruth adored Candy and would do anything to protect her. Having lost one child, she was twice as fearful of losing another. Ruth, though, did not hide her daughter from the world.

HERMAN AND RUTH ALSO MANAGED to indulge their child's dreams and desires without spoiling her. They took her on trips here and abroad, and introduced her to famous people. In addition to Candy's *50-50 Club* appearances, Ruth would even arrange for her daughter to be in a movie with one of Hollywood's biggest stars. The Newmans did their best to shelter their daughter from the evils of society. The liquor cabinet was off-limits, as was tobacco, although Ruth was a cigarette smoker. (The use of recreational drugs, fortunately, had not yet become widespread among teens.) In short, Candy touched parts of the world that her mother and father wanted her to touch.

Did she know she was adopted? That's almost certain. Ruth and Herman might not have informed Candy about the stillborn child, but they were too honest not to have told her that she was adopted, and smart enough to know that a bright person like their daughter would find out soon enough. There were already rumors by the time Candy was 12. The three were so close that revealing her origins to Candy really would not have made any difference in her relationship with her adoptive parents. To Candy, Herman Newman and Ruth Lyons were her parents. Period.

Ruth's sister had been stricken once before with cancer and survived, so there was hope when Rose's condition began to improve during the course of another round of treatment. Ruth, however, lost one of her broadcast "family" in January, 1957, when Willie Thall left *The 50-50 Club* to host a similar show on WKRC-TV with his wife. Mrs. Thall and a WKRC producer persuaded Willie to take the leap, confident he could take Ruth's viewers with him. Perhaps the management at WLW's rival station thought Thall could win a ratings duel with Ruth Lyons because he had a certain cachet from working on *The 50-50 Club* for seven years and was well-known from all the years he spent as emcee of *Midwestern Hayride*. But it didn't happen. WKRC dumped Willie Thall after less than a year on the air. Ruth's former sidekick would continue working in television, hosting short-lived shows, producing and doing commercials well into the 1970s.

When Willie told Ruth he was leaving, she joked that she would no longer have eye problems and headaches from the glare of the studio lights reflecting off his balding head. But joking aside, she was hurt by Thall's departure. They were, as Bob Braun once said, the perfect complement for one another. Ruth had grown close to Willie over the years, and she wasn't going to find another partner like him. Instead of making a rash decision on his replacement, Ruth auditioned several male announcers and one woman as guests on *The 50-50 Club*. She didn't want to replace Thall too soon, she explained, "for I felt that in the minds of my viewers he was still very much a part of the show." In the end, she selected three men to serve as her assistants—Peter Grant, Bob Braun, and Sid Daugherty. Never again, she vowed, would she depend on just one man for the show.

PETER GRANT WAS A LEGENDARY NEWSMAN. He came from St. Louis to Cincinnati in 1932 to work at WLW. His voice as the nightly news anchor had become familiar to tens of millions of listeners across the country when WLW radio was broadcasting at 500,000 watts in the 1930s. He also had served as announcer for a variety of local and network radio programs, noteworthy among them *The Red Skelton Show*. His career continued in television with WLWT, where he delivered the evening news and developed a Crosley network news program called *Tri-City Final* that was broadcast at 11 p.m. over WLWT, WLW-D in Dayton, and WLW-C in Columbus.

Grant was an easygoing man whose only activity outside the studio was riding his horse. "Peter . . . was a recluse until Miss Lyons got him to go on her show," noted Bonnie Lou, who split time between *The 50-50 Club* and *The Paul Dixon Show*. "He was very reserved, but when he came on her show he really was something." Delivering the news or talking informally, Grant was poised, serious, and reserved. On Ruth's show, he was game for just about anything—ad-libbing commercials, joking with the cast, even singing on occasion. He possessed a fine speaking voice, of course, but he couldn't croon any better than Ruth could. Still, Grant put on an act in which he sang "Thank Heaven for Little Girls," affecting a fake French accent a la Maurice Chevalier. He also played along with Ruth's endless attempts to get him married off, but like bandleader Cliff Lash, remained a bachelor his entire life.

Bob Braun, formerly of WCPO, came to WLW after winning a competition on the CBS program, *Arthur Godfrey's Talent Scouts*, in January, 1957. The program was famous for giving a number of big stars early exposure, among them Tony Bennett, Leslie Uggams, Eddie Fisher, Johnny Nash, Connie Francis, Barbara McNair, and Vic Damone. Braun beat out some tough competition on Godfrey's national TV and radio program. He won $1,000 and was booked for the week on the show, along with the Andrews Sisters, Pat Boone, and others. It was a million dollars' worth of exposure, as well as testimony to Braun's talent and hard work perfecting his singing.

Braun, who was working for $125 a week at WCPO, felt that winning the talent contest was a signal; it was time to take the next step in his career. In February of 1957, shortly after his return from New York, he worked out the terms of his separation from WCPO and took the job with WLWT. He easily could have found employment in New York, perhaps with one of the networks, but the offer from his hometown's top-rated TV station was too tempting to turn down.

Poised, handsome, and with a permanent friendly tone in his voice, Braun was perfect for television. He had honed his TV skills on both sides of the camera at WCPO, including hosting *Captain Video* in his army uniform, singing, and emceeing. One of the models on a swimsuit fashion show he hosted would become his wife. Braun also appeared on the ABC television network program *Pantomime Hit Parade*, which starred a beautiful singer named Dottie Mack, Cincinnati television's first "glamour girl." So-called "pantomime" shows were peculiar to early television. They featured telegenic performers, usually standing in front of a painted backdrop, lip-synching popular recordings. Sometimes the "singers" also acted out the story in a song. But lip-synching wasn't easy, and Braun admitted having problems with it; he was better at real singing.

WLWT made good use of Braun's vocal gifts. He appeared on *The Paul Dixon Show*, as well as on evening shows hosted by singers Marian Spelman and Ruby Wright. He also did some commercial announcing on the shows. Ruth Lyons was impressed by his on-air presence and invited him on *The 50-50 Club*. Braun was so excited, he showed up at the studio two hours early, cooling his heels at a nearby coffee shop until Ruth arrived. His first guest appearance—Wednesday, February 19, 1957—went smoothly. He sang the song that won the Godfrey talent contest for him, "All the Things that You Are." He did commercials and helped hand out prizes as Ruth interviewed women in the studio audience. He was so busy and having so much fun, it seemed as if the show was over just as it was getting started. Ruth asked him to return on Friday. He had no idea that he had secured a permanent position on the show.

Braun and Grant were welcome additions to *The 50-50 Club*. Braun gave the show a permanent male singer, balancing out the alternating female singers Bonnie Lou, Marian Spelman, and Ruby Wright. Ruth also felt he would attract younger viewers. Both men could do commercials, which was a plus. Ruth didn't like doing all of the commercials all of the time. Grant, with his stentorian voice and good looks, lent extra authority to his commercials while providing comedic relief as well. He appeared on *The 50-50 Club* three days a week, largely because he was a known entity to the audience. Staff announcer Sid Daugherty, who became Ruth's third assistant, joined Braun on the show the other two days of the week. After a few weeks, however, Daugherty dropped out.

Bob Braun and Peter Grant would remain with Ruth until she retired. Over time, Braun became the strongest presence on *The 50-50 Club*. He continued working with Spelman and Wright on their evening musical programs. In addition to his other tasks, he spent his weekday afternoons as a disk jockey on

WLW radio and as the co-host of a movie segment on WLWT with Judy Perkins, the same host who had taken over *Petticoat Partyline* after Ruth started *The 50-50 Club*. On Saturday afternoons, he deejayed a dance party show called *Bandstand* on the radio, broadcasting from a local department store. Within a few months, the show was being televised on Sunday afternoons. Andy Williams and many other young recording stars made stops in Cincinnati to appear on Bob Braun's *Bandstand*.

The conglomeration of shows had Braun working seven days a week. Crosley's tradition of squeezing as much as possible out of each employee was alive and well.

COLOR TELEVISION WAS FIRST DEMONSTRATED in 1929. It was a mechanical system then, soon to be superseded by electronic scanning systems similar to today's television. Both RCA and the CBS network had color TV systems working in 1940, as did NBC in 1941. As with black and white TV, each used a different technology, none compatible with the others. Experimentation ceased, however, when the United States entered WWII. After the war, the same companies waged their own battle, vying with one another to have their respective technologies approved by the Federal Communications Commission as the national standard for color broadcasts. As a result, the first coast-to-coast color broadcast did not take place until December, 1953, over the NBC network.

NBC broadcast a half-dozen shows in color in 1954, but CBS and ABC were slow to jump on the bandwagon. NBC was owned by RCA, which manufactured color sets, while CBS and ABC were not affiliated with television manufacturers. Crosley Broadcasting, always at the leading edge of technology, rushed to establish color broadcasting facilities after its network affiliate, NBC, began transmitting color shows. Crosley spent $500,000 on equipment and by the summer of 1954, WLWT was carrying nine hours of color programs every week.

A completely new set was built for *The 50-50 Club*, most of it painted in shades of blue. The pink piano received a new, lighter coat of pastel pink. The furniture was still Early American. The rocking love seat occupied center stage. Cast members paid special attention to their attire and how it would blend in—or clash—with the new studio décor. The video engineers worked out the problem of adequately lighting those on camera without turning the entire studio into an oven. There was some concern over make-up, but Ruth sensibly pointed out that if the cast used anything other than their street make-up, they would look odd compared with the audience. Her office was decorated in blue with Early American furniture, a coffee percolator, a record player, a fireplace, and, of course, a color TV.

The first production color television sets cost over $1,000, but lower-cost sets soon followed. Thousands of Cincinnatians bought new TVs to watch what would be the first locally produced color program in Ohio: *The 50-50 Club*. Those who didn't have color receivers gathered in local taverns (mostly men) or in appliance or department stores (mostly women) at noon on Friday, August 9, 1957, to watch the show. Crosley had nearly two dozen sets placed in a downtown hotel conference room so advertisers, the press, and city officials could see *The 50-50 Club* in living color. (*The Paul Dixon Show* and *Midwestern Hayride* soon would be broadcast in color as well.) New videotape machines in the studio allowed audience members to see what they looked like in color. "I conceived the idea of having the audience wave to the folks back home," Ruth said, "then playing it back so the women could see themselves on our color monitors after the show was over."

Local TV sales grew at an ever-increasing rate. The penetration of color television in Cincinnati households reached 30 percent, compared to 3 or 4 percent nationwide, earning the city the nickname, "Color Town, USA." A regional sales manager for RCA, whose receivers were advertised on *The 50-50 Club*, attributed color TV's initial growth spurt to Ruth Lyons and her show.

Ruth's longtime secretary, Mickey Fisher, joined WLWT shortly after the station began its color broadcasts. Mickey, who had originally applied for a job in the stenographer pool, recalled her exact words when the personnel director asked if she would be interested in interviewing for a position in Ruth Lyons's office. "I said, 'Are you kidding? My mother watches her every day. I would love to work for her!'"

She interviewed with Ruth's assistant, Elsa Heisel, who asked her to take some dictation and gave her two fan letters to answer. "In the letter [Elsa] dictated," said Mickey, "she used the word 'apropos.' When I got to that word, I couldn't spell it. So I asked [her] how to spell it and she said, 'A-P-P-R-O-P-P-O-S.' I got the job, but Elsa told me that when Ruth looked at my letter, she said, 'She does fine, but she spelled the word apropos wrong.' And Elsa said, 'Well, don't blame her. She asked me how to spell it.'"

At the time, Mickey's name was Mildred Walker. "I was known as 'Millie' in school," she explained. "The first day I was (at WLWT), Elsa looked at me and she said, 'You're not a Mildred, you're not a Millie, you're a Mickey.' And so I became Mickey. It was my first day on the job, and I was introduced to everyone as Mickey Walker." She became Mickey Fisher in a later marriage.

Mickey grew up wanting to be secretary to Alan Ladd or Lana Turner. But with Ruth Lyons, she said, "I think I got a better boss."

THE 50-50 CLUB WAS ON TOP, drawing more viewers to the Crosley TV network than some popular prime-time NBC shows. There was a long waiting list of sponsors, eager to pay the premium rate for the opportunity to advertise on Ruth Lyons's program, and the biggest names in show business—Bob Hope, Perry Como, Ethel Waters, Angie Dickenson, Carol Channing, Henny Youngman, Jimmy Durante, Victor Borge, and others—made their way to the WLWT studio. Crosley Broadcasting even bought a six-seater Aero Commander to fly in entertainers from Detroit, Pittsburgh, Cleveland, and other nearby cities for guest appearances on *The 50-50 Club*. (The airplane carried tail number N700KC, which stood for 700 kilocycles, WLW radio's frequency. It was powered by Lycoming engines, made by a division of AVCO.) With the show bringing in about $2 million a year, the private aircraft was well worth the expense.

Ruth worked harder than ever. She felt it necessary to make sure everything was going right and to be part of every element of the show. She met with sponsors, advised them on how to present their products, and even suggested improvements. She was involved with the sales department as a liaison with programming, and was on WLWT's management committee. After each show, she spent many hours preparing for the next day's program, working with her staff, and even hiring new people.

With everybody else, she worked long days for two to three months after Christmas, making sure the monies from the Ruth Lyons Children's Christmas Fund were properly distributed. She also created and managed a year-around "TV fund," with donations used to buy televisions for nursing homes, veterans' hospitals, county hospitals, and schools for handicapped children.

Nevertheless, when Ruth left the studio, said her secretary Mickey Fisher, "she was Mrs. Herman Newman and mother of Candy."

travels & adventures

Ruth took an early vacation to New Orleans in 1957. At the railway station in Cincinnati, as she waited to board the train, she saw an African-American woman trying to warm a baby bottle between her hands. When she asked the woman why she didn't warm the bottle at the nearby soda fountain, the woman said she wasn't permitted to do so, for obvious reasons. Angry, Ruth grabbed the bottle and marched over to the fountain, asking the girl behind the counter to please warm it for her.

After a moment's hesitation, the girl complied and Ruth returned the bottle to the mother.

Years later, she wrote about what happened next:

"Then everything broke loose! A man came rushing up to me, saying that he was the station superintendent and that I had broken one of the rules of the station. I have never been more furious in my life, and I proceeded to let him know it. I concluded by walking deliberately over to one of the two drinking fountains, the one labeled COLORED, and saying in a loud voice as I turned it on, 'Why, this water isn't colored at all. This is false advertising.'

Ruth's stock was high in New York; the Big Apple pondered a Lyons show on its turf.

"We almost missed our train, but with the station manager following along behind making all sorts of threats in a loud voice, we made it."

In his autobiography, *Here's Bob*, Bob Braun recalled a luncheon hosted by Ohio Gov. John O'Neill and his wife at the governor's mansion in 1957, attended by the cast of *The 50-50 Club*. Their party numbered nearly fifty people. At one point during the table conversation, Ruth asked, "Governor, why don't you use saucers with your coffee cups?"

O'Neill chuckled. "We don't have enough saucers to go with all of these cups," he replied.

After Ruth related the conversation the next day on her show, saucers began arriving in Columbus—approximately 10,000 in all, according to Braun—more than enough to properly serve coffee at the governor's mansion.

Later that year, the Newmans toured the Mediterranean and met Pope John XXIII at the Vatican, a meeting arranged by one of Herman's connections from his 1934 tour of Europe.

EVEN AFTER SIGNING a seven-year contract with NBC and then "firing" the network, as she characterized their split in 1952, Ruth's stock remained high in New York. A few years later, a New York City ad agency sent a female representative to Cincinnati to sell WLWT on the idea of a Ruth Lyons show from the Big Apple. The woman told WLWT general manager John Murphy, "She can make as much as $75,000 a year."

Murphy replied mildly, "She makes twice as much here."

Fan mail poured in at the rate of half a million pieces a year.

Undeterred, the New York rep pitched the plan to Ruth, showing her a treatment for the show. The first page listed a dozen or more names.

"Who are these people—the cast?" Ruth asked.

"The producers, assistant producers, and the directors," the woman replied.

"Well," said Ruth, "I don't need that many bosses. One [WLWT's general manager] is enough for me."

In April, 1958, NBC made one more advance, inviting Ruth to substitute for *Today* show regular Helen O'Connell, who was on maternity leave. Bob Braun and Peter Grant hosted *The 50-50 Club* while Ruth spent a week in New York. Her co-hosts, Dave Garroway and Jack Lescoulie (who sometimes hosted documentaries for Crosley/AVCO Broadcasting), were as nice and helpful as she could have wanted. Ruth did her part, reading news headlines, interjecting a comment when appropriate, and doing a commercial for a nursery in which she peeked out at the audience from behind potted palm trees.

The hometown audience was stunned. Their Ruth Lyons was always in charge of whatever show she was on. Ruth's fans expected her to walk on the *Today* set and take over, with Garroway and Lescoulie doing her bidding. The men would help with commercials and trade witty bon mots with Ruth. She would hold forth on the most provocative of the news headlines, deftly weave conversations into commercials, and in general charm the national early-morning audience. All of America would learn what a tremendous treasure Cincinnati and the Midwest had.

Yet there was no time for Ruth to do anything notable on *Today*. Show segments and commercials rotated through quarter-hours with the precision of an atomic clock, timed to the second. The script ruled everything. Ad-libbing was avoided like dead air. Ruth's talents were set aside. Her fans had expected "Ruth Lyons Week" on NBC. Instead, what they got was the *Today* show as usual. They were outraged. How could NBC insult Ruth Lyons by hiding her from viewers?

Ruth, though, was not outraged; she understood what happened. "My viewers had expected that I would chat with Dave Garroway in the same way in which they were accustomed to seeing and hearing me on my own show. Obviously they were disappointed, and I was shocked to find on my return to Cincinnati the furor that my visit had set up. For days, and even weeks, the newspapers and hundreds of letters from viewers—some sent to NBC— protested that I had been treated very shabbily by the entire network. Many such expressions came from around the country from friends I had made during the short period of time that I had been on the network with *The 50-50 Club*."

When Ruth tried to explain that she wasn't really snubbed, her fans thought she was just being gracious. "In vain," she said, "I tried to explain to my audience that Dave and the entire cast, as well as representatives of NBC, were wonderful to me, but it was all to no avail." There was no way she would ever get her viewers to understand that she wasn't brought in to run the show, but to perform in a supporting role, to temporarily fill an empty seat.

While her fans were unhappy, Ruth had a most pleasant experience during her week-long sojourn in New York. As soon as she knew she would be in the city for a week, she wrote to Eleanor Roosevelt and asked if she might call on her, as she was among the former first lady's most ardent admirers. Mrs. Roosevelt invited Ruth to a luncheon at her apartment, where everything was as elegant, delightful, and perfect as Ruth imagined it would be—that is, until she spilled a small vase of violets she brought as a present.

Ruth was mortified. But Mrs. Roosevelt was more than graceful about the mishap, which required sopping a bit of water from the floor. It was forgotten within minutes. Several other guests attended the luncheon, and Ruth was somewhat amazed by the fact that Mrs. Roosevelt served the guests herself.

After Ruth's brief *Today* show tryout, NBC never troubled her again. Meanwhile, *The 50-50 Club* continued to grow. A typical contest on the show might bring in 75,000 entries. Fan mail poured in at the rate of half a million pieces a year. WLWT hired more people to handle the onslaught of ticket requests.

Gloria Rush remembered the phone call from her friend Ruth Lyons. "She asked me to come and work for her as a secretary. I couldn't say no to that. I knew that was a fun office. . . . When I went in on Monday, I had to go to the personnel office and fill out a questionnaire and sign up for withholding. And then I had to take a typing test. . . . If anyone ever looked at my typing test they would wonder why I had a job there. Of course, Ruth knew I could write a good letter, she knew I would be true-blue to her forever, and I had good telephone tact."

Ruth didn't necessarily want a highly-trained employee—just the person who was right for the position and someone she could trust as a friend, which is why Gloria Rush got the job. The same was true for anyone Ruth hired.

ONE DAY AS HERMAN DROVE HOME from the University of Cincinnati campus, he noticed a hearse in the driveway of 5205 Colerain Avenue—the house that he and Ruth coveted. He gave her the news as soon as he walked in the door and they both kept an eye out for a *For Sale* sign. That was in February.

By June, the Newmans had moved into their new residence. Built in 1865, the house was set on four and one-half acres. It stood well back from the road and was approached by a long, curving driveway that widened for parking on the house's southern side. Behind the house was a two-car garage. There was also a large in-ground swimming pool. With four bedrooms, two baths, living room, sitting room, kitchen, and dining room—plus two fireplaces—the house had everything the family could want.

Newspapers in the WLW listening area, and later in the Crosley Television

Network cities—Cincinnati, Dayton, Columbus, and Indianapolis—frequently carried features on Ruth Lyons and her shows throughout the 1930s, '40s, '50s, and '60s. Ruth was no stranger to national publicity, either, featured in many radio and TV magazines.

Dial magazine tagged her a "Jill of All Trades" in a 1939 article, and gave her age as five years younger than she was. But her eleven-month run on NBC during the 1951-52 season brought her to the attention of mainstream magazines like *Cosmopolitan*, which tagged her the Midwest's "Million-Dollar Dynamo" (a reference to *The 50-50 Club's* annual revenue).

The March 19, 1953 national edition of *Grit* magazine lauded her tremendous drawing power—60,000 women in the studio audience each year, along with a TV and radio audience in 300 counties across six states. The November 1, 1953 issue of *Coronet* featured a lengthy story, written by Ruth's friend and Cincinnati TV and radio critic Mary Wood, detailing the good work of the Ruth Lyons Children's Christmas Fund. In 1954, *Look* described *The 50-50 Club* as "the zaniest, most popular, and most profitable program in the Midwest," and called Ruth a female Arthur Godfrey. Others joined in applying the "female Godfrey" or "girl Godfrey" tag.

In 1957, *The Saturday Evening Post* commissioned a full-length feature titled "The Lady Lays Down the Law." Sprawling across six pages of the high-circulation slick magazine, Ruth was portrayed as a tough businesswoman by the article's author, James Maxwell. "Ruth Lyons seems more the president of a highly lucrative business than either television performer or housewife," Maxwell wrote. "She handles all contacts with her sponsors, plans with them all the advertising details for her program, makes the arrangements for the many prizes which are given away daily at the conclusion of her show, arbitrates problems between members of her staff, answers an enormous amount of fan mail and, for about three months of the year, operates a one-woman Christmas Club campaign to raise money for toys, movie projectors, televisions and similar entertainment facilities for children's hospitals and wards.

"In addition to the responsibilities connected with her own show," the article continued, "Ruth also acts as liaison between Crosley's programming and sales departments, and is a member of the top planning group of the station." (In reality, Bill McCluskey was the sponsor-programming liaison—although it's likely that Ruth kibitzed.)

"She unquestionably has great power within the Crosley organization," Maxwell wrote, "but how she uses it is often a matter of bitter debate between her admirers and detractors. She has many of both."

One unidentified source painted Ruth as a deadly dictator. Another—probably Elsa Sule—conceded that Ruth cracked the whip occasionally but that no one would take notice were she a man.

In March, 1958, *Grit* profiled her career in radio and television, marveling at her ability to work without a script. A month later, *The American Home* magazine showcased her home in a six-page spread with seven large photographs, some in color. Describing it as "a completely remodeled 140 year-old farmhouse" (it was actually ninety-three years old), the reporter noted the strawberry theme of the décor—on china, in old prints, and on the walls—as well as a rocking chair in every room and a color TV set in every room except the living room. Ruth and Herman had recently re-decorated the kitchen and added a family room, complete with a full-size pool table that cleverly converted to a buffet table. The article took readers on a tour through the rest of the house and detailed Ruth's collection of knick-knacks and *objects d'art* from around the world.

Although the publisher sent several thousand extra copies to Cincinnati, the April, 1958, issue of *The American Home* sold out almost immediately. More copies had to be shipped in from other cities. Albers (at this time still an advertiser on *The 50-50 Club*) had reserved ad space five months earlier. Ruth also gave her audience advance notice, tipping them off in January about the magazine's upcoming story, and on the Monday after the photographers visited her house, she told her radio and TV friends all about the photo session.

"Well, as you know, Saturday was the great picture taking!" Ruth exclaimed. "It was wonderful. It was adorable. I've never met such nice people. They didn't really change things around too much as I told you I'd been told they would. That's the truth.

"But of course they brought the photographers from Chicago and everything. If they took a picture of a table, the telephone would be here and then the photographer would look into the camera and say, 'Move the telephone one half inch to the left. . . . Now move the flowers one quarter inch northeast!'

"I mean, you have never gone through such . . . . They didn't change any of the fundamental things. I'd have killed them if they did, killed them deader than doornails. Of course, you've seen the magazine, *The American Home*, and you've seen how beautiful everything looks. But now I know all the tricks. For instance, the drapes in the dining room and pool room . . . they taped the bottom of the drapes so they'd set right. You know, I left the tape on 'cause they never did hang too well."

The magazine's reporter went on to detail each room in the Newman residence, along with the furnishings (Early American again), collectibles, antiques, photos, and whatnots carefully placed around the house. With the extra-large photos, the spread would have satisfied just about anyone who wondered about how Ruth lived. Readers also met some of the Newman menagerie—five of the dogs, the cat, and the canary. Oddly, the only thing lacking was an exterior photo of the house.

RUTH, HERMAN, AND CANDY HAD GONE on several cruises since they traveled to England for Queen Elizabeth's coronation in 1953. They traveled to Bermuda aboard the *Queen of Bermuda* in January, 1954, and stayed for three weeks. Early 1955 saw them travel across the U.S. by rail, then take a cruise to Hawaii. In September of the same year, it was back to Bermuda aboard the *Ocean Monarch*. The next year there were vacation trips to Florida and Canada. Judging from Ruth's itineraries, it would appear that she successfully negotiated for six weeks of vacation every year in her contract. Management probably didn't like it when she was gone for extended periods, no matter who took her place on the show.

In August, 1958, the family went on a landmark cruise to Russia—the first permitted since before World War II. After taking the *Queen Elizabeth* to Ireland and Scotland, Ruth, Candy, and Herman boarded a ship named *Meteor* for a whirlwind tour of the Scandinavian countries. Their ultimate goal was Russia—specifically, Leningrad and Moscow. In both cities they saw what came to be the typical tourist sites—the Kremlin, the embalmed bodies of Stalin and Lenin side by side, the Czar's jewels and Fabergé creations, the Winter Palace, the nearly empty GUM department store in Moscow, and endless museums and works of art. It was an alien world to all of the Americans on the cruise

The *Meteor* docked in Poland and the group took a train to Warsaw, which was still being rebuilt after being devastated by three armies during the war. Ruth's brief account of the return journey across Europe by water and rail leaves the impression that she felt as if she was fleeing to safety.

In due time, the family boarded a cruise liner to New York and received a grand welcome at Union Terminal on their return to Cincinnati. To Americans, Russia was a dark mystery, so Ruth was extensively interviewed about the trip (as was everyone on the cruise), and Herman wrote a description of the tour for the University of Cincinnati's alumnus newsletter.

A more pleasant experience awaited Ruth at the end of the year. On December 26, the American Institute of Public Opinion's Gallup Poll included her on its 1958 national list of "Most Admired Women." She was ranked second in the "Literature, Journalism, Art" category, keeping good company with the likes of Pauline Fredericks (first), Pearl S. Buck, and Grandma Moses.

FOR THE NEW YEAR'S HOLIDAY, the Newmans did something different; they took a Caribbean cruise to Jamaica, Puerto Rico, and Trinidad. The ship also sailed to Cuba, where Ruth noticed one of "Castro's men," heavily armed, positioned at each store entrance in Havana.

"I felt fear for the first time," she admitted, ". . . and to add to my fear, I stole a white straw belt in Cuba. It was an accident, I assure you. We were shopping for all the people back home, and I was trying on belts for size. I put one on myself, over the belt I was already wearing. We completed our shopping there and hastily grabbed a cab for the hotel, where Fidel Castro was supposed to land on the roof in a helicopter within the hour. I was still wearing two belts, my own and one with a tag attached. Senor Castro did not appear, and we finally gave up. I didn't discover what I had done until I undressed. Thank goodness we left the following day—on the last boat ever to carry a cruise to Cuba."

Back home, Ruth began planning her first business venture outside of broadcasting: a line of dresses to be called the Ruth Lyons Autograph Collection. Offered by department stores in her viewing area, including Shillito's in Cincinnati, the collection ranged from sheath and belted sheath dresses to shirtwaist dresses with flaring, bouffant skirts or cluster-pleated skirts. (Shirtwaist dresses were declared "in" by *The New York Times* and other fashion arbiters that season.)

Text from a typical illustrated newspaper ad read:

RUTH LYONS AUTOGRAPH DRESSES are exclusive designs, from the drawing board of a famous French-American couturiere—designs either inspired initially by Ruth Lyons herself, or approved by her personally. As Ruth says, "Designed by me—with YOU in mind!" Beauty of design, quality of fabric, and artistry of craftsmanship are the cornerstones of the RUTH LYONS Dress Collection.

The "queen" of television invites discriminating women to share her ideals in fashions.

The dresses were available in sizes 10 to 20 and $12^1/_2$ to $20^1/_2$. Each carried a tag with a replica of Ruth's signature, though the designer was not named. *The 50-50 Club* carried ads for Ruth's dresses, but Ruth got ninety minutes of free advertising on WLWT each day she or any of the women in the cast wore a dress from her clothing line.

The Ruth Lyons Autograph Collection lasted through the fall season, even though it had the best possible advertising. Premium pricing might have caused some customer resistance; the dresses in Ruth's line cost half again as much as off-the-rack dresses. Typical Ruth Lyons Autograph dresses were priced around $30-$35 (there was a silk number for $25), while similar dresses at Bonwit Teller were priced at about $20. The change of season was also a consideration.

fame & friendship

Near the end of 1959, Troy Donahue came to *The 50-50 Club* to promote *A Summer Place*, the first movie in which he had a starring role, alongside Connie Stevens. Donahue and Candy Newman immediately hit it off, because Troy said she looked like his younger sister, Eve. Candy called him her "big brother," and Donahue appeared on the show several times over the next two years. The friendship was to lead to an important event in Candy's life.

In January, 1960, the Cincinnati Royals basketball team played the New

The *Ladies Home Journal* revealed that Ruth had a combined radio-television audience of seven million.

York Knickerbockers at Cincinnati, and Ruth made one last appearance on network television. At halftime, Ruth and several other cast members from *The 50-50 Club* ran out onto the court and held a charity basket-tossing competition. During the weeks following, Ruth received mail from fans all over the country, who remembered her from the *Today* show and her own show during the 1951-1952 season.

In 1960 Ruth got national exposure in the pages of popular magazines, as well. The April 1 issue of *Ladies' Home Journal* offered up an illustrated feature about Ruth. "Ruth Lyons is an attractive, vital blonde with a bad slouch such as teenagers get lectured for," wrote Betty Hannah Hoffman, "and a sandpaper voice that gets her the highest rating of any daytime TV performer in the country." In describing Ruth's features, Hoffman wrote, "In repose, Miss Lyons' face, with its high blunt cheekbones, firm chin, and steely blue eyes is pure American Gothic." The story also revealed that Ruth's combined radio and television audience totaled seven million.

For the same issue, Ruth wrote an autobiography titled "Life Has a Lovely Way of Living" (a line from a song she wrote). "The results were amazing," Ruth said. "It was almost impossible to buy a copy of the magazine anywhere in our area. Copies were shipped in to Cincinnati from Chicago, Cleveland, and other places to help fulfill the demand." It was a repeat of what happened when Ruth's home was profiled in *The American Home* two years before. "It was," Ruth added, "the largest magazine sale that the journal had ever had." The stories also generated mail from across the United States.

Then the July 19 issue of *Look* magazine ran a multi-page pictorial, headlined "TV Powerhouse: Her Show is the Highest Rated in Daytime TV." Her show pulled a rating of 28 to 31, which was very high. (The rating was consistent for Ruth, which is why she wasn't worried when ABC television put the Frances Langford-Don Ameche show opposite her back in the 1950s. It never pulled more than a 2 rating, and didn't last the season.)

Ruth was lauded as a bookseller in *The Sporting News* later that year.

"She wasn't a television star or a radio star—she was a friend."—Elsa Sule

The story talked about how Joe Garagiola appeared on *The 50-50 Club* to promote his new book, *Baseball is a Funny Game*. Needless to say, Ruth had fun with Joe (she was a big baseball fan but loyal to the Cincinnati Reds), and told her audience to go right out and buy a copy.

Which they did. That afternoon Garagiola signed 305 books in four hours in Dayton, and 114 in one hour at the Shillito's department store in Cincinnati. (Most authors would have been pleased to sell thirty books in an hour.) In Cincinnati, people were buying the book for weeks afterward. The first sports book ever to make *The New York Times* bestseller list, *Baseball is a Funny Game* sold over 41,000 copies, all very high numbers in 1960—and today.

The Ruth Lyons Autograph series wasn't the success she had hoped it would be, but Ruth had no problems selling records—hers as well as records by others.

Perhaps the most famous tune she penned was "Let's Light the Christmas Tree," which was a minor hit for singer Ruby Wright in 1958. "Hey, Nonny Nonny" was another holiday favorite. Johnny Mathis and Peter Nero recorded her song, "Wasn't the Summer Short?" and over the years several other artists covered her songs. According to DJ Dusty Rhodes, "Wasn't the Summer Short?" was a big regional hit.

In 1959, Ruth put together a Christmas album titled *Ten Tunes of Christmas*, and it quickly sold 50,000 copies in Cincinnati, Columbus, and Dayton. One woman who didn't own a record player bought a Christmas album because Ruth said to buy it. It eventually sold 250,000 copies, and it was also released as a boxed set of four extended play records.

Ruth created a record label, CANDEE Records, and incorporated Candee Enterprises to handle its business affairs in 1959. After *Ten Tunes of Christmas*, came *Our Best to You* (1960), a few of its songs written by the likes of Cole Porter and Lerner & Lowe, as well as Ruth. Ruth's final album was *It's Christmastime Again* (1963). Most of the songs featured Ruth on organ. Singers on the albums included Ruth, Bonnie Lou, Marian Spelman, Ruby Wright, Bob Braun, and even Peter Grant (who was less of a singer than Ruth was). The CANDEE label also put out singles by Bob Braun and Ruby Wright.

In 1960, Columbia Records put out a single with two of Ruth's songs: "All Because It's Christmas" and "Everywhere the Bells are Ringing." And in 1995 WVXU, the public radio station formerly operated by Cincinnati's Xavier University, issued CD and cassette tape versions of some of Ruth's best Christmas songs. An indication of how well-loved her records were can be found in the liner notes, which describe the difficulty the producers had in finding— among the thousands of copies produced and sold—"clean" copies from which to record. They tried 130 copies of Ruth's Christmas recordings, but there were none that did not have audible wear in the grooves. It was quite a bit of work to restore the audio quality to an acceptable level.

Almost all of the cuts were recorded at Cincinnati's famous King Records studio, where James Brown and an endless roster of hillbilly, rockabilly, and soul groups recorded some of their biggest hits. King Records was in one of Cincinnati's grittier neighborhoods, but King's owner, Syd Nathan, and his cousin Howard Kessel, who ran the record-pressing plant, really liked Ruth's show, and so did their wives, according to music historian Randy McNutt, author of *The*

Cincinnati Sound. So they worked hard to persuade Ruth Lyons to record at King.

"It must have been a real coup for them to have her come into their studio to record," McNutt speculated. "As if it wasn't enough culture shock to mix up in one studio performers like James Brown, Hank Ballard and the Midnighters, and a bunch of Appalachian singers, Syd Nathan goes and brings in Ruth Lyons, Cliff Lash, and Marian Spelman." Lash added strings (including a harp) to some of the arrangements, giving them a truly compelling sound.

Ruth wrote most of the songs used on her albums and owned the copyrights. But everyone who played or sang on an album with Ruth got a share in the royalties, unusual in the cutthroat music business. The typical arrangement is that backing musicians receive an hourly rate for the time spent in the studio, as are some singers. The royalties are taken by the star singer and those who own the music.

Ruth's personal sense of honor would not allow her to do that. With albums selling in the tens of thousands, there was money for everyone. Besides, Ruth could not abide the thought of cheating a friend, which is how she regarded all of her co-workers in any project. This same sense of friendship extended to her audience, and she would never betray them by taking money to convince them to buy products in which she did not believe. To Ruth, the women in the audience really *were* her friends. *The 50-50 Club* assistant director, Elsa Sule, put it more succinctly in a 1991 interview: "She was everybody's next-door neighbor. She wasn't a television star or a radio star. She was a *friend.*"

"She got to know each of us personally," said Jerry Imsicke, the former page, noting that Ruth paid attention to even those at the lowest level.

CROSLEY SQUARE was in some ways a good place to operate TV and radio studios. In other ways it was strange, with the two television studios on different floors, and offices strewn here and there without regard to where the occupants might need to go. Storage was similarly scattered. The weather and news people were stuffed into the basement, as was Bob Braun's disk jockey studio.

Getting the Paul Dixon and Ruth Lyons shows organized was an exercise in controlled chaos. Both prop boys and pages had to hustle, judging by Van Cottengim's description of a typical day. He worked as a page in the early 1960s. "We'd start about 8:30 in the morning because we had *The Paul Dixon Show* to set up on the fifth floor (Studio A), and we had to take the audience up a dozen at a time in the elevator." Dixon's show ran from 9 a.m. to 10 a.m. in the beginning, and was later extended to 10:30.

"We'd get the Dixon audience up by 9 to his studio (Studio A, on the fifth floor), and then about 10:30 in the morning, the Lyons audience started coming into the lobby, because they had to be upstairs for lunch by 11, which was held in the third floor studio.

"The Dixon show would end up about 10, and they'd have a drawing after the show, so about 10:15 we'd start taking the Dixon audience from Studio A down to the lobby, and pick up a load of Lyons's ladies going up to lunch in Studio B (on the third floor) for lunch. The prop guys would be setting up the third floor temporary dining room every day from 8:30 a.m. to 10 a.m." WLWT employed three waitresses for this event, and a Cincinnati caterer brought in the food.

"Lyons's show was on five," Cottengim explained, "the same studio as Dixon's. So setup had about forty-five minutes to change the set from Dixon to Lyons. It was our job as pages to hustle the audiences around. They couldn't get on a self-operating elevator and just go to three. We had to take 'em up there. It was as if the ladies were blinded by the fact that they were going to see Mother.

"About 11:30 or so we'd start taking the Lyons group from the third floor and up to the Studio A on five, where *The 50-50 Club* was. All this time we were hustling ladies all around the place, and we never misplaced one. Except from time to time we would hit the wrong button and drop off a load on one—which was the basement. At Crosley Square, two was the Lobby.

"When this happened, they would blindly push out of the elevator and start walking all over the place, wondering where they were. It would take about five minutes to gather them all up and take them up one floor. All this time they thought we had kidnapped them."

The cast and Ruth's staff were busy in the hours before the show, as well. "Ruth's office was right directly behind the stage," Cottengim said, "more or less partitioned, with walls about two inches thick. You could hear the band practicing through the wall. They usually came in about 10, often tired from playing a late gig the night before.

"Ruth and Mickey Fisher and Elsa Sule were in their private domain back there. Elsa would get any food they had to cook that day, and materials for commercials. There were fresh flowers every day to decorate the set, and there was a cake from Excell Bakery. Pages also worked as drivers, and took care of the audiences and picked up talent at the airports, and went out to pick up and deliver cakes and flowers to the shows."

The prop boys attended to any number of details. "Another prop guy and I set up the many tables and chairs in the third floor studio and placed product samples of featured products on them, for the ladies who had lunch before the show," said Eric Schneider, who worked his way up to floor director after starting as a prop boy.

"It was always very important to me to go into Mother's office to see what color dress she wore, to help choose the right color flowers to tape onto her microphone." Schneider went on to produce shows by Bob Braun, Nick Clooney, and others before pursuing a television career in Europe.

"After each show there were drawings for prizes," Schneider recalled. "Ruth had every prize in the world to give away." There was one staffer whose job it was to stock, inventory, and dispense items from the "prize room," where everything from television sets to electric knives was housed.

After the drawings, Ruth headed for her office. Sometimes there were meetings with advertising clients or management, but Ruth and her staff would often just play bridge. According to Elsa Sule, "We played bridge practically every day there wasn't a meeting with a client. It kind of brought Ruth down from her high, so we played bridge for forty-five minutes or so."

Sometimes client liaison Bill McCluskey would play, as well. Business talk like "How big is this company?" and "Do they have good distribution?" would be interspersed into the games, along with "Bid four hearts!" and "Slam!"

Sule also explained that no matter how good or poor a player was, Ruth usually won—with a little help. "Gloria Rush loved Ruth and didn't want her to lose. Gloria would slip Ruth her high cards under the table. It didn't make for much of a game. And she would much rather have Ruth win than win herself. But Mickey and I didn't feel that way; Mickey and I were in there ready to fight."

When Ruth was ready to go, one of the pages had to have the elevator waiting for her. Van Cottengim often had this job. "I remember one time I was taking her down from the fifth floor," he said, "and she had a cigarette in her mouth. One of us told her there were still women in the lobby. 'Oh, damn!' she said, and threw her cigarette down in the elevator and put it out with her foot. She didn't want to get caught smoking."

Having grown up during a time when it was either daring or trashy for women to smoke cigarettes—depending on who was making the judgment—Ruth probably had a bit of residual guilt over smoking. But she enjoyed the habit. Salem menthol cigarettes were her favorite.

Cottengim also remembers working on the show one day when a guest made Ruth angry. "Annette Funicello from the Walt Disney TV show on NBC came in as a guest, and she didn't know who Ruth was. She couldn't understand why in the world she had to go to this old lady's show.

"Annette put Ruth down on the air, said something to her on the show about her age, implying that she was a washed-up old woman running a talk show. And Ruth just lit into her, came right back at her with something.

"Ruth got off the stage at the end, walked out with the theme song playing. She hurried to the side entrance and yelled down the hall, 'Mickey—get Walt on the phone! Get Walt on the phone now!'

"She really gave Walt Disney an earful, and told him never to send Annette to his show again."

Annette Funicello thus joined a small club that included Gloria Swanson and Jerry Lester.

Such problem cases aside, Ruth welcomed anyone, as long as they were interesting. She was wary of authors. "Although they might have written an excellent book," she said, "when they appeared on television with a live audience before them, they were, as a rule, very nervous. I considered it my job, having read their books, to put them at their ease by disagreeing on some issues with them, thus stimulating the conversation. An exciting interview was often the result."

It may have helped had she told them that any mistakes they made wouldn't come back to haunt them, because in general she refused to allow her show to be taped or otherwise recorded. If she made a mistake, she figured, people would forget about it faster if they couldn't replay it. (Elsa kept a set of notes as to what went on during each show, should the FCC ever want to know what they had been doing.)

Ruth also had practical motives in forbidding the taping of her show. She didn't want people profiting from her work without her involvement. Nor did she care for the image of herself as a ghost-like presence, chattering at people in their living rooms long after she was gone. (This happened to Paul Dixon, who died of a heart attack in 1974. A decade after his death, Channel 5 was running his old shows to fill in the wee hours of the morning.)

HERMAN NEWMAN was Ruth's rock. His love for her never faltered. His sense of justice and duty and responsibility were equally solid. He lived a personal philosophy that evolved from his experiences as a student, minister, and teacher. The only aspect of his character that varied was his religious faith, which grew strong in his youth and rose to the pinnacle of commitment when he was ordained. But at some point, religion relaxed its hold on him. No one but Herman knew when that was or what caused it, but it appears to have been a gradual process.

All of which is not to say that Herman Newman was not a spiritual person. While religion slipped away from him with a quiet tread, spiritual belief traveled right alongside him. But he had no zeal for organized religion. "A believing freethinker" might have described Herman some years after he left the ministry. He did not disdain practitioners of any religion, nor men of the cloth, and he respected everyone's beliefs, maintaining friendships with ministers, priests, and rabbis.

None of this particularly troubled Ruth. Her religious roots were deep, but family and work often took precedence over practicing religion. Her personal beliefs were not a subject for public consumption, in any event—though Herman opened her mind in that area. This was for the better; if she favored no particular religion, she angered no one. Thus, she was able to speak equally with Billy Graham, Dr. Nelson Glueck of Cincinnati's Hebrew Union College, the Catholic Archbishop, and representatives of any other group.

Ruth summed up her feelings for Herman this way: "He is as handsome as I once thought Clark Gable to be, more intelligent than I will ever give him credit for being, and as stubborn as any descendant of German forebears inevitably would be."

As Ruth's co-workers observed, Ruth seemed to be the main force in the family. "She ruled the roost" was something several of her friends and co-workers said of her. Most of the time this was true, most likely because she and Herman thought so much alike that a decision made by Ruth was the same decision that Herman would have made. But if there was a conflict over something about which Herman felt strongly, he had the ability to persuade Ruth to come over to his side. (Ruth wasn't joking about his stubbornness.)

One example of this was in politics. Ruth had grown up to be a moderate Republican (raised by a faithful Republican). After marrying Herman, she took on his liberal attitudes, and to some of those around her she started talking like a Democrat. Never on the air, of course; she could sell almost anything, but she refused to try to sway anyone in their political opinions.

"She listened to Herman," Elsa Sule said. "Her politics even changed because of Herman. She was a big Republican, and Herman convinced her that the Democrats lived. He had a tremendous influence on her in many, many ways. She changed a lot of her philosophy because of Herman."

coming out

Ruth was responsible for jump-starting the careers of several recording artists. One was Al Hirt, who had studied at the Cincinnati Conservatory of Music in 1940. Hirt was a frequent guest on *The 50-50 Club* and introduced his first album on the show. In the early 1960s, Ruth's support helped put albums like *Honey in the Horn* in the Top 10.

Another act Ruth helped get going was the Limelighters, a West Coast group whose new album did poorly until they performed on Ruth's show. Within a few months the record sold 80,000 copies in the Midwest, where previously they had been all but unknown.

Candy's many childhood pets stirred her ambition to become a veterinarian.

Award-winning pianist Peter Nero's career was just beginning when he appeared on *The 50-50 Club* for the first time in 1961, not long after his first album, *Piano Forte*, was released in April. (Nero would receive a Grammy as the Best New Recording Artist of 1961. He was the second artist to receive the award; Bobby Darrin was first.)

Ruth Lyons was understandably impressed by the album, which showcased Nero's trademark style, labeled by one reviewer as "a glossy shading of popular music with classic overtones." In fact, she couldn't wait to get her hands on his music—literally. According to Nero, "She was quite a good organist and before I would get to Cinci, she would pick off the orchestral arrangement to one of the cuts on my latest recording and play the orchestra part while I played piano." Ruth's perfect pitch no doubt helped her along.

Ruth invited Peter back to *The 50-50 Club* again when his next album, *New Piano in Town* (a Grammy nominee) was released in September. Thereafter, he was a frequent guest on the show, more often than anyone but Bob Hope. He appeared on *The 50-50 Club* "at least three times per year for as long as she was on. I released three new recordings per year and I appeared each time." (He recorded a total of sixty-seven albums.)

Ruth's support played a major role in Peter Nero's career for several years. "She was probably the most important force in the first three years of my career," he affirmed. "She made me in her markets." Those included not only Cincinnati, Dayton, Columbus, Indianapolis—but also the other states into which WLW radio reached with its *50-50 Club* simulcast.

"At the end of a show in which I would appear, she told her audience to meet me across the street at Shillito's (where I would autograph albums) and buy a recording even if they didn't have a phonograph."

All it took was for Ruth to say, "Peter Nero's going to be over at Shillito's Department Store, signing albums."

Nero came to know Ruth more as a friend than a sponsor or mentor. "One of the things I enjoyed the most," he remembers, "was the time spent with her in the 'green room' backstage after the show; her in her rocking chair and me and some friends seated in her Early American style living room. She was a wonderfully clear thinker and I was fascinated by her views on human nature, racial equality, and her belief in the goodness of mankind."

"She was an extraordinary woman and had the same skill as a communicator that Oprah does today."—Earl Hamner, Jr.

What stood out among his memories of Ruth, he said, was "her strength in keeping her integrity. For instance, sponsors waited in line for two years to get their products on her show but she would take them on only if she used and liked their product. The same held true for performing and recording artists."

Other famous guests were similarly impressed. Lorne Greene was surprised by her ability to get him to talk. "I've never really enjoyed an interview so much," he said, which was saying a lot as Greene was interviewed often during the years *Bonanza* was in production. "It was like nothing else I've ever done on TV. I felt like a member of Ruth's family and talked about things I've never talked about on TV before. How does she do it?" Milton Berle made similar remarks.

Earl Hamner, Jr., creator of *The Waltons* and *Falconcrest* and himself a veteran WLW radio writer, recalls his visit to *The 50-50 Club* fondly. Ruth's communication abilities impressed him the most. "She was an extraordinary woman," he said, "and had the same skill as a communicator that Oprah does today."

Singer Eydie Gormet marveled at how Ruth kept a running patter of talk and commercials, never getting lost and without a dull moment. "How she can ad-lib for ninety minutes and never run dry is a modern wonder," she said. Ruth was in part responsible for Steve Lawrence and Edyie Gormet getting married—at least the timing. Each had been on *The 50-50 Club*, but never together. One afternoon following the show in 1957, Steve Lawrence was bemoaning the fact that while he had thought about marrying Edyie, they could never get together. They were each constantly touring on different schedules.

Ruth suggested to Lawrence that they change their schedules and go on tour together. Surprised that he hadn't thought of that himself, Lawrence called Gormet from Ruth's office and the two were soon married.

THE YEAR 1961 WAS A GOOD ONE for the Cincinnati Reds, who hadn't won the National League pennant since 1939—the last year they won the World Series. Late in the summer of 1961 it became clear to Ruth and everyone else that the team was headed for the pennant, and she wrote a special song, "Rally 'Round the Reds." She sang the song literally every day on *The 50-50 Club*, and soon much of Cincinnati was singing it, too.

Ruth boosted the team from its Crosley Field dugout when she could, always wearing a Reds baseball cap, which she jokingly referred to as "more of a coaching strategy than a good luck piece." She was great friends with manager Fred Hutchinson. Despite Ruth's good efforts, the Reds fell short of winning the series—a special goal since team owner Powel Crosley, Jr., had passed away just before baseball season started.

Ruth had achieved more startling results as a Reds booster back in 1957, when she "fixed" the election of the National League All-Star team. The team was selected by fan vote, and in 1956 members of the Cincinnati Reds scored five positions in the starting lineup, plus a few second-string spots. Ruth decided that Cincinnati Reds players ought to fill all the positions on the All-Star team. And she knew how to make it happen. She let her audience know how to vote and encouraged them daily to get their friends to send in ballots for the Reds, too. A half-million votes from the Cincinnati area filled the All-Star team with Cincinnati Reds. All that without the Internet.

It wasn't allowed to stand, however. Baseball Commissioner Ford Frick started receiving complaints about ballot-box stuffing, looked into the matter, and bumped several Reds off the team. The All-Star team was not selected by fans' votes for several years after that.

Ruth's favorite basketball team, the University of Cincinnati Bearcats, had a better year in 1961, winning the NCAA championship. The team was led by Oscar Robertson ("the Big O"), who came from Indianapolis.

Ruth had all the Reds players on the show in celebration, and the Bearcats, too. Back home in Indy, Oscar's mother, Mazell Robertson, was thrilled to see her son on the television show that she watched every day. As Robertson recounted in his autobiography, *The Big O*, *The 50-50 Club* played a major role in his decision to attend the University of Cincinnati. He was being recruited by several schools, among them UC, and his mother was approached behind the scenes by people representing UC. It turned out that she was a gospel songwriter, and she hoped for the opportunity for someone with clout to listen to her music. And she had always wanted to be on Ruth's show.

The recruiter returned to Cincinnati and got in touch with Herman Newman, who talked to his wife. Soon, a demo recording session was arranged for Mrs. Robertson at King Records, and she appeared on *The 50-50 Club*. Mrs. Robertson in turn steered her son toward UC. Oscar was not aware of any of what had transpired until years later. So it was that Mrs. Mazell Robertson and Mrs. Herman Newman helped assure Oscar Robertson's future with the Bearcats and the Cincinnati Royals.

In 1962, Bob Braun had a huge hit record. "Til Death Do Us Part" on the Decca label stayed on the Top 100 chart for four months. The romantic ballad sold 500,000 copies.

Suddenly, Bob Braun was getting lots of national attention. And WLWT started thinking about the possibility of Braun getting offers to work elsewhere. It was well-known that his dream was to have his own show, yet after five years he was still second-fiddle to Ruth on her show. Yes, he was loyal, but he just might jump ship for the right offer.

Crosley Broadcasting management knew that Braun wanted his own weekday show. For this reason he was offered a morning radio show in 1963. The format for what came to be called *The Good Morning Show* was "similar to *The 50-50 Club* but without pictures," as Braun described it. It was sponsored by and broadcast from McAlpin's Department Store—the same store from which Braun's Saturday *Bandstand* program originated—in downtown Cincinnati from 9 to 10 a.m.

With all the planning and preparation required, plus a month of rehearsals, *The Good Morning Show* did not make its debut until September. It wasn't a television show, but Braun was pleased. It was his first vehicle for an adult audience.

Braun found the days when he had to take Ruth's place and handle other on-air work a bit pressing, but at the same time doing both shows in one day bolstered his confidence.

CANDY NEWMAN WASN'T as enthusiastic about baseball or basketball as her mother, but she was involved in competitive swimming, which allowed her at least some exposure to her peers. She had learned to swim at the age of three, and loved having a pool at home. She shared many other interests with each of her parents—paramount among them a love of travel. She had her own interests, too. She loved reading historical biographies and collected ceramic figurines. In a newspaper interview before she entered college, she talked about her hobbies of cooking and quilting. "I quilt like I'm eighty-five years old," she said. Ruth bragged about her work, noting that she was a deft left-handed quilter and carried quilting pieces wherever she went, even on overseas journeys. She also made dresses, as well as aprons, for the maids, Callie and Pauline.

She began her freshman year at the University of Cincinnati in the fall of 1962. She rode back and forth from school with Herman. It was a practical matter because they had the same destination and similar schedules. It also added another layer of parental protectiveness.

Candy still cherished an ambition to be a veterinarian. Her many adored pets gave her plenty of experience in animal care: she had accumulated six Japanese Spaniels, an Irish setter, a canary, and an ancient, overweight cat. But after meeting Troy Donahue she was drawn to acting. The stars she had met on *The 50-50 Club* opened her eyes to the real people behind the glamour—to her, regular folks blessed with good luck and reward for their work, more than born with some inherent magic (though she also saw a few of those, as well).

MOST STARS, WHEN SHE SAW THEM in person, might be someone who came from her own hometown of Cincinnati, as did Tyrone Power and Theda Bera. To be a part of the glittering world of film they had to go off to California. Some of the glitter brushed off when they visited her small city. Candy wanted more of the glitter, the ersatz magic. It was not necessarily because she believed she was beautiful, no matter what her mother said, but because she knew that she could put in the work. She had seen television from the inside, and she had met Troy Donahue, Tony Randall, Stephanie Powers, Jayne Mansfield, and many others, and saw how hard actors really worked.

Judging by a letter she wrote to Candy during Candy's senior year in high school, Ruth didn't see Candy as a future media star. Intended for Candy to read later in her adult life, Ruth wrote:

I hope you will discover some field in education where you will be happy. I also hope that you will learn shorthand and typing, which I believe are always helpful in getting a job.

It is ironic that the powerful and entrepreneurial Ruth thus cast Candy in the role of a stereotypical female of the time, someone who should train in a traditional, low-paying woman's occupation. Did Ruth want her daughter to live a different and more peaceful life? Or was this another way for Ruth to keep Candy young, pointing out a path for her young adulthood—a path that wouldn't have enabled her to be a completely independent woman?

Indeed, there was little chance that Candy would ever have to earn her own way in the world. Ruth and Herman provided everything: Candy had a wonderful home life, a menagerie of pets that could only be exceeded by a zookeeper's daughter, and more possessions than she needed or probably wanted. Her parents also gave her money and taught her how to manage it.

Herman and Ruth were dutiful, attentive, and caring parents. They taught her manners and moderation, the difference between good and bad, along with helpfulness and appreciation. They also made it possible for her to exercise her mind and keep it at its fullest potential. She was responsible for a token amount of housework, enough to provide her with a sense of responsibility.

They also shielded Candy from much of life's pain and many of its realities. Except for one school year, she wasn't subjected to the immature cruelties of other children, which are a part of most childhoods. She never toiled at an unpleasant job for pocket money. She was protected, insofar as it was possible, from exposure to crude or rude people, and she almost never left home without at least one of her parents. In Candy's world, everyone was intelligent, accomplished, and mannerly, just as she was herself.

Most of her friends were adults, most of them connected with her mother's show. The younger people Candy saw were daughters or sons of Ruth's friends or co-workers. By the time she was 18, Candy Newman had seen Europe, Russia, the Caribbean, and the Mediterranean, as well as Hawaii and most of the continental United States. Yet it is unlikely that Candy Newman ever took the bus downtown on a Saturday to go shopping with girls her age. She probably never went to a record hop or teen dance with a live band, let alone on a date. Dropping in on Bob Braun's *Bandstand* at WLWT may have been the limit of her teenage activities.

Though she had no musical talent, Candy was an avid listener. According to Ruth, her favorite album was the soundtrack from *The Sound of Music*, which she played over and over. Candy and Ruth together saw the London premier of the film and the Broadway production twice, and met Mary Martin.

Ruth didn't seem to care for the new rock music that was emerging when Candy started college; few of the new singers or groups that appealed to Candy's age group were ever on her show. Paul Anka and Bobby Rydell were notable exceptions. Dick Clark visited the show, too.

Candy may not have had much of a taste for rock, either. As in many other respects, Candy tastes were formed by her parents, perhaps because her interaction with peers was minimal.

There was an obvious gap in her life, that span between the innocence of childhood and the sophistication of adulthood where she could experiment with independence. At 18 she was intelligent, charming, and acted like an adult, though her blond hair—kept in a classic, smooth page-boy cut—left her looking much younger than her age, innocent and "girlish." Now at 5'4" an inch taller than Ruth, Candy was slender and delicate, of light complexion with a soft, round face that was pretty without makeup.

Mickey Fisher saw Candy as "older than her age. She was so sweet, she was too sweet. I perish the thought about how she would ever make it in the world. She was so sweet, and so giving."

Bob Braun, who thought of Candy as a little sister, noted that even at 12 she was very adult for her age. "Yet," he wrote, "in many other ways Candy was still very much a little girl."

The little girl quality may well have been fostered by Ruth. Bonnie Lou remarked that Ruth "kept Candy a child. She wanted Candy to *be* a child." This is true of many parents, but few have the power and resources of Ruth.

On the other hand, children achieve a certain level of wisdom on their own, and always see and hear more than adults give them credit for—even though adults were once children themselves. If she lacked some important life experiences at 18, Candy may have been more worldly than she appeared. An observant teenager with a sharp mind could draw a lot of conclusions. Candy may have been sheltered, but she was certainly no dullard.

IN HER SYNDICATED "Hollywood Today" column on February 6, 1963, Hedda Hopper wrote:

When I was on Ruth Lyons's TV show a few weeks ago, I met her daughter, Candy, who has a giant-sized crush on Troy Donahue.

Candy has been given a two-day walk-on part in his next picture, Palm Springs Weekend. She arrives there with mother the first week in March for filming, then comes to Hollywood. Ruth is a human dynamo.

The person who had actually made the part possible was Frank Casey, a Chicago representative of Warner Brothers. The suggestions were made after Troy Donahue's first visit to the Ruth Lyons show, and Candy was offered a part in the film, with Casey likely doing all the legwork.

And so it was that Ruth and Candy traveled by train to Palm Springs, California, the first week in March. The film was a romantic comedy, written by

Earl Hamner, Jr., and one of the first "Spring Break" films. Candy chose "Candace Laird" as her stage name. Her part involved a festive party scene in a kitchen, where she and some other girls are sitting on the countertop. Candy flashes on the screen for less than two seconds, laughing with the rest and obviously having a good time.

Three months later, the Newmans were in Europe, touring Germany. They visited the Brandenburg Gate and East Germany, where Ruth witnessed life in yet another Communist country, which she found deplorable. They went on from Germany to Austria and Paris, Ruth's favorite city, and returned home in July.

Palm Springs Weekend opened on November 5, 1963, in California. The Cincinnati opening was November 22—not a good first day for anything, as it turned out, though Troy Donahue came to Cincinnati for the premiere.

As an extra in the role of an anonymous "party guest," Candy was not credited, but neither were more than two dozen other walk-ons, including Linda Gray, Dawn Wells (of *Gilligan's Island*), The Modern Folk Quartet, and Mel Blanc (as a Bugs Bunny doll).

looking for miracles

The year 1964 was a good one until June, and then it went downhill fast. By the time the counting was completed in March, the Ruth Lyons Children's Christmas Fund for 1963 topped $390,000, another record year. The money was shared out by the Fund's board of directors, headed by John Murphy. (All of the proceeds went to hospitals—more than eighty of them by now—and WLW paid the salaries of the people who worked on the Fund.)

In April, Ruth learned that she was to be the recipient of McCall's Golden Mike Award, an honor for women in broadcasting. It was to be presented at a dinner hosted by the American Women in Radio and Television in Tulsa, Oklahoma.

The date for the award presentation was May 2, but Ruth was not attending. Her ex-husband, Johnny Lyons, lived in Tulsa, and she did not want to chance meeting him. It wasn't proper. Who knew how he might behave if he met her, or what demands he might make? Therefore, she sent a representative from AVCO to accept the award.

In 1964, the years of cumulative stress finally caught up with Ruth. Even worse, Candy was ill.

The stress of her sister's illness was wearing on Ruth. Rose Lupton had been in and out of Cincinnati's Christ Hospital for months, still fighting cancer, her condition deteriorating. Ruth had to substitute for Rose in her daughter's wedding, but still she hoped for the best. Rose had, after all, survived cancer before.

Despite Ruth's hopes, her sister wasted away. She visited Rose at the hospital daily, and missed the show frequently. Facing the death of her sister, even Ruth

Lyons had difficulty being bright and energetic day after day.

When Rose died on June 24, it was no surprise. She passed away suddenly in the middle of the day. She was 53. Just as she was starting her show, Ruth received a message to come to the hospital. She knew what was waiting. Her sister was, as Ruth wrote, "at peace at long last."

As always, Ruth sought solace in her work, diving into the daily routine of the show. New talent like the Osmond Brothers, John Gary, and the Four Saints graced *The 50-50 Club*. Popular favorites came to the show, too, including Imogene Coca, Frankie Laine, Celeste Holm, Cab Calloway, Carol Channing (who sang "Hello, Ruthie"), and Charlton Heston. Ruth passed the weekends at home, holding to Candy and Herman all the tighter.

Later in the year, the three of them took a month and a half and toured the length and breadth of Scotland and England by car. The sojourn was relaxing. But without the hustle and bustle of work, Ruth had more time to think about Rose, and to grieve. Fate had been so unfair to Rose, first taking her husband, then taking her life before her time.

Ruth went back to work immediately upon her return to Cincinnati (greeted, as always, by a huge crowd of admirers at Union Terminal). She focused on taking the Christmas Fund beyond 1963's total. She kicked off the fundraising on her birthday—Thursday,

"I didn't want to be a Playboy bunny, anyway."—Candy Newman

October 4—as usual. Two days later she wrote to a friend about how exhausted she was, and toyed with the idea of not returning to the show Monday—not for the first time. But she returned, as usual. She had to be there for the children.

The fundraising had just gotten off to a good start when her friend Fred Hutchinson—just 45—died of cancer on November 12. It was another blow so soon after her sister's passing.

Back in the mid-1950s, when a dizzy spell sent Ruth staggering off the stage in the middle of a show, Ruth's doctors had warned her to slow down. She had a checkup and was advised that she was working too much, driving herself too hard, and that she needed to take it easy.

So she took a few days off, Willie Thall hosting *The 50-50 Club* in her absence. Ruth, of course, didn't know how to take it easy and didn't think she needed to, anyway. Except for having the appendectomy in 1932, her health had always been good, no matter how much she drove herself. To her, the dizzy spell was a minor event, a temporary impediment.

She recovered and went on as before. However, she failed to realize that sustained stress exacts a subtle but steady toll, the cumulative total of which can bankrupt emotional and physical health. Or if she did, she denied it.

NOVEMBER SLIPPED INTO DECEMBER as Ruth quietly mourned the loss of her sister and her friend. It was then that the stress she had borne through decades of work, worry, and anxiety finally caught up with her.

Van Cottengim was a news photographer for WLWT that year, working on the nightly news. He was in the film editing room on Wednesday, December 9 when the station's still photographer, Art Voss, came in from the adjacent darkroom with a freshly developed photo. He had taken a series of publicity stills of Ruth that afternoon.

"Look at her face," he said to Cottengim. "Look at the pull."

Cottengim could plainly see that Ruth's face was pulled to one side. "I had photographed her before, and she didn't have a bad side on her face," Cottengim said. "We were looking at it when Gene McPherson, the news director at the time, walked by, and I said, 'Gene, look at this!'

"Voss showed him the print and said, 'I just shot this about 5:30 this afternoon. She doesn't look right.'

"Gene looked at it, then looked at me and said, 'My God—the woman's had a stroke!'

"Gene told us to keep our mouths shut and he went into his office and made a few phone calls. He learned that they had taken her to the hospital that night and nobody even knew it." Whoever McPherson called asked him how he knew that Ruth had a stroke. McPherson told them about the photo.

Bob Braun had noticed on the show that afternoon that Ruth seemed to be having difficulty speaking. At one point, she touched his hand and said, "Bobby, take over. I've got a problem."

"As I recall," Cliff Lash remembered, "Oscar Robinson was on the show. I went back to the office and I could tell something had happened, because she couldn't talk."

After the show, Ruth complained that part of her lip felt numb, but otherwise acted as if things were normal. Later that afternoon she attended a Cincinnati Symphony concert that featured Marian Spelman singing some of Ruth's Christmas songs. Mickey Fisher, Elsa Sule, Herman, and Candy were with her in one of the boxes. It was here Voss had taken the photos.

Fisher noticed that something was wrong, but what had happened still wasn't obvious. "Elsa and I noticed Mother's mouth," Fisher said. "When she talked, it was pulling over to the right. We mentioned it to Herman and said, 'This doesn't look good. What do you think?' But they didn't leave, they stayed through the concert.

"The next day Herman called in and said that Ruth would not be in. They went to the doctor and of course they made up some kind of a story about a virus and stuff, but she'd had a stroke."

No one publicly admitted that Ruth had suffered a stroke. WLWT management did not want the truth to get out. If Ruth's fans learned of it they might assume she would be off the air for good, and stop watching. *Associated Press* newspaper stories passed along a station announcement that Ruth Lyons was suffering from "complete emotional and physical exhaustion" and that she was "just worn out" and would recuperate at home. In her memoirs, Ruth simply said that she was "very ill" that afternoon. "The following day," she said, "I went to a specialist, who told me I was suffering from complete nervous exhaustion and that I should take two months off and rest.

"But I couldn't—at this time of year," she continued, "with the Christmas Fund to raise! So after several days at home I went back to work."

It was a short-lived rebellion against the reality of her situation. Ruth was back in the hospital on December 17. She didn't want to alarm her viewers, so still nothing was said about a stroke. She claimed she was in the hospital "for some tests. All of them pointed to the same diagnosis—nervous exhaustion." (Five years later Ruth continued to cling to the fiction that she hadn't had a stroke—just "nervous exhaustion.")

Ruth described one of the tests administered at the hospital as involving an injection of albumin, which she fought against. She later said that she had an immediate reaction to the substance, which shut down the blood supply to her brain. One wonders whether this was Ruth still bravely denying the stroke, or if perhaps she experienced a second stroke at that point.

On December 21, the Christmas Fund reached $401,386.85. Ruth was still hospitalized and prepared a statement of thanks for Candy to read on the air. On December 24, John T. Murphy issued another statement, stating that in addition to having worn herself out, Ruth had "vascular problems." Others said she had a "vascular occlusion." Such claims danced around the truth.

When they released her from Holmes Hospital, Ruth's doctors were adamant about her resting at home. So was Herman, and that settled it. She went home on Christmas Day and told everyone she was returning to *The 50-50 Club* on January 1, 1965. A few days later she reset her sights on returning to the show in February.

In the meantime, WLWT hired Vivienne Della Chiesa to host the show until Ruth returned. Della Chiesa was an opera and pop singer of Italian descent who had hosted radio shows in the 1930s and 1940s. A tall, pretty blonde with a husky voice, she was a frequent guest on *Texaco Star Theater* and other popular television shows. Della Chiesa was a doing a regular show in Las Vegas when she was contacted about filling in for Ruth, and likely welcomed the opportunity to do something different.

There was much speculation that Ruth was going to retire. It wasn't true, but without her the staff of *The 50-50 Club* was stretched far too thin. Bob Braun was working hard on *The Good Morning Show* and he and Peter Grant were each covering *The 50-50 Club* two days a week while Candy and Braun hosted on Friday. What was needed was a stable, mature presence to host the show throughout the week, and give Braun some relief. Thus, Vivienne Della Chiesa.

As it was to develop, Ruth would not return to *The 50-50 Club* for some time.

SEVERAL WEEKS BEFORE RUTH planned to return to *The 50-50 Club*, Candy Newman discovered a lump in one breast. She saw Dr. Charles M. Barrett, a radiologist and cancer researcher, and was admitted to Holmes Hospital almost immediately. Ruth had expected a lumpectomy, at worst. Herman had a bleaker outlook, but said nothing to Ruth about his fears.

On January 15, 1965, exploratory surgery revealed malignant tumors. At the age of 20, Candy underwent a mastectomy. Herman was at the hospital for the surgery, but Ruth wasn't; it would have been too much for her. He telephoned her as soon as the surgery was over.

Gloria Rush received a call that evening from a friend at the hospital, a nurse, who told her what had been done.

"I simply had to call Ruth, knowing that the maids had gone home and she would be alone. We cried together and prayed together. I asked her if she wanted me to come and stay the night with her. She said she was all right, and the next day she went to Candy and stayed with her at Holmes until Candy could come home."

Cobalt treatments followed the surgery. Herman took a leave of absence from the University of Cincinnati, and he was at the hospital every waking moment, along with Ruth.

As might be expected, Ruth was devastated. But Candy's light-hearted nature came shining through as she tried to cheer her mother. Gloria Rush remembers, "Candy, always so cute and so funny, said 'Oh, Mother, don't worry. I didn't want to be a Playboy bunny, anyway!'"

Ruth and Herman were devastated. How could this happen, when Ruth was still recovering from her own illness? And why Candy, who was so young and innocent and filled with potential? Ruth spoke of retiring, but Candy wouldn't hear of her giving up *The 50-50 Club*. She urged her mother to get better so she could go back to the show. Herman backed her up, and Ruth gave in and agreed to return.

A few days after Candy went into the hospital, WLWT had issued a press release stating that Ruth Lyons would not be returning in February as planned: "Miss Lyons will remain at home because of the illness of her daughter, Candy Newman. Miss Newman was stricken with a virus infection and pneumonia a month ago, shortly before she was to have left with her parents on a month-long Mediterranean vacation. She still is in a hospital here."

As with earlier news about Ruth's health, this announcement avoided reality. People already worried that Ruth might retire, and this was reinforced every day she was at home. WLWT management feared that if the public learned how serious Candy's condition really was, *The 50-50 Club* might lose both sponsors and viewers. As long as the audience and sponsors believed that the problems were minor, they were willing to wait for Ruth's return.

the darkest time

Ruth stayed at the hospital with Candy until her treatments were finished. They were back home by March, 1965, and took a short trip to California. To help counter rumors and reassure fans, Ruth began telephoning Bob Braun on the show. Doing this also helped Ruth feel that she was still a part of things.

The conversations were trying at first, because the FCC required a seven-second delay on a telephone tie-in to a broadcast. WLWT engineers set up a remote system so that Ruth could just talk into a microphone, with no delay involved. Gloria Rush took one of the artificial microphone flowers to Ruth at home, so she would feel closer to the show.

Ruth joined *The 50-50 Club* via her home microphone often, a disembodied voice that issued from the studio speakers without warning. As Braun described it, "She would cut in with her customary, 'Bobby.'" (Braun disliked being called "Bobby," and Ruth was the only one who did it.) It sometimes threw off the show's rhythm.

When Candy was very ill, she still wanted one more trip— to the warm Mediterranean.

Every day that Ruth wasn't in the studio, *50-50 Club* sponsors grew more agitated. They were paying $660 per minute for Ruth Lyons, but got Bob Braun. Braun was uncomfortable with this, just as he was uncomfortable with the fact that he advertised for competing sponsors on *The Good Morning Show* and *The 50-50 Club*.

On April 9, Braun was just through the first half-hour of *The 50-50 Club* and wondering when Ruth was going to break in. Normally, she would have called by now. Braun began to worry that something was wrong when Ruth walked through a door into the set with Candy and John Murphy (by then president of AVCO Broadcasting).

The audience was of course delighted. They stood and applauded for several minutes. Braun set his microphone on a table and rushed to greet Ruth, forgetting that he needed it to speak on the air. Ruth and Candy stayed for the rest of that day's show, and Ruth promised that she would return permanently to *The 50-50 Club* in May.

Ruth's return lightened Braun's workload. Still hosting *The Good Morning Show* and maintaining the rest of his schedule (including *Bandstand*), he cut back to appearing on *The 50-50 Club* three days a week. Peter Grant was on twice weekly. Ruth was on the show Monday through Thursday. Candy was on the air with Ruth one day of the week, and she hosted the show with Bob Braun on Fridays. The

"Candy's death was a tragedy that I will never quite accept." —Ruth Lyons Newman.

three other days she was in the studio, Candy greeted guests, served coffee, and helped with the Christmas Fund. Like everyone else, Candy did commercials. "I've used most of the products at home," she said, "so it's easy for me to talk about them from the standpoint of a consumer."

In September, Candy was added to the show as a paid cast member. It was almost as if Candy was "learning the business," being prepared to take over *The 50-50 Club* at some future date. The audience liked Candy. She was cheerful and outgoing, though she had nowhere near the exuberance of Ruth. That was fine; her personality was her own.

"Candy was really almost back to herself," Mickey Fisher said. "But she started losing her hair and they got her wigs."

Everyone did their best to make Candy comfortable. As might be expected, she was showing the effects of her illness, but Elsa Sule described how they were able to compensate for that. "We had a makeup man named Dana Bruce who was a good friend of ours. And he got Candy all fixed up so she didn't look sick. He supplied us with wigs and wiglets, which were in style at that time, too."

Bruce was originally brought in for Lena Horne when she appeared on *The 50-50 Club* in October, 1965. He extended his skills to all the women in the cast. One day he returned to the show and did a special transformation of Candy that included a blond wig, false eyelashes, and heavy eyeliner. Ruth was somewhat stunned by the effect. "Hundreds of letters, many of them from college students (male) poured in," she remembered. "Of course, it was an exaggerated makeup, but Candy did look lovely, and quite different." The proud mother couldn't help but add to her recollection of the day that "many commented upon the striking resemblance to the late Marilyn Monroe."

Candy always fostered hope of recovering. She began a quilt, and found a new project that kept her looking to the future—typing up recipes for a cookbook, which she hoped to see published.

Come October, it was time for the Christmas Fund, which eventually reached $474,000. On December 19, *The 50-50 Club* cast did their annual "Holiday Hello" show, a tradition established in 1963. It was a two-hour Sunday afternoon special that tied in with the Christmas Fund.

The next day, Ruth and family left on a cruise to London, England. They passed a pleasant six weeks in and around the city. Candy was not always feeling her best, so they paced their activities to match her condition on a given day.

SOON AFTER THE NEWMANS return to Cincinnati, Candy was back in Holmes Hospital, and in great pain. Ruth was off the show again to be with her. As Ruth wrote later, she was "doing everything possible to help the dear, sweet child and keep her unaware of how ill she really was."

In truth, it was Ruth who was unaware of how bad the situation was. Herman had talked with a specialist (probably Dr. Barrett) who told him that Candy's situation was hopeless. Herman knew the news that their daughter's condition was terminal would crush Ruth, and for a time he put off telling her.

The doctor suggested a change of climate to make her more comfortable, so Ruth and Candy went to southern California for two weeks. The pleasant climate had Candy feeling better after a few days, and made her long for the similar climate of the Mediterranean. After her return from California—and with the help of a friend at the Provident Bank Travel Department—Candy planned out a trip to Italy and beyond.

On June 3, 1966, Ruth, Candy, and Herman sailed for Genoa, Italy, on the

S.S. Michelangelo. Candy was in terrible pain, but insisted on traveling. More than anyone else, Candy knew how bad her condition was, and that she might have but just this one last chance to travel, one of the great joys of her life. Elsa Sule saw this clearly. "The one thing Candy wanted to do," she said, "was go to Europe one more time."

Candy's doctors warned Herman and Ruth that their daughter might not survive the journey—not because of the traveling, but because her time was running out. They embarked with a foreboding that Elsa Sule sensed. "They started out for Europe and I think Ruth and Herman knew in their hearts that Candy would never come back," she said.

Candy Newman spent most of the week-long cruise resting and trying to deal with increasing pain. She could not swim or use any of the other recreational facilities, but she rallied enough to attend the Captain's Reception and, remarkably, enjoyed it.

Candy's condition went downhill all week. When the ship docked in Genoa on June 11, she was taken immediately to the Internationale Hospital in the city. Herman and Ruth remained with her at the hospital day and night, exhausted by strain and worry. The hospital staff could do little for Candy, beyond making her comfortable.

There was no possibility of continuing the trip Candy had planned—on to Cannes and then Paris. When the *S.S. Michelangelo* left Genoa on its scheduled cruise to New York on July 15, the Newman family was aboard. Candy was placed in the ship's infirmary. The *Michelangelo's* doctors—Dr. Luigi Guerrini and Dr. Carlo Manfredi, who would become distinguished researchers and medical professors—did what they could to sustain her and reduce her suffering.

Candy slipped rapidly over the next four days. Ruth and Herman stayed at her bedside, hoping in the midst of sorrow. The inevitable end came near sunset on Sunday, June 19—Father's Day for Americans. She was 21.

Ruth later called the hours after Candy's death "the saddest of all nights that I shall ever know." She sat far into the ocean night and tried to translate the anguish of her emotions into words:

My darling is gone, my love—my heart. Always so understanding—so peacefully companionable—so quick to laugh—so beautifully dignified. So willing to serve in any way—so anxious never to offend. So instinctively honest . . . So gentle—so trusting—so

*loyal to those she loved. So obedient without being servile . . . So beautiful, with her
lovely brown eyes and hair, her peaches and cream complexion, her graceful slim waist .
. . She moved in beauty and dignity, and ever—our "little princess"—so quietly joyous.*

*And in her father's words—An "unfinished quilt" of uncommon magnificence—our
dearly beloved Candy.*

RUTH AND HERMAN WERE SHATTERED. The pain was literally too much
to bear. It was incomprehensible that such a loss—one that should never happen
to any parent—was preceded by so much suffering. It was beyond the ability of
the human mind to process.

Along with shock and sadness came anger. Ruth subdued the anger she must
have felt, or she channeled it into other emotions. Herman was immeasurably
angry, and he directed his anger at what others would have sought at such a time.
Mostly agnostic for years, he stepped firmly into atheism.

Ruth never recovered from the heartbreak of losing Candy. Nearly everything
around her made her think of Candy—and thinking of Candy only reopened the
wound. "Candy's death," she wrote years later, "is a tragedy that I will never quite
accept. There are endless little reminders of her: her countless favorite ways of
doing things, the songs she loved, the memory of her sweet smile, her charming
giggle, her companionship—and most of all, her great consideration of others."

Nor did Herman Newman ever get over Candy's death. He did not share his
emotions in public, but they were always with him.

Ruth sent a terse cable to John T. Murphy in New York City that night.
Murphy released the news immediately. In hundreds of newspapers on Monday,
June 20, 1966, the *AP* and *UPI* reported Candy's death. The story that she had
been afflicted with a virus persisted to the very end, as the final lines from a *UPI*
story headlined "Candy Newman Dies At Sea" indicated:

*Her parents, Miss Lyons and Herman Newman, assistant professor at the
University of Cincinnati, had taken her to Europe in hope the voyage might strengthen
her after a recent illness.*

*Miss Newman was treated in Holmes Hospital here earlier this year for what was
termed a virus infection.*

The *S.S. Michelangelo* arrived at New York's West 50th Street dock on the morning of June 23. Arrangements had already been made. Candace Laird Newman was cremated in New York, and a private service was held.

Ruth attended the latter, but not the former. Herman did not want her to go with him and the undertaker; he thought it would be too hard on her. Later she told friends that she very much regretted not having gone.

Herman and Ruth returned home with Candy's ashes in an urn, which was placed on the mantle of the living room. There was, of course, no coffin when the couple arrived at Cincinnati's Union Terminal, which led to the rumor that Candy had committed suicide by jumping off the ship in the middle of the Atlantic. The rumor persists today, more than forty years after her death.

There were Ruth's losses, her own illnesses, and finally Candy's suffering and death, things experienced by most people but seldom so many of them at one time. Even more rarely is death accompanied by such pitiless irony: twenty-one years before, Herman and Ruth lost a child. Still grieving, they were given another, only to lose her, too. It was perhaps a more painful loss because Candy had fulfilled them for more than two decades, then she was cruelly taken away just as she was ready to find her own fulfillment.

THAT MONDAY *The 50-50 Club* went on the air at its usual time. Bob Braun hosted the show, but he knew he would have trouble talking about Ruth. So he taped the announcement of Candy's death to run before the show and taped another announcement to run at the show's end.

Thousands of letters, telephone calls, and telegrams came into Crosley Square, in sympathy for Ruth and Herman. Everyone at WLWT shared page Eric Schneider's reaction, "We were all so shocked, she was such a great person."

And they wondered about Ruth. Would she return? Would she be the same? One thing they did know was that it would be some time before she could think beyond her grief.

Ruth communicated with a very few friends. What she had to say to one friend a few weeks after Candy's death illustrated her outlook at the time. "We're trying to do what Candy would have wanted us to do," she said, "to go on with our wonderful memories to entertain us." Rather than engage with the world, she wanted to relax in more pleasant times past with her memories of Candy. It's more likely that Candy, who cared so much for her parents, would have wanted them to continue with their lives.

Being the most visible and talented of Ruth's assistants, Bob Braun was scheduled to host the show until Ruth's return, whenever that might be. Peter Grant went back to doing news. Vivienne Della Chiesa was available to take Bob's place when he went on vacation.

As the main host on *The 50-50 Club* for the indeterminate future, it was a stretch to expect Bob Braun to continue other duties. WLW began searching for a replacement for Braun on *The Good Morning Show*. Several hosts auditioned before Braun remembered a young man named Nick Clooney, who hosted a show in Lexington, Kentucky, similar to *Bandstand*. WLW radio's general manager and program director traveled to Lexington to have a look at him in action, liked what they saw, and made him an offer.

Clooney accepted it a few weeks later and was soon in Cincinnati, where his sisters Betty and Rosemary Clooney began their careers in the 1940s. He started assisting Braun on *The 50-50 Club* in April or May. He also worked as Braun's assistant on *Bandstand*, but he took over the show by summer. (Clooney would go on to have his own show on WCPO-TV and work as news anchor on WKRC-TV, among other positions. He was also a host and writer for the American Movie Classics (AMC) cable channel. Out of all the radio and television work he has done, television news was his favorite. "News is my passion," he once said.)

DURING A PRESENTATION to advertisers and agencies in mid-August, WLWT general manager Walter Bartlett and John Murphy made the announcement that Ruth would be returning to *The 50-50 Club* on October 10. Bob Braun announced this the following week on the show, and the audience was elated by the news. Some wept.

At home, Ruth began to sway in her decision to return to the show. Herman was having a difficult time persuading her to go back to what she'd agreed on. He went so far as to write to Ruth's good friend Lee Wilson on September 3, saying, "Please call Ruth and encourage her to return. She needs bolstering so very, very much."

One or both of them persuaded Ruth to go back to work. Another reason she ultimately changed her mind was the Christmas Fund. She decided that she wanted to see it through one more time and, as Nick Clooney explained, "She wanted to make sure the Children's Christmas Fund would remain. She decided to come back even though she was impaired and was not thrilled with her performance. Ruth herself, however, even in her impaired condition, was quite remarkable, very bright."

But Ruth wasn't on the show on Monday, October 10. NBC was running a special program that cut into part of *The 50-50 Club*. Happily, Tuesday saw Ruth back on the air, much to the relief of her fans, Herman, and WLWT management.

She was, according to Bob Braun, every bit her old self—lots of energy and kidding around, and she quickly took over the show. It looked as if she was there to stay. The 1966 Christmas Fund, in memory of Candy, reached $474,000. And the show's base advertising rate was up to $700 per minute.

Over the ensuing weeks, however, Braun noticed that the show was becoming a strain for Ruth. Eric Schneider noted that Ruth was beginning to have her problems with the show. "We always knew right away when Ruth arrived in her office if she was in a good or bad mood," he recalled. "If we didn't, she let us know."

After a time, she was having a difficult time talking. "She was so articulate before," said Nick Clooney, "and this was absolute purgatory for her to have to reach for the word." When she got stuck for a word, everyone on the set pushed for her, sometimes whispering the word she was groping for, or talking over her.

Quite a few viewers and some of the staff were upset with this, thinking that Braun or whoever was trying to help was being rude. "We would try to cover it, by overtalking her or changing the subject," Nick Clooney explained. "Several of us became quite good at this," he added. "The mind was still there, but the body was not willing."

Ruth began missing days here and there, and took a vacation at the beginning of January.

BOB BRAUN WAS SURPRISED one day when Ruth told him she was going to bring Peter Grant back on the show one day a week, and Nick Clooney was coming in as Ruth's assistant on another day.

"When she did," Clooney related, "I became one of a rotating group who were her assistants—Peter Grant and Bob Braun of course principal among them. I think I worked with her once a week for a while, and then twice a week."

This left Bob Braun with lots of time on his hands, and it worried him. He had lost *The Good Morning Show*, and now it looked as if he was being demoted to a shared second place on *The 50-50 Club*.

Braun made up his mind that he wasn't going to go on with such an arrangement. It came down to getting his own show or leaving Cincinnati. Braun and his wife did not want to leave the area, though, so he decided to plead his case to Murphy.

Before he could get to John Murphy, the executive called him in for a meeting. Murphy offered Braun his own show from 4:00 to 5:30 in the afternoon. This was more like it. Since starting with WLWT, his goal had been his own television show. The show, appropriately enough, would be called *The Bob Braun Show*.

Three other shows had been tried in that time slot and failed, but Braun was confident that he could make it work. With the help of several musicians he put together a band for the show and added singer Rosemary Kelly (another WLWT staffer) as his assistant. He needed one more girl singer to round out the program—Bonnie Lou, who sang on *The Paul Dixon Show* and sometimes on *The 50-50 Club*, signed on. Colleen Sharp, a recent addition to *The Paul Dixon Show*, was available to sing on both shows.

"It was all his," Nick Clooney said about Braun's program. "He wasn't in Ruth's shadow. And there was a lot of excitement to the show. He had his own band, a younger band. And he had his own audience . . . a younger audience."

Braun continued working with *The 50-50 Club* three days a week as he prepared for the January premiere of *The Bob Braun Show*. The show made its debut on Monday, January 23. It went without a hitch, and a number of special guests were on hand. Tuesday's show was just as good.

The afternoon of January 25, 1967, Braun was rehearsing a song for his show when Mickey Fisher appeared and told him that Ruth wanted to see him in her office. When Braun entered her office, Ruth dropped a bombshell. She was retiring.

Her words left him speechless at first. When he was able to speak, he asked, "When, Ruth?"

"Today was my last day," she replied. She added that she had told management and the girls in the office. Presumably she had told general manager Walter Bartlett, who got on the phone fast to Mexico City, where John Murphy was attending a convention.

Further, Ruth wanted him to take over *The 50-50 Club*.

Nick Clooney was Ruth's assistant on that final show. (No one knew it was to be her final show, of course.) He noticed nothing unusual. "She left [the stage]," Clooney recalled, "and we all went back to her office, which is what usually happened. We all sat around and talked for a while, and rehashed the show. And then she went back to the ante-room with some of her closest friends, then came back out and then left in mid-afternoon. When I got back to my home, I got a telephone call and was told that Ruth had decided to retire. At that time she was only working Monday, Wednesday, and Friday.

"Either that Wednesday night or that Thursday night, Bob called me and asked me to come to his house.

"He told me that the hierarchy at WLW had said to him that he had his choice: he could either stay with his own program and they would make every attempt to move it into the other markets. Or, he could take over the already hugely successful *50-50 Club* and be the host.

"We talked very late into the night. It was one or two in the morning and we were sitting there talking over what he should do. When I left, my advice to him was to take his chances on his own show. I felt that if he took over *The 50-50 Club* from Ruth it would never really be his own program. It would always be *The Ruth Lyons 50-50 Club with Bob Braun*. That was my take on it, whether I was right or not.

"But he felt that, too. When I left he said 'Okay, I'm telling them I'm going to take my own show. I'm gonna take my chances with it.'

"For one reason or another, when he went in the next day, either he changed his mind or they changed his mind for him. I thought it was interesting during that very brief interim period his instinct—and I think it was a correct instinct— was to do his own show. It's very interesting to think of what that might have been like, had he indeed gone on to do his own show."

History shows that Braun went against his instinct. Perhaps it was a long-distance phone call from Mexico City that persuaded him, or a talk with Walter Bartlett. But in the end it was Braun's decision, and some part of him felt that taking over the show was the right thing to do.

a queen's farewell

From Wednesday afternoon on, events moved rapidly for those who knew that Ruth was retiring. There were no press releases, and no one said anything on the air about it. Unknown to the public, Ruth had telephoned Mickey Fisher and dictated her farewell on Thursday evening.

Braun described *The 50-50* Club on Friday, January 27, as nothing unusual. "We opened as usual and I came on, but I said at the beginning of the program that we had a special announcement which would be made before the end of the show." At 1:15, Bob Braun introduced Walter Bartlett, who read the letter Ruth had dictated the night before:

Said Ruth: "If I knew I was living through an era, I would have paid more attention...."

After being with you daily for eighteen years, I will never forget many of you who have done so much for me.

1. First of all, the AVCO Broadcasting Corporation and all its employees, with a special thank you to Mr. John T. Murphy, and Mr. Walter Bartlett, for their understanding and consideration, and especially their generous support of the Ruth Lyons Christmas Fund.

2. To the many wonderful sponsors who have shown their faith in me year after year. But most especially you, the great audience out there, who watched for so long and supported my every endeavor and have written thousands of letters of inspiration and sympathetic understanding to sustain me many times when I needed them so much. And you who have also contributed through the years to the Ruth Lyons Christmas Fund, my most cherished endeavor.

3. I want to express my love and appreciation to my four girls, Elsa, Mickey, Gloria, and Andrea, without whose loyalty and help I would have been unable to continue for as long as I have.

4. To Clifford and those fine boys in the band for all they have contributed to my enjoyment as well as yours.

5. To Bill Gustin, my kind and untiring producer.

6. To the dedicated and talented vocalists, Ruby Wright, Bonnie Lou, Marian Spelman, and Colleen Sharp, who have sung so beautifully for all of you, to my great delight, and to the other boys and girls, in their various capacities who have helped make this show one of which I can ever be proud.

7. To all the fine engineers who have treated me so kindly through the years as good friends.

8. To Mr. Bill McCluskey, "Bonnie Man" whom I have so long admired and relied on.

9. To Peter Grant for his great help, his delightful sense of humor, and his true friendship.

10. To Nick Clooney for his youthful enthusiasm and his delightful charm.

11. And to Bob Braun for his unfailing willingness to stand beside me for these past ten years offering encouragement and help, when I know that at many times it must have been difficult for him to do. May I ask that you, the great viewing and listening audience, continue to help and encourage him in every way as you have done for me.

And now I say goodbye, with my love and appreciation for each and every one of you—and I hope that you will never forget as it says in the Second Book of Timothy— "I have fought a good fight—I have run my course—I have kept the faith!"

Sincerely,

Ruth Lyons

THAT WAS IT— after nearly four decades in broadcasting, Ruth Lyons had officially retired. There wasn't a dry eye in the studio. The same was true in many homes. Afterwards, Bartlett read a letter of appreciation from John Murphy for Ruth and for Bob Braun.

Some accounts imply that Ruth Lyons lived in retirement as a recluse, perhaps bitter and angry. In reality, she enjoyed life as much as she could, though the ghost of Candy was never far away. After she retired, she and Herman went on a vacation trip to Paris. Ruth expressed some anxiety by telephoning friends from New York both when the ship left and returned. She was unenthusiastic about the cruise because "it just wasn't the same without Candy."

The couple went out to dinner occasionally, although it was sometimes complicated by people who recognized Ruth and wanted to talk. Ruth's one scheduled weekly contact with the outside world was a woman she called "Little Mary," who came in to do her hair and nails. And there were doctor appointments. Herman visited the horse track a little more often.

Ruth entertained friends at home, too. Gloria Rush was one of the people who visited Ruth often. "She read a lot and always had the television on— keeping up with the news of the world—and always had her own opinion of what was going on," Gloria Rush related. She even watched a soap opera or two, and she did try to watch *The 50-50 Club*, especially during the Christmas Fund drive, hoping each day would bring a great total. And she listened to the Cincinnati Reds." Herman and Ruth also came to visit Rush at her home east of Cincinnati, where she ran an antique shop.

Mickey Fisher, Mary Wood, Sue Bressler, Marian Spelman, and Ruby Wright were frequent visitors. Mickey, Elsa, and Gloria often went to Ruth's home for an afternoon of bridge. Herman went to the race track, "to visit his money," Ruth would chuckle. Ruth occasionally played the piano when Gloria or someone else asked her to, which may have helped her condition.

Memories of Candy were in every room at Four Chimneys, looking out from photos on the wall, attached to favorite possessions and shared furnishings. It eventually became too much. Ruth and Herman sold their house (for just $75,000) and bought a smaller one. During the moving period, Gloria Rush bought a number of the antiques that filled the Newmans' home. After two years they moved on to another house in the Watch Hill area of Cincinnati, a far eastern suburb. Finally, after a number of years, they moved into the luxury Edgecliff high-rise apartment building.

The Edgecliff—the only building of its kind for miles—towered over Columbia Parkway, and Ruth could see Eastern Avenue and the Ohio River from their apartment. When her maids retired, Ruth hired just one, a woman named Joyce, who like her predecessors was a companion as well as a helper.

50-50 Club guests who had become Ruth's friends telephoned and always remembered her birthday. Some visited her whenever they were in Cincinnati, among them Carol Channing, Joe Garagiola, Bob Hope, Celeste Holm, and Peter Nero.

"I was lucky enough to be one of the few to be allowed to visit her and Herman in her apartment," Peter Nero said. "But it was so sad to see her incapacitated. Yet she understood everything being discussed and was still able to spew pearls of wisdom which shall forever remain with me. She was a vital force in my life, and while she considered me like the son she never had, I considered her as a mother that nurtured me and my career."

Once—perhaps because of the emotions he held inside—Herman asked some of her former co-workers to stop reminiscing with Ruth, but they never did. Telling and retelling the old stories and laughing seemed to mean so much to Ruth. But sometimes she might start thinking of Candy a bit too much and say something like, "Candy would be 36."

In the early days of her retirement, Ruth was out of touch with the public. "For quite some time she remained completely out of the picture," Nick Clooney related. "Which I think is a wise thing; you can diminish your legacy if you hang on."

Later she started calling Bob Braun and at first he put her on the air, but talking with her was difficult because of her impediment, and Braun accepted the calls less and less often.

NICK CLOONEY CONTINUED to work for WLWT after Ruth's retirement. He eventually left and later returned to do a new program on WCPO, opposite *The 50-50 Club*. "It was only briefly successful," Clooney explained. "But it was a distraction for *The 50-50 Club* for a while."

Ruth telephoned Clooney's show several times, perhaps because she couldn't get on the air with *The 50-50 Club*. She asked Nick if she could go on the air to talk about a specific charity, Clooney said, and he put her on three or four times.

"Bob was irritated about that and I talked to him. We had remained friends. But of course it's a competitive business, and Bob thought that Ruth was diminishing his credibility by showing up on the other program. I explained to him that I had already said 'No' when she intimated to me on the phone that she wouldn't mind saying that she preferred my style to his.

"I said to Ruth, 'Well, that's not fair. Let's not talk about that.' But then I did put her on when she wanted to talk about the specific charity she had an interest in."

In talking about Ruth after retirement, Clooney said, "Ruth had become disenchanted, as often happens in retirement, with anybody who took over from her. Whoever that would have been, she would have been irritated with what was going on, and probably always felt that she would have done it better."

Clooney also compliments Ruth for knowing something that so many network shows missed. "The studio audience was just as important as the performers at the proscenium of the stage. The home viewers were not just watching the TV show of Ruth, Peter Grant, Bob Braun, Ruby Wright, Bonnie Lou, Nick Clooney—they weren't watching that. They were watching the interaction of those performers with an audience. And therefore anything that became a barricade or an obstacle for that interaction was harming what the people at home were being able to eavesdrop on.

"Everyone who thought they knew television—all the network moguls— what they missed was the fact that this was the biggest local television show in the nation."

Paul Dixon followed Ruth's lead in making the studio audience part of the show, and Dave Letterman carried on the tradition, devoting a part of every show to interacting with his audience. As a child, he watched Ruth closely, and later he worked as a floor boy for WLW-I when *The Paul Dixon Show* came to Indianapolis to do a remote. Dave tossing canned hams to the audience and stepping into the audience to talk with them are direct knockoffs of Paul Dixon—who threw Oscherwitz salamis—and Ruth Lyons, gratefully acknowledged by Letterman.

And the local hosts who followed Ruth—from Bob Braun to Phil Donahue (who began at WLW-D) to Jerry Springer (whose talk show started at WLWT), followed in her footsteps, using the same techniques. Donahue and Springer eventually became strong national forces, and later television talk show hosts like Oprah Winfrey took their lead from them—and the entire trail leads directly to Ruth Lyons, the originator of the interactive television talk show.

Today, Oprah's style mimics that of Ruth Lyons; they share a consummate skill in communications, timing, wit, and empathy. Both developed themselves from humble beginnings, kept a "common touch," and once they caught on in television there was no stopping them.

Oprah is known for her emotional, ad-lib delivery, as was Ruth Lyons. Oprah's guests, like Ruth's guests a generation before, according to *Time* magazine, "find themselves revealing things they would not imagine telling anyone . . . ." Others confessed to similar feelings.

Like Ruth, Oprah began with a part-time job in radio. Both lost a child, and each had a grandmother who made a strong imprint on her character. The similarities go on from there. Winfrey and Lyons earned high salaries, both became television executives and philanthropists, and they worked directly with advertisers. While Ruth Lyons married, she intentionally spent a decade building the foundation of her career without a man in her life.

Celebrities clamored to be on both shows, but neither Ruth nor Oprah booked a star on the basis of his or her popularity; they had to be someone who interested them and who they believed would really interest the audience. If you were pushing a book or a record album, appearing on *The 50-50 Club* sent your sales skyrocketing the very same day; the same thing happens with *Oprah* today. (And probably some *Oprah* viewers who don't have CD players have bought CDs, just as it happened with Ruth's viewers who didn't have record players.)

At the same time, a negative word or pulling advertising could spell disaster for a product or business. Albers Super Markets tumbled into oblivion when they stopped advertising on *The 50-50 Club,* and in the 1960s sales dropped to nothing when Ruth didn't like a particular gelatin flavor, just as the sales of beef plummeted when Oprah said of mad-cow disease, "It has just stopped me cold from eating another burger."

Each in her own time was named on nationwide lists of admired people. Self-driven hard workers, these women worked themselves to exhaustion. Both had famous friends. And both embraced socially unpopular minorities—Ruth when she danced with African-American singer Arthur Simpkins during her show—speaking out as they spoke out against injustice in general. Their respective shows went to multiple media outlets. Each earned Emmys and other awards. Ruth wrote a bestseller; Oprah made several. Successful programs were spun off both women's shows.

There are so many fascinating stories about her. There was the little boy who, when asked on the air what he liked about Ruth's show, said "It doesn't have 'merrcials!" And another boy who hadn't been able to walk as the result of an accident, walked for the first time in nearly two years. As she often did, Ruth had the band strike up her "Christmas Marching Song," and with children from the studio audience parading around the set, she said to the viewers at home, "Get up! Get up and march around your couch!" The boy got up from his wheelchair and marched around the couch in his family's living room. Marian Spelman and others were near tears a quarter-century later when they described how his grateful mother called after the show. Spooky, but glorious!

Ruth rarely failed at anything. Perhaps her only failures on the show were being unable to marry off Cliff Lash or Peter Grant, and trying to make singers out of people who just couldn't sing. She tried this first with Grant, and later with Nick Clooney, "because my sisters were singers." No dice—but each gave it a try for Ruth, and more than once. If you can find a copy of Ruth's albums, *It's Christmas Time Again* and *Our Best to You*, you can hear Peter Grant singing (or trying to sing) "All Because It's Christmas" (with Bonnie Lou) and "Que Sera, Sera" (with a grand backup chorus).

Whenever there was a remote broadcast of *The 50-50 Club*, from Indianapolis, Columbus, Cincinnati, or Dayton, the show received at least ten times more ticket requests than there was room in the theater or auditorium. People lined up for blocks to get into the show.

RUTH LYONS NEWMAN died at home on the afternoon of Monday, November 7, 1988. Herman and her housekeeper, Joyce, were with her. She was 83. Newspapers and television reports stated her age as 81, which would have pleased Ruth.

She was cremated, and Herman placed her and Candy in a niche at Hillside Chapel in Cincinnati, as they had planned. In the niche is a stained-glass window modeled after a Hummel figurine of a little girl sweeping. The original figure occupied a place of honor on a table beneath a photo of Candy in the Newman home.

Within months of Ruth's death, Herman entered an extended care facility, The Arbors, having taken care of Ruth throughout their marriage. He remained at The Arbors until his death in 1991. His remains joined those of Ruth and Candy.

Part of the estate went to charities, with the remainder to Ruth's niece—with one exception. In his will, Herman directed that the rights to Ruth's music be assigned to Jewish Hospital, where Candy was born.

Ruth left an important legacy in the Ruth Lyons Children's Christmas Fund.

It continues to raise money to benefit hospitalized children directly, as well as answer some of the more prosaic needs of twenty hospitals throughout Ohio, Indiana, and Kentucky. It's been seventy years since that first $1002 was raised; today the Fund collects and disperses hundreds of thousands of dollars annually. WLWT and WLW radio, though no longer operated by the same company, partner in fund-raising. Numerous corporate as well as individual donations bring in six figures every year.

Ruth also left behind hundreds of thousands of fans who talk about her today as if they'd seen her show just last week. Most of them—unselfconsciously—call her "Mother."

And many are the broadcast professionals and celebrities who recall Ruth Lyons fondly. Erma Bombeck was a Ruth Lyons fan when she lived in Dayton, and got inspiration from listening to *The 50-50 Club*. Phil Donahue, once Bombeck's neighbor, told an interviewer, "If there had not been a Crosley Broadcasting with a commitment to local programming, and if there had not been a Ruth Lyons, I probably wouldn't be here."

Carol Channing said of Ruth, "She was an extraordinary woman, and had the same skills in communications that Oprah does today. Radio in the Midwest was synonymous with her name."

After having observed Ruth Lyons's entire career and having worked with her, Nick Clooney stated simply: "From the 1950s through the late 1960s, she was the primal force in Cincinnati broadcasting." He first met Ruth in 1942, when his sisters, Betty and Rosemary, were on her show. "She had a gift," he said. "She talked in paragraphs. Most of us talk in jagged little sentences, but Ruth spoke in neat paragraphs."

Darryl Parks, general manager of WLW, says of Ruth: "In television today, there are many performers that owe their careers to Ruth Lyons. From Rachel Ray, Ellen DeGeneres, and Oprah, I hope they know who Ruth Lyons is and what she has meant to their careers. Ms. Lyons was the original. All others imitate."

Janeen Coyle, top air personality on Cincinnati's WGRR-FM, always felt that Ruth Lyons never really got the credit she deserved as a broadcaster. "Had she been Ruth Lyons in New York City," Coyle says, "she would have gotten a lot more attention.

"But she really was a trailblazer. It's fascinating to see—having started in radio myself in the early '80s—just to see all the jobs she held in the '30s that women just didn't hold until the year 2000: jobs like program director and music director. Even today you don't really see that. And Ruth was doing it back around the Depression and during the war.

"What I think is, if I could just use my own style as an example—I certainly could never be compared to her—but when I learned that she was the kind of person who would talk about 'I almost got hit by a car on the way to work this morning,' that's kind of what I do. And I think that endears you to people, so I can really see why people loved her so much; she was one of them!"

MARIANNE BOYD, WHO WORKED at Crosley Broadcasting in the 1950s, can testify to the difficulty women experienced back then when they tried to get jobs with more responsibility. Her husband, Bill Myers, explains:

"Marianne Boyd, the young lady who later was to become my wife, decided to leave her job in WLW radio and television's Special Broadcast Services Department to pursue a broadcasting career in New York. It was Ruth Lyons who provided her with letters of introduction which opened many important doors for her. She did this because she liked young 'Billy Myers' who was on her staff and handed up the props for her commercials from under her desk in his first job as set-up boy at Channel 4 [WLWT's first channel assignment].

"To Marianne Boyd Myers, Ruth was the first woman success story she had witnessed up close who wasn't an entertainer. Here was a tough saleswoman, producer, and star of her own show, absolutely fearless, but with a heart of gold. Her charisma attracted every big-name talent who came to town wanting to promote their show or book or lecture. These stars didn't realize it was quite a large simulcast network that reached five states, and many felt so comfortable in this local station that you could see they were relaxed, frequently revealing their true selves to our benefit. Ruth had that gift and it was copied by many network stars who were aware of her success."

"It was the '50s and '60s and I couldn't even be hired as an assistant producer," Marianne said. "I knew one female director. No engineers—only secretaries and public relations assistants. The only women you saw on your screen were glamorous singers, musicians, dancers, or cooks. There was one spokeswoman from the U.N. ...

"You saw no females in news till weather girls were introduced 'for show' years later. Today is just the opposite. Ruth Lyons was a pioneer and we had her here in Cincinnati, Ohio, at the Nation's Station—first on the air locally, and the first NBC network affiliate. How proud to be associated with WLW and WLWT, and all you had to do was mention those call letters and the doors in the big time opened immediately—it was all you had to say! Thank you, Ruth.

"She was the Queen of Television and not just for her early arrival, her longevity, her power, and being a sponsor's dream, but she was herself. We enjoyed the talent of her songwriting—beautiful words and music that still are classics the world has never heard—her advanced knowledge of the new America evolving. Ruth was 'herself,' a new breed of independent women who followed their dream, well before Mary Tyler Moore."

FOLLOWING AN ACT LIKE THAT was Bob Braun's job, and he faced a difficult time, knowing that *The 50-50 Club* wanted Ruth. He couldn't deliver her, but he could do his best. And his best gradually brought the show's advertising rates back up from where they had fallen after Ruth retired, and maintained a good rating, even bringing new people to the audience.

Braun kept things going on *The Bob Braun Show* (later renamed *Braun & Company*) until 1984. He was constantly improving the show, bringing in fresh, younger singers like Rob Reider, Mary Ellen Tanner, and Colleen Sharp, and adding viewers from a younger pool. Probably the biggest reason the show eventually ended was the phenomenon of more and more women going to work fulltime in the 1980s.

Just about anyone in Cincinnati will say it: "There will never be another Ruth Lyons." There won't, but it's not because people like John T. Murphy took steps to prevent someone from achieving her level of power at WLWT. It's the fact that Ruth was a unique woman in unique circumstances, someone whom everyone could like for herself and who was both an accomplished entertainer and a tough businesswoman. It was a unique time, too—those early days of television when programming was still being invented.

In a way, however, we still get to see some of Ruth every day on television, as we watch *Oprah*, *Ellen*, and the myriad other TV talk show hosts. The formats, techniques, and—well, the talk—they are all Ruth's legacy to the world.

Acknowledgments

My thanks to all those who helped this book along. Mickey Fisher, Gloria Rush, Bonnie Lou and Mel Okum, Nick Clooney, Lana Albright, Bill Myers, Marianne Boyd Myers, Van Cottengim, Jerry Insicke, Eric Schneider, Ron Whitaker, Len Goorian, Bill Nimmo, Peter Nero, and Charles K. Murdock were particularly helpful in sharing their memories, as were the many fans of Ruth Lyons who told me their stories.

Contemporary Cincinnati broadcasters Darryl Parks, Janeen Coyle, and Gary Burbank provided useful insight and comments. Debbie Morner helped by proofreading several chapters and telling me when I was off-course. Special thanks to Randy McNutt, Charles Stinger, Cliff Adams, Jason MacDonald, Anita Holmes, Doug Ross, and Mike Martini for sharing artifacts and information from the past.

I am grateful to the staff at Orange Frazer Press, including Sarah Hawley, Marcy Hawley, and John Baskin for their work on book design, production, marketing, and the rest of the heavy lifting.

The staff of the Newspapers & Magazines department and the Genealogy & Local History department of the Public Library of Cincinnati & Hamilton County were their usual efficient selves. Valerie Edwards Elliot of the Smith History Library in Oxford, Ohio, was especially helpful with historic sources.

Timeline

1905
Ruth Evelyne Reeves is born on Eastern Avenue.

1906
Herman Andrew Newman is born in Cincinnati's Fairview section.

1911
Rose Jayne Reeves (Ruth's sister) is born. Ruth enters grade school, begins piano lessons.

1919
Cincinnati radio station WMH goes on the air. Ruth enters Cincinnati's new (and incomplete) East High School, later named Withrow. The Reeves family moves from the East End to Madisonville, another Cincinnati suburb.

1922
Crosley Broadcasting and WLW are founded. At the end of the year, Crosley buys and shuts down WMH.

1923
WSAI is founded by the U.S. Playing Card Company. The Reeves family moves back to the East End and Ruth meets Johnny Lyons. Ruth graduates from Withrow High School, but not before she writes her first musical, which inaugurates an annual tradition for the school. In the fall Ruth begins her freshman year at the University of Cincinnati. Delta Delta Delta rushes her, and she writes the entire musical

score for a freshman comedy troupe's play. She and Johnny drift apart as she meets new men.

1924
Instead of signing up for her sophomore year of college, Ruth takes a sales position with Willis Music in Cincinnati, where she meets several professional musicians who help shape her ambition. Taking the job is ostensibly to spare her father the expense of another year's education, but in reality she is saving for dental work. Herman Newman graduates from Hughes High School.

1925
Ruth gains valuable experience as a piano accompanist at society parties. In March, she is heard on radio for the first time when she backs up singer Ann James on a new incarnation of station WMH (soon to become WKRC).

1926
Ruth has her teeth capped and renews her social life, especially with regards to Johnny Lyons. Ruth tries work as a librarian. After several months she begins training for an advanced position, but finds that she doesn't like the idea. She goes to work for her father as a clerk-typist with Provident Bank's Travel Department. Johnny Lyons leaves his father's shoe business and takes a job as a clerk with an insurance company. Financial circumstances in the Reeves and Lyons

families are such that Ruth and Johnny are forced to provide most of their support, so they postpone marriage. Later in the year, she is invited to play regularly on WSAI.

1926
Crosley Broadcasting buys WSAI, causing Ruth's friend Howard Hafford to leave and join a relatively new station, WKRC. Ruth is hired full-time as assistant music director at WKRC by Howard Hafford, who had given her a start at WSAI. She plays piano and organ, and does odd jobs.

1928
Herman Newman receives his B.A. from the University of Cincinnati, and begins law school.

1929
When the host of a program called A Woman's Hour calls in sick, Ruth asked to substitute. The sponsor is so impressed with her ad-lib approach that he asks her to take over the program. WKRC is upgraded to 5,000 watts and sold to a front for the CBS radio network. Black Friday collapses the stock market and Samuel Lyons— along with millions of other investors—loses most of his money. Despite the Depression, radio grows. Herman Newman leaves law school to work fulltime, in order to fund seminary studies.

1930
WKRC is sold to another company owned by the CBS radio network. The new management cleans house, but Ruth is retained as a valuable employee. Johnny Lyons moves into management with his employer, the Pearl Insurance Co.

1931
Ruth takes on new programs and assignments, including live remote broadcasts. She is soon working 6 days a week, plus some evenings. She begins featuring guests on A Woman's Hour. Ruth's father is promoted, lightening her financial load.

1932
Ruth takes a road trip to California with Tyrone Power and Lee Wilson, returning without Power. Back in Cincinnati, she hones her radio skills, often by substituting for male employees who skip out of work. She is promoted from assistant music director to music director. Her already heavy load is expanded by two evening programs. John Lyons, Sr., closes his shoe store. Ruth and Johnny marry. The couple honeymoons in Canada, after which they take an apartment in Walnut Hills, near WKRC. Ruth has an appendectomy and spends part of the holiday season recovering.

1933
Herman Newman is ordained a Universalist minister in Illinois, and leaves for England, where he will study at Oxford University. Prohibition is repealed. Johnny and Ruth Lyons move to a new apartment in eastern Cincinnati. They rarely see one another. Ruth buys her own car.

1934
Johnny Lyons moves to Cleveland with his employer. Ruth and Johnny try unsuccessfully to maintain a "commuter marriage." Ruth's father takes ill, and she moves in with her parents and sister. Herman Newman completes his studies and spends the summer touring Europe before returning to the United States, where he takes the pulpit of a Universalist church in Erie, Pennsylvania.

1935
Ruth and Johnny continue the commuter marriage, meeting in Cincinnati or (more

often) Cleveland every weekend. Ruth gamely tries to find a radio job in Cleveland, but nothing is in the offing. WKRC begins work on new studios. Ruth's father, still ailing, retires from his job, and Ruth moves her family into a rented four-bedroom home.

1936
WKRC completes its new studios, and Ruth continues to develop programs. She brings more women into radio.

1937
Weeks of rain force the Ohio River far beyond its banks, creating a disaster situation in Cincinnati. Ruth proves to be the heroine of the hour, staying on the air for several days straight and providing emergency instructions and information to citizens. She is promoted to program director of WKRC. WKRC is sold to hometown Taft Broadcasting. Crosley Broadcasting obtains an experimental television license, W8XCT.

1938
Ruth turns down an offer to see her songs turned into guaranteed hits by the country's biggest bandleader. As program director at WKRC, she has nearly two dozen people reporting directly to her and controls more than $60,000 in annual salaries. Margaret Reeves, Ruth's mother, contracts pleurisy and dies.

1939
Ruth divorces Johnny Lyons, but keeps the Lyons name. The Ruth Lyons Children's Christmas Fund is inaugurated on *A Woman's Hour*. Crosley Broadcasting demonstrates closed-circuit television at Cincinnati's Carew Tower and the Crosley Pavilion at the New York World's Fair. RCA does the same at the Fair, but gets all the publicity.

1940
Herman Newman resigns his ministry and returns to Cincinnati to find work.

1941
Ruth attends the third inauguration of FDR, then travels to New York to get some of her songs published. Ruth's father, Samuel Reeves, is hospitalized, then moved into a nursing home. She enrolls in classes at UC and the CCM. The Japanese attack on Pearl Harbor brings the US into World War II.

1942
Herman Newman and Ruth Lyons meet in May and marry in October. Ruth retains Lyons as her stage name. She moves to Crosley Broadcasting (WSAI and WLW) for a ten-dollar per week raise and starts a new women's program on WSAI, *Petticoat Partyline*. She also takes over an existing WLW program, *Consumer's Foundation*. Ruth's father dies at 71. WLW and WSAI move from the Crosley factory in an industrial district to "Crosley Square" at 9th and Elm, downtown. Ruth is named "Mayor for a Day" of Cincinnati.

1943
Ruth and Herman are quarantined in their new house because Herman has scarlet fever. Ruth does her shows from home. A wheelchair-bound woman walks on *Petticoat Partyline*. Ruth develops new shows, including *Your Morning Matinee* on WSAI. Rose Reeves and Herb Lupton are married. Frazier Thomas joins Ruth as her sidekick on a new WSAI show, *Your Morning Matinee*.

1944
Ruth learns she is pregnant. Rose Lupton gives birth to a girl. Crosley sells WSAI to Marshall Field III, and *Your Morning Matinee* moves to WLW. Ruth's child is stillborn. The

Newmans adopt a newborn girl and name her Candace Laird Newman.

1945

AVCO buys Crosley Broadcasting; operation continues unchanged. Ruth inaugurates *The 50 Club* at WLW.

1946

Ruth further develops *The 50 Club* on WLW. Crosley Broadcasting broadcasts the first television signals in Cincinnati.

1947

Your Morning Matinee, with Ruth as host, is broadcast on WINS radio in New York, in addition to WLW. Crosley Broadcasting begins regular television broadcasts: one hour per week as W8XCT.

1948

Commercial television makes its debut in Cincinnati. Crosley Broadcasting builds "Mt. Olympus" in Clifton, as the home of WLWT's studio, offices, transmitter, and tower. WLWT signs up as the first affiliate of the NBC television network. Herman Newman joins the faculty of U.C.'s engineering college.

1949

Ruth Lyons is made program director of WLWT. *The 50 Club* moves to television for one week in May. John T. Murphy is hired to be WLWT's program director. WLWC and WLWD go on the air. *The 50 Club* returns to television. (Broadcast of *The 50 Club* on WLW radio discontinued.) Ruth wins her first battle with Procter & Gamble, displacing popular soap operas. Ruth hosts Christmastime shows for children in hospitals in Cincinnati, Dayton, and Louisville.

1950

Candy Lyons begins school with tutors at home. Herman Newman criticizes Harry Truman's English usage in the national press. *The 50 Club* appears on WLWC and WLWD, with Gene Walz as the show's director. WLWT abandons Mt. Olympus for Crosley Square. Willie Thall replaces Frazier Thomas as Ruth's sidekick.

1951/52

The first half-hour of *The 50 Club* is broadcast nationally by NBC. Ruth receives 200,000 pieces of mail. Ruth selects Judy Perkins to take her place on *Your Morning Matinee*. At the end of the summer of 1952, Ruth cancels her contract with NBC over a problem with advertising sales. Big-name stars such as Bob Hope and Milton Berle appear regularly on *The 50 Club*. Ruth is criticized for dancing with an African-American singer on her show; Ruth criticizes America's racial attitudes.

1953

Ruth, Herman, and Candy sail to England for Queen Elizabeth II's Coronation. Ruth, who is in the Cathedral, sends home tape-recorded reports to the *Cincinnati Enquirer*. Ruth and *The 50 Club* are profiled in the national newspaper, *Grit*. The Newman family tours Europe for the first time. The show expands to 90 minutes at times. The audience accommodations are more than doubled, which results in the show being renamed *The 50-50 Club*

1954/55

Ruth is profiled in *Look* magazine. Ruth adds a floral bouquet to spruce up a microphone, and it becomes her trademark. Around the same time she mentions that a woman is not fully dressed-up without white gloves. This results in the ladies in the studio audience wearing white gloves to the show for years. Ruth, Herman, and Candy vacation in England both years. WLW radio begins simulcasting *The 50-50 Club*. Paul Dixon comes to WLWT.

1956
Your Morning Matinee is replaced by *Mel Taylor's Breakfast Club*. Candy is permitted to attend public school, but difficulties with other children caused by Ruth's status result in her going back to home-schooling.

1957
Cincinnatian Bob Braun wins the Arthur Godfrey Talent Scouts competition on national TV. A few weeks later he leaves WCPO TV for WLW and WLWT. The Cincinnati Post publishes a souvenir Ruth Lyons edition. America's Number 1 general interest magazine, *The Saturday Evening Post*, runs a full-length feature article about Ruth Lyons. WLW-I in Indianapolis goes on the air. Cincinnati Mayor Charles P. Taft proclaims May 17 "Ruth Lyons Day." Willie Thall leaves *The 50-50 Club* to start his own show on WKRC. Ruth tries several substitutes. Peter Grant and Bob Braun replace Thall. *The 50-50 Club* is the first local show to be broadcast in color in Cincinnati. More color TV sets are sold in Cincinnati than anywhere else. Mickey Fisher joins WLWT as Ruth's secretary. Ruth is so influential that, at her urging, fans vote a majority of Cincinnati Reds to the All-Star Team. The voting rules are changed the following year.

1958
Ruth substitutes for Helen O'Connell on the *Today* Show, turns down an offer from CBS for her own show. The Newman's home is featured in *The American Home*. Candy, Ruth, and Herman travel to Leningrad and Moscow aboard the first passenger liner permitted into

Russia since World War II. Ruth Lyons is listed in the Gallop Poll as one of the country's "Most Admired Women."

1959
The Newmans take a Caribbean cruise and wind up fleeing Havana as Fidel Castro takes over the country. They sail aboard the last cruise ship to travel to Cuba. Ruth, Candy, and Herman incorporate CANDEE Records. The Ruth Lyons Autograph Collection of dresses makes its debut in the fall, and quietly disappears. Troy Donahue guests on *The 50-50 Club* and becomes Candy's "big brother." Ruth's first record album, *Ten Tunes of Christmas* is released.

1960
Ruth shows up in *Ladies' Home Journal*, *Look*, *The Sporting News*, and on NBC. Joe Garagiola promotes *Baseball is a Funny Game* on *The 50-50 Club*; he signs over 400 copies that afternoon in Cincinnati and Dayton. Ruth's second album, *Our Best to You*, comes out.

1961
Peter Nero makes the first of many guest appearances on *The 50-50 Club*. Ruth writes a song to urge the Cincinnati Reds on to the National League Pennant, titled "Rally 'Round the Reds." The Reds win the Pennant but lose the World Series.

1962
Candy Newman starts college at the University of Cincinnati and becomes a member of Delta Delta Delta, like her mother. Bob Braun has a major national hit record with *Till Death Do Us Part*, and is given a morning show on WLWT.

1963
Under the name "Candace Laird," Candy Newman has a bit part in the movie *Palm Springs Weekend*, with Troy Donahue and Connie Stevens. Candy and Ruth travel to California for filming Candy's scene. The movie opens in November. Ruth's final album, It's Christmas Time Again is released on the CANDEE label.

1964
Ruth's sister, Rose Lupton, dies of cancer. In December, Ruth is named the recipient of McCall's magazine's Golden Mike Award for outstanding contributions to broadcasting. Ruth is hospitalized after suffering a small stroke. Singer Vivienne Della Chiesa is hired to fill in for Ruth while she convalesces at home.

1965
Ruth is presented the Governor's Award by the Ohio Newspaper Association on February 5. Candy Newman is diagnosed with breast cancer and has a mastectomy. The family sails for Europe after Candy's follow-up treatments. CANDEE Enterprises is dissolved. Ruth returns to *The 50-50 Club* and Candy is officially added to the show's cast. Candy begins work on a cookbook.

1966
Governor James Rhodes declares February 18 (the 20th anniversary of *The 50-50 Club*) Ruth Lyons Day. Candace Laird Newman dies in a cruise ship's infirmary in the mid-Atlantic, on Father's Day. She is cremated in New York. The lack of a coffin when Herman and Ruth arrive in Cincinnati sparks a long-lived rumor that Candy committed suicide by jumping into the ocean. Ruth does not return to her show for four months.

1967
Having seen the Christmas Fund through one more time, Ruth retires for good. Walter Bartlett reads Ruth's farewell letter during the show on January 17. After struggling with the decision, Bob Braun assumes the role of host of *The 50-50 Club*. The Ruth Lyons Children's Christmas Fund continues.

1969
Ruth's memoirs, *Remember With Me*, are published in hardcover by Doubleday. It will sell 90,000 copies.

1972
Ruth agrees to be the honorary chairperson for the "Save the Terminal" committee, a group dedicated to saving Cincinnati's 1929 Art Deco railroad terminal. Later in the year, she is announced as the recipient of the International Humanitarian Service award from the Overseas Association of the American Red Cross. She makes no personal appearances.

1974
Paul Dixon, a great supporter of the Ruth Lyons Children's Christmas Fund before and after her retirement, and part of her television legacy, dies of a heart attack.

1983
Cincinnati's City Council names a downtown street "Ruth Lyons Way." There is some public discontent over the fact that the "street" is a short alley.

1984
Bob Braun departs WLW to pursue new opportunities in California.

1986
Nominated by Cincinnati Enquirer television critic John Kiesewetter, Ruth Lyons receives

the Cincinnati Chamber of Commerce's Great Living Cincinnatian Award.

1988
On November 7, just weeks after her 83rd birthday, Ruth passes away quietly at home. Herman soon moves into an extended care facility.

1991
Herman Newman dies at the age of 84. *Cincinnati Radio: The War Years (1941 – 1945)* is released on CD, under the auspices of the X-Star Radio Netowrk, a public radio network. Ruth Lyons figures prominently in this chronicle Cincinnati radio during the Second World War.

1993
Bob Braun inducted into the Cincinnati Radio Hall of Fame.

1995
CD and cassette tape compilations of Ruth Lyons Christmas songs are released under the auspices of WVXU with the title Christmas Music of Ruth Lyons.

1999
Bob Braun retires, six years after returning to Cincinnati to host a regional radio show.

2002
The X-Star Network and Media Heritage, Inc. release *Cincinnati Radio: The Nation's Station (1921- 1941)*. Ruth Lyons is profiled in this chronicle of WLW's first 20 years.

2004
Ruth Lyons is inducted into the hall of fame of the Ohio Valley Chapter of the National Academy of Television Arts and Sciences.

Donate to the Ruth Lyons Children's Christmas Fund

More than seventy years after it was established, the Ruth Lyons Children's Christmas Fund continues Ruth's work at hospitals throughout the region. The Fund is a combined project of WLW radio, WLWT television, and other sponsors. Donations are accepted all year around.

Contact:

Ruth Lyons Children's Fund
P.O. Box 59
Cincinnati, OH 45201
(513) 412-5007

Bibliography & resources

Books

Banks, Michael A., *Crosley* (Cincinnati, Ohio: Clerisy Press, 2006)
Braun, Bob, *Here's Bob* (New York, Doubleday & Co., 1969)
Dixon, Paul, *Paul, Baby!* (Cleveland, Ohio: The World Publishing Co., 1968)
Friedman, Jim, *Cincinnati Television* (Charleston, South Carolina: Arcadia Publishing, 2007)
Keller, Cynthia, *Remembering Ruth Lyons: 1905-1988* (Cincinnati: Cincinnati Historical Society, 1995)
Kelly, Mary Ann, *The Trouble is Not in Your Set* (Cincinnati: C.J. Krehbiel Co., 1990)
Lyons, Ruth, *The Ruth Lyons Songbook* (1969)
Lyons, Ruth, *Remember with Me* (New York: Doubleday & Co., 1969)
Lyons, Ruth, *Sing a Song* sheet music collection (Cincinnati: Willis Music Co., 1969)
McNutt, Randy, *The Cincinnati Sound* (Charleston, South Carolina: Arcadia Publishing, 2007)
Perry, Dick, *Not Just a Sound: The Story of WLW* (Englewood Cliffs, New Jersey: Prentice Hall, 1971)
Perry, Dick, *Vas You Effer in Zinzinnati?* (Garden City, New York: Doubleday & Co., 1966)
Wood, Mary, *Just Lucky, I Guess* (Garden City, New York: Doubleday & Co., 1967)

Recordings

Vinyl Records

1959: Lyons, Ruth, et al *Ten Tunes of Christmas* (Cincinnati: Candee Records, 33-1/3 album and boxed set of 45-rpm records with lyrics on sleeves)
1960: Lyons, Ruth & Wright, Ruby, *All Because It's Christmas* and Everywhere the Bells Are Ringing (New York: Columbia Records, 45-rpm single)
Christmas Marching Song (CANDEE/ASCAP)
This is Christmas (CANDEE/ASCAP)
1960: Lyons, Ruth, et al *Our Best to You* (Cincinnati: Candee Records, album)
1963: Lyons, Ruth, et al *It's Christmastime Again* (Cincinnati: Candee Records, album)
Lyons, *Ruth, Christmas Marching Song/This is Christmas* (Cincinnati: Candee Records, 44-rpm single)

Audio Cassette

Lyons, Ruth, et al, *Christmas Music of Ruth Lyons* **(Cincinnati: X-Star Radio Network, 1995)**
        Audio Cassette (available from WGUC radio)
Pauley, Jane, et al, *Let Me Entertain You: A Ruth Lyons Memoir* **(Cincinnati: X-Star Radio**
        Network, 1995) Audio Cassette (available from WGUC radio)

Compact Disc (CD)

Pauley, Jane, et al, *Let Me Entertain You: A Ruth Lyons Memoir* **(Cincinnati: X Star Radio**
        Network, 1995) Compact Disc (available from WGUC radio)
Lyons, Ruth, et al, *Christmas Music of Ruth Lyons* **(Cincinnati: X-Star Radio Network, 1995)**
        Compact Disc (available from WGUC radio)
X-Star Radio Network & Media Heritage, Inc, et al, *Cincinnati Radio: The Nation's Station*
        (Cincinnati: WVXU, 2002)
X-Star Radio Network, et al, *Cincinnati Radio: The War Years* **(Cincinnati: WVXU, 1991)**

Songs Written by Ruth Lyons (Partial List)

All Because It's Christmas
Bungalow Blues (music only, 1924)
Christmas Marching Song
Everywhere the Bells Are Ringing
Fooled
Have a Merry Merry Merry Merry Christmas
Hey, Nonny Nonny
Let's Light the Christmas Tree
The Marching Song
Nu-Maid Song
Quarantine Blues
Rally 'Round the Reds
This is Christmas
Wasn't the Summer Short?

Web Sites

Cincinnati Radio–*http://www.cincyradio.com*

Media Heritage–*www.historyofbroadcasting.com*

WCPO Television–*http://www.wcpo.com*

WGUC Radio—*http://www.wguc.org*

WKRC Radio—*http://www.55krc.com*

WKRC Television—*HTTP://WWW.LOCAL12.COM*

WLW Radio—*http://www.700wlw.com*

WLWT Television—*http://www.wlwt.com/video/5053493/index.html*

WSAI Radio—*http://www.wsai.com*

Index